Birth of a Dancing Star

Daniel J. McGrath
B.A. Dip.Ed. Dip.R.E. Cert. Soc. & Pas. Min. M.S.D.I
Spiritual Direction/Accompaniment

4 Rymalton,
Pathhead Village
Kirkcaldy, KY1 2PL

Home: 01592 640 286
Mob: 07913 482 748
Car: 07910 855 515
mcgrath.daniel@sky.com

*Let the song be sung
that the journey is
An inner one,
and
its mountain top
is in the heart.*

Murray Bodo

"In the end what you don't surrender
Well the world just strips away."
Bruce Springsteen, "Human Touch"

"Love and do what you will"
Saint Augustine, *Sermon on John 4:4–12*

Birth of a Dancing Star

From Cradle Catholic to Cyborg Christian

Ilia Delio, OSF

ORBIS BOOKS
Maryknoll, New York 10545

Founded in 1970, Orbis Books endeavors to publish works that enlighten the mind, nourish the spirit, and challenge the conscience. The publishing arm of the Maryknoll Fathers and Brothers, Orbis seeks to explore the global dimensions of the Christian faith and mission, to invite dialogue with diverse cultures and religious traditions, and to serve the cause of reconciliation and peace. The books published reflect the views of their authors and do not represent the official position of the Maryknoll Society. To learn more about Maryknoll and Orbis Books, please visit our website at www.maryknollsociety.org.

Library of Congress Cataloging-in-Publication Data

Names: Delio, Ilia, author.
Title: Birth of a dancing star : from cradle Catholic to cyborg Christian / Ilia Delio, OSF.
Description: Maryknoll, NY : Orbis Books, [2019] | Includes bibliographical references and index.
Identifiers: LCCN 2019017780 (print) | LCCN 2019980548 (ebook) | ISBN 9781626983472 (print) | ISBN 9781608338115 (ebook)
Subjects: LCSH: Delio, Ilia. | Catholic women—United States—Biography.
Classification: LCC BX4705.D29443 A3 2019 (print) | LCC BX4705.D29443 (ebook) | DDC 271/.973092 [B]—dc23
LC record available at https://lccn.loc.gov/2019017780
LC ebook record available at https://lccn.loc.gov/2019980548

Contents

Introduction

SEVERAL YEARS AGO I had the privilege of visiting the University of Canterbury Mount John Observatory in New Zealand. I was fortunate to be the guest of the New Zealand Mercy Sisters who arranged for me and another sister to visit Lake Tekapo in the South Island. Since Mount John Observatory was nearby, we signed up for the nighttime excursion that would begin at eleven thirty in the evening. We had to wear heavy insulated jackets designed for life at the South Pole because the midnight air on the top of the mountain could be brutally cold. Embarking on the bus was like going on a pilgrimage to the Holy Land. We climbed in with ten or so other star pilgrims and began our trek in the dead silence of the night. Halfway up the mountain, the bus driver turned off the headlights so that the artificial lights of the bus would not disturb the light of the nighttime stars shining overhead. When we arrived at the top of the mountain, it was pitch black, and the only visible light was coming from the stars and galaxies. I looked up into this sea of dazzling lights flickering and dancing in the sky, peering at galaxies whose names I never heard of, and all at once I was part of this immense cosmic dance of light. I lost myself amidst the stars of the Milky Way, becoming myself a little star, as I twinkled with delight at this most amazing expanse of lights born of dust and gas, cooked in the pressure of convergence, and bursting forth from the density of fire. There were hundreds of billions of stars that evening, young and old, large and small, quiet and violent, various intensities of light dappling the night sky, like fireflies swirling across the cosmos. For a moment I forgot that I was on Earth and felt myself expanding in the immensity of the cosmos, as if heaven and earth were one endless flow of light-filled wonder.

Was it I who was gazing at the stars, or were the stars gazing at me? Was it I who was observing the heavens, or were the heavens observing me? As I stood on the mountain of the observatory I realized it is all about perspective. Gazing up at the night sky, I was seeing my own history born billions of years ago in the furnaces of stars and only in that moment awakening in my conscious mind. We humans can easily lose perspective on our humble place in the universe. We get locked up in our heads, prisoners of our limited ideas and thoughts, cutting ourselves off from the wider world of experience. We forget or are simply unaware that we are part of an immense cosmic history that continues to stretch into a vast unknown future. Our time here is a blink of the cosmic eye, as the psalmist wrote: "Our days may come to seventy years, or eighty, if our strength endures; yet the best of them are but trouble and sorrow, for they quickly pass, and we fly away" (Ps 90:10). Brief is our time and fragile are our lives, and yet we are here in this moment, in this space of time, part of an immense flow of energies, consolidated into the particularity of *this* life, my life, to do one thing and to do it well, to radiate the love that moves the sun and all the other stars.

The Jesuit priest and scientist Pierre Teilhard de Chardin spoke of love as the core energy of the universe, the most mysterious and unknown energy that endures beyond all evil and darkness, beyond all destructive powers, beyond every human fear and every tear shed from hearts broken by grief. Love forges stars out of the chaos of the elements; love writes the lines for the nighttime sky; love alone endures through the darkness of the night into the brightness of a new day. It is love that takes what is deepest in the center of everything that exists and unites it with another center, creating a force and bond of enduring character that leads to nothing less than a new higher consciousness open to the future fullness of life. Love alone, Teilhard thought, can bring us to another universe, for the power of love is God, and God is forever the maker of everything new in love. This is a story about my journey into the heart of love, into God.

When I was a child I thought of God as a parent, like a benevolent father. But when I grew older, I put aside this image for another image, God as a fountain fullness of love, an irrepressible endless flow of love that lies at the center of my life and everything that exists. God is not only that than which no greater can be thought, God is that than which no greater can be loved. God is an incomprehensible power of love, a power of infinite nearness, hidden in the flesh of the world, so closely united with everything that exists that the lines between divinity and humanity are often blurred. The power of God is not what we think or imagine, as in the power of a ruler or monarch. God is the paradox of power—not power over us but the power within us and in everything that exists. Christ attests to the impotence of patriarchal power and reveals the truth of divine power as the omnipotence of love. Everything flows from this deep power of love, the things of science and religion, church and world, the joys and sorrows of every life; everything flows from divine love unto the fullness of love. Teilhard saw this powerful attraction of love in the hardness of rocks and in the dirt dug up by well-worn hands. He was a paleontologist who searched for old bones in the yawning earth, trying to understand the story of human origins. Closely observing bone fragments from millions of years ago, he saw and believed that this physical cosmos, this earthly place we call home, is not mere matter passing away. Rather, this cosmic home is profoundly sacred, imbued with divine presence—a home made of water, dirt, sweat, and toil, constantly being filled with divine presence, incarnational love, and becoming ever more personal in love. He spoke of this love-forming universe as christification. Evolution is the rise of transpersonal life, one cosmic person in formation whom Christians call the Christ. Teilhard's vision is my vision as well.

My story begins with my traditional Italian American family in New Jersey, steeped in Catholic practice and ritual, where Sunday Mass and pasta dinners bounded our lives and where the world of science was completely foreign to us. I found my way to a Catholic boarding school, from which I narrowly escaped being expelled but where I experienced my first sense of a mystical presence of God. I pursued an academic career in science, earning a doctorate in pharmacology, without any inkling of how my scientific knowledge could connect with God, nor was I even remotely interested in relating science and faith. I liked school enough to make it a full-time occupation with the intent of solving a major disease and winning a Nobel Prize. I was inwardly religious but outwardly secular, as religion seemed irrelevant to the world of science. God was actively engaged in my life, however, arriving unannounced and luring me into the desert. From the world of science, I entered a traditional Carmelite monastery and found myself steeped in contemplation and manual labor. After several years of intense prayer and rigorous physical labor, my constricted spirit propelled me in reverse direction. Just when I thought I had settled on my vocation, I found myself reentering the world and living in a Franciscan community. Even here however I could not settle down (for various reasons as the reader will see) but found myself pursuing a graduate theological education while in formation as a Franciscan sister. Every time I thought I had arrived at my destination, God showed up in novel ways and I was impelled to get up and follow this mysterious God of breathless love, traveling into new patterns of life.

My story has a lot of detours and mishaps, but it is good to know up front that I was a traditional Catholic who avoided Vatican II and the documents that proceeded from this council. I rebelled against a liberal church engaged in history and had strong convictions about Christian life as being over and against the world. As a traditionalist, I held fast to the three-tiered universe with heaven above, life on earth, and hell for those who die in mortal sin. When I eventually entered religious life, after a prolonged and mischievous adolescence, I opted for the most traditional community where strict asceticism and prayer could nurture a life of holiness. The most significant sign of religious life for me was the habit since it provided a religious identity in a godless world. Even today I empathize (although no longer agree) with those who resist or reject the worldly gospel of Pope Francis; I too once rejected a secularization of gospel. I opted instead for a smaller, purified church untainted by the evils of the world and rejected all liberal forms of Christian life.

Although I was initially trained as a scientist before entering a monastery, I maintained a staunch divide between science and religion as nonoverlapping domains of knowledge. The idea of bridging these two areas or seeing a mutual relationship between them seemed absurd. At the same time, my understanding of religion was weak and limited. I accepted the Christian story as it was conveyed in homilies, feast-day celebrations, the prayers we recited and the songs we sang at Mass. There was absolutely no reason to question this story and the faith handed down to me by my parents and grandparents (really my grandmother) for it was a comfort and a cushion on which I could rest my fragile life. If someone had spoken to me about God and evolution in 1985, I would have thought they were on the road to perdition, and I would be on the same road if I continued to listen to them. I not only kept science and religion far from each other, but I was one who held that faith is about God and heaven while science is about knowledge and facts. I remember seeing a documentary on Darwin's evolution in high school and thinking that such ideas could not account for the immortal soul created directly by God. Since the human person had an immortal soul distinct from the rest of creation, the human person must be created uniquely by God and not by way of evolution.

I had strong opinions about liberal Christianity, yet as my path unfolded, the very people I rebelled against, especially the religious women of Vatican II, became my teachers and guides (because God works in paradoxical ways and God has a great sense of humor). Teaching at a post–Vatican II graduate school of theology and ministry at the turn of the twenty-first century, I gained invaluable insights on religious life, gender and personhood, church and world. As a vowed religious sister I had to grapple with who and what I am and whether or not the body holds real significance for me. I came face to face with questions on gender and celibacy and was confronted by my own gendered identity. As I began to engage theology with modern science through the influence of Teilhard de Chardin and Ewert Cousins among others, I began to see that these avenues of knowledge must be brought together for a new level of global consciousness in the twenty-first century. From a static, fixed understanding of Catholic life in New Jersey, God burst forth in my life in such a way that I began to see the dynamism of God in our midst and a new type of person emerging in the twenty-first century.

The idea for this book arose from a question many people continue to ask me, "How did you arrive at an integration of science and religion?" There is no quick answer to this question, and I would be remiss if not outright deceptive to suggest that science and religion are like two electrical wires that can be soldered together. After teaching courses in science and religion for the last twenty years, I can attest that the integration of these disciplines is not "out there," written in a book or in a formula. Rather science and religion are two forms of knowledge that emerge fundamentally from the pursuit of self-knowledge, rather than some type of objective relationship. My story is not so much an evolution of knowledge but an evolution of the heart, as I moved from the *Baltimore Catechism* to science and theology and the integration of these paths of knowing in relation to God and evolution. I will explore this evolution as a growth and development of consciousness, from the suburban malls of New Jersey through the halls of scientific research to the monastic cloister and into the Franciscan view of the cosmos as the place of God's self-revelation and self-becoming. Woven into the text are significant relationships that have changed my views on self, God, and world. Some of the most profound influences have come through great and humble persons who took me under their wings, so to speak, and taught me how to walk and speak in the ways of wisdom.

My life from cradle Catholic to the edge of cyborg Christian life is something of an adventure in love but one that includes sorrow and pain as part of the overall drama of my life. My journey into God is an unyielding mystery at the core of my life, a life I cannot fully fathom apart from the power of God's love. It has taken me years to realize that love is the very breath of God and that this love is also the breath of my life; for it is love who awakens me in the morning, love opens my eyes and draws me forth into the light of a new day, but it is also love who bears the weight of my sorrows and feels my inner pain when I am crushed or weighed down by life's difficulties: "for darkness is as light with you," the psalmist writes (Ps 139:12). This power of God's love is not a power over me, like a cloud to which I aspire to reach, but a power deep within me, like a bright star constantly struggling to emerge from the inner tensions of my life. God's mysterious depth of love is at once so intimate and close, as if being held in a sacred womb, and yet "so high beyond my reach" (Ps 139:6) that my mind can hardly fathom it. "You search me, O God, and you know me, you know my resting and my rising; you search my thoughts from afar" (Ps 139:1–2).

My story has had twists and turns and some dead ends, as I began to realize the outer space within, as Teilhard did and as the poet Maria Rainer Rilke so eloquently expressed: "Through every being single space extends, outer space within."[1] One God empowers one flow of love

---

1. Cited in Meins G. S. Coetsier, *The Existential Philosophy of Etty Hillesum: An Analysis of Her Diaries and Letters* (Leiden: Brill, 2014), 47; Maria Rainer Rilke, *Gedichte, 1906–1926, Sämlichte Werke II* (Frankfurt am Main: Insel Verlag, 1955–1988), 92.

through the one cosmos of life. What an injustice we have inflicted on the cosmos by separating science and religion as two separate spheres of unrelated knowledge or better yet by removing ourselves from the equation of love. All our questions on how science and religion relate are really one question on being itself: what is our connection to the whole inner–outer flow of life? In Rilke's words:

Ah, not to be cut off,
not through the slightest partition
shut out from the law of the stars.
The inner—what is it?
if not intensified sky,
hurled through with birds and deep
with the winds of homecoming.[2]

This inner–outer movement of life is divine love forever moving toward us, becoming one with us, evoking a longing within us, inspiring our perpetual movement toward God: "You have made us for Yourself, O God, and our hearts are restless until they rest in You."[3] As my views shifted from a static God to a dynamically engaged God, I began to experience God as unchanged change or eternal creativity, and thus the source of novelty and future. It was in the midst of life's changes that I began to realize God is not waiting for me to get things right; rather, God is right in the midst of my chaotic life. When I realized that God lives in the flux and flow of life, I found an irrepressible freedom. Evolution became less a fact of science than the core description of life itself, and I began to see God not as the unmoved mover but as the unpredictable, chaotic source of life. It was by opening up to a new understanding of God that I began to see the world of technology and artificial intelligence in new ways as well, integral to God and not outside the sphere of God's love. By engaging evolution as the flow of life's energies, I began to let go and engage new ideas, new ways of think-

---

2. Maria Rainer Rilke, "Ah, not to be cut off," in *Ahead of All Parting: The Selected Poetry and Prose of Rainer Maria Rilke*, trans. Stephen Mitchell (New York: Modern Library, 1995).

3. Saint Augustine, *Confessions* 1:1. trans. John K. Ryan, *The Confessions of St. Augustine* (New York: Image, 1960), 1.

ing and new structures of relationships. Like the caterpillar changing into the butterfly, my views on God and world underwent a profound metamorphosis.

I often think of that night on Mount John because for a moment heaven and earth were turned upside down and I saw my life in the cosmos in an entirely new way. And I knew then as I know now that change is possible, that we are not consigned to a world of sorrow or a vale of tears, that life is open to transformation and novelty in ways that we have yet to imagine. I continue to find myself in new relationships and new ways of seeing the world that I once would have considered impossible. Over and over I die, and over and over I am born again; and I have yet to fully embrace life's creative flow. But I know that only out of chaos can a star be born. It is a tumultuous birth where flowing gases condense in a massive darkness that eventually explode into light, into the birth of a star, dancing amidst billions of stars, light that is love itself, the light of Christ shining in the world and in our hearts; the diaphanous presence of God radiating through everything that exists. I have come to see this light of heaven within me, and it is the story I want to share with you: my journey into light or, rather, into the brilliance of love.

1

A Blessed Event

WHEN I WAS BORN, the world was a very different place. Elvis Presley and Mickey Mouse were prominent American icons, and the average cost of a new house was about ten thousand dollars or less. My father, Dominick Delio, used to drive for miles so that he would not have to pay more than twenty-three cents for a gallon of gas (of course he used that much just to drive to the cheapest gas station!). Life was local, family oriented, and lodged in ethnic communities. My own local ethnic community was an Italian-American family. My father was born in the Greenpoint section of Brooklyn, New York, which in 1912 was a poor, rough neighborhood, from what I am told. His grandparents emigrated from southern Italy, reportedly, the area of Naples or Salerno. His twin brother died at childbirth, and his biological father died at the age of twenty-eight, shortly after my father was born. His mother soon remarried, but the new husband did not want my father around, so he was sent to live with his grandparents in a small tenement apartment in Greenpoint.

I did not know my father all that well. He was a quiet and reserved man who worked hard and rarely spoke of his childhood. But I loved being with him. He was kind-hearted, gentle, and contagiously funny. He could tell a joke in such a way that his audience would often wind up in tears of laughter. He was an excellent cook and enjoyed a good dish of pasta and gravy every Sunday, which of course, was the Italian-American ritual in the late fifties. He seemed to accept life as it rolled out across the carpet of life's pains and sufferings. After he died, I found in his wallet a worn and faded picture of the face of the Shroud of Turin face of Jesus, a darkness surrounded Jesus's eyes of pain. With the many illnesses my father suffered in his later years due to the effects of diabetes, I saw his face in that picture as well. We never really know the pain of the ones we love.

A Dance for Life

While my father was born in Brooklyn, my mother, Anne ("Anne" with an "e" she would always say), was born in the rough, mountainous village of San Fratello, Sicily, a small commune about six hundred fifty meters above sea level and nested on the crown of the Nebrodi Mountains that run along the Thyrrenian coast. San Fratello is in the metropolitan city of Messina in the Italian region Sicily, located about sixty-eight miles east of Palermo and about fifty-six miles west of Messina. The village was founded in the eleventh century by Adelaide del Vasto, a noble of present-day French Normandy who conquered Sicily. Adelaide came to Sicily together with colonists and introduced the Gallo-Italic dialect, which is still spoken in the village. My mother and grandmother spoke the Fratellese dialect, which was like an Italian wedding soup that bore little resemblance to classical Italian.

Geography informs biography, and there is something about the mountainous region of San Fratello and the magnificent view of the Mediterranean from high up that was embedded particularly in the fiery strong-willed women of San Fratello. My grandmother, Maria Salanitro, was married early in life to a man she did not love and forced to live in a country she did not like. When my grandfather brought her to America at the age of eighteen, confined to the hull of a ship for three weeks with two small children, she landed on Ellis Island in bitterness and regret, wanting nothing more than to return to her homeland. My mother was one of those two small children, and she suffered the internal conflicts of a hostile mother for most of her life. My mother was small and petite, very attractive and stylish in attire. Even at the ripe age of ninety-one, she wore petite dresses as if attending a nightclub. Perhaps it was the long boat ride as an infant or the crowded living conditions in the Bay Ridge section of Brooklyn, New York, but my mother was frail as a child and subject to illness. She bore signs of tuberculosis at the age of twelve and was sent to a TB camp for healing. She often said that being sent away was a blessing, releasing her from the stress of her overcrowded family living conditions and a stern Sicilian mother.

Anne Delio was, for all practical purposes, an intellectual who loved to read books and dream big ideas. Even in her advanced years, she would pull out her books on Plato and Aristotle and ask her philosophical questions of why this and not that? Or what is God? Usually no answer could satisfy the infinite longing within her, and she was persistent in her questions. She told me that as a high school student she wanted to be a Dominican nun. She was smitten by the Amityville Dominicans in their long, white flowing habits and dreamed of one day joining them. However, my devoutly religious grandmother did not have the two-thousand-dollar dowry required to enter the Dominicans. Hence my mother forfeited her dream and chose to go to nursing school instead. She loved nursing, and it was on a nurses' "night out," on a dance floor to be specific, that she met my father. She claimed that he pursued her relentlessly, but she never quite owned up to the fact that she was attracted to him—probably because he was funny and she was dead serious. The comedian and the philosopher on the floor doing the tango—quite a dance team.

My parents started a family soon after they married in 1936, and my three siblings were born within six years of each other. Money was tight in the young family, and I am told that my mother had to pawn her wedding ring for a turkey one Thanksgiving. My eldest brother, Vincent, was restless and always on the edge of mischief. My sister Anne Marie was born two years after Vincent and became my mother's constant helper and companion. She was also the big sister to my second brother, Richard, who was born four years after Anne Marie. Unlike Vincent, Richard was a quiet baby who enjoyed the attention of being the youngest. Anne Marie looked after him like a little mother and pushed his baby cart around town like a responsible elder, until, I am told, she pushed his cart down the stairs one day. (The motive has never been entirely resolved, whether it was spite or her small stature that caused the mishap.)

Life took a turn for the family when my parents moved from Brooklyn to Lyndhurst, New Jersey. My mother found a big, white stucco house in Lyndhurst that had an add-on structure and a large backyard.

She was a creative thinker who quickly envisioned a nursery school on the grounds of the new home. She opened the Hickory Dock Nursery School in 1947, and it became a very successful endeavor. The reputation of the Hickory Dock School spread in the local area, and, within a few years, the school was full of waddling toddlers. My mother went to Rutgers University at night for early childhood education while my father drove the children to and from their homes, while working for the Erie Lackawana Railway. From what I understand, it was a frenetic time of constant work but a fruitful time of growth, as the school brought in extra income to the family and afforded my parents the opportunity to build their American dream.

A Fire in Our Midst

By the time I was conceived in 1955, life in the Delio clan was settled into the suburban neighborhood of Lyndhurst. I was not a planned birth, as the family was nicely packaged with three children and a set of parents. When my mother was diagnosed as "pregnant" at the age of forty-three, a shock wave was felt around the house. Vincent had already joined the Air Force and Anne Marie had started nursing school at Holy Name Hospital in Teaneck, New Jersey. Richard was twelve years old, and at that ripe age the news of a new baby began to rock his privileged place as the youngest in the family.

We do not choose our families or our destinies. These foundational factors that form our lives are born in the stars or in the heavens or simply in the eternal mind of God. Why *this* family and not that one? Why *this* home and not that one? Why *this* gender and not that one? We simply have no choice in the poker game of genes. The dice are rolled, the union made, and our lives are conceived as tiny seeds of God's love expressed in unique and particular processes of life we call "human persons." And so, my life began in this Italian-American conglomerate of the Delio family.

My parents were not sure if the newborn would be a boy or girl. So they considered names like John, Marguerite, and Bernice until they came face to face with a tragic unexpected event. The name I received at birth, Denise, emerged out of the ashes of a dreadful fire. A few months before my August birth, my parents received a frantic phone call from their best friends, Pat and Della Giaconne. Pat and Della had three children, and the oldest, Denis, was a Boy Scout. One day Pat, Della, and the two younger children took a ride to visit some friends; Denis stayed home so he could complete his Boy Scout project, which was a new type of ant trap. As the story goes, the ant trap required a tunnel, so Denis carved out the tunnel in the earth and covered it with kerosene. He lit the kerosene tunnel but got too close to it and caught fire; in no time the fire was consuming his clothing. Since no one was home, he ran down the street frantically screaming for help. By the time a neighbor saw him, he was scorched with third-degree burns.

Pat and Della rushed home to find their son in the burn unit of the hospital. In the mid-fifties, burn units did not have the technology or medical therapies that are available today. Extensive third-degree burns usually resulted in death. Pat and Della called my parents to convey the news: Denis was in the hospital dying from third-degree burns. My parents rushed to see him in the hospital, and my mother was in her seventh month of pregnancy with me. Their hearts were deeply torn by Denis's suffering body. He was in terrible pain but conscious enough to see that my mother was expecting a baby. He looked at her with sorrowful eyes and asked, what will be the baby's name? My mother's heart was so moved that she replied, if it is boy, we shall name him Denis, and if it is a girl, we shall name her Denise. "In any event," she said, "we shall name the baby after you." My father agreed without hesitation. Denis died in the summer of 1955, and I was born and given a name that emerged out of a fire of destruction, a name that would establish a new life, beginning in Lyndhurst, New Jersey.

What is in a name? The prophet Isaiah wrote, "I have called you by name and you are mine" (Isaiah 43:1). I have called you by fire, I have called you by death, I have called you into a new life—Denise. Years later when I was doing my doctoral work in theology at Fordham University, I was introduced to the master of mystical theology, Denis the Areopagite, or Pseudo-Dionysius. I was immediately struck by the name "Denis"—the mysterious person who wrote the most exquisite words stretching into the mystery of the incomprehensible God. "Higher, higher," he wrote, "higher than the Trinity."[1] God is the name

---

1. Pseudo-Dionysius, "Mystical Theology," in *Pseudo-Dionysius: The Complete Works*, trans. Colm Luibhard (New York: Paulist Press, 1987), 135.

of absolute divine mystery beyond any speech or thought or movement. God's love is so tremendous, this mystical writer claimed, that God is like a sober drunk, falling over himself in the desire to share divine life.

God, the *eros* of divine love
God, *agape*, giving Godself away
God, *ek-static, standing outside Godself,* in the creation of the world
God, the volcanic eruption of divine *life.*

Because God's *eros* is cosmic, Dionysius claimed, the whole universe is drawn to God, who is always utterly transcendent. God is both hidden and revealed, and there is no access to the hidden God except by way of God manifested in creation. We long for God because God longs for us; God eternally desires to give Godself away in love so we can give ourselves in love; love always stands outside itself in the other. To be united to God we must "break through" the sensible world and pass beyond the human condition to move beyond knowing to unknowing, from knowledge to love. In his *De mystica theologia* Denis wrote: "As we plunge into that darkness which is beyond intellect, we shall find ourselves not simply running short of words but actually speechless and unknowing."[2]

I was given the name Denise—after Denis of the fire, Denis of the mystery of God, the name that reflects fire and divine love intertwined in the hidden chamber of the human heart. Fire can either burn and destroy or forge together and illuminate. The universe is created out of fire because the universe is created out of love. Eventually I would realize that my genes are not simply DNA molecules; they are forged from an incomprehensible mystery of fire and love.

Born to Run

I came into the world on a lazy Saturday morning around 11:00 a.m., which is still about the time I like to get up, when possible. It is not insignificant that the hospital where I was born, Columbus hospital in Newark, New Jersey, burned to the ground several years after my birth. Born with the mystical name of divine *eros*, Denise, I like to think that the outer fire of Denis Giaconne's life became a new inner fire, the fire

---

2. Pseudo-Dionysius, "Mystical Theology," 139.

of my life, and with no record of the room in which I was born—due to a fire—my life was set with the seal of God's love hidden in the mystery of Christ even before I took my first breath.

My eldest brother likes to recount how my father spoke of me as a newborn bundle of blessings—"a blessed event" he would say. My Sicilian grandmother quickly assessed my tiny feet and said, "She will be tall and special" (I think most Italian grandmothers say this). Judging from early photos, my mother hovered over me, and my father doted on me. I was born into an academic milieu, so to speak, since my parents ran the Hickory Dock Nursery School. One of my earliest memories is playing pegs on the floor at the age of two. My father would clear out all the children so that I could play unimpeded by noise or disruption. He did the same for me at the playground. He would shoo away all the children so that I could go down the sliding pond at my leisure without interruption. The gift of solitude was made possible by a set of devoted parents.

I was an adorable dumpling of a baby with dark locks of hair and huge brown eyes—cute enough to win a baby contest at the age of two. In a last minute decision, my mother decided to enter me into a baby contest at Lake Neepaulin in Sussex, New Jersey, where my parents had a summer home. The outfit I wore belonged to another kid who got sick right before the contest; luckily my baby fat could squeeze into the ruffled dress. I have vague memories of waddling around a large room with twenty-seven other toddlers but no recollection of actually winning the contest. Apparently, it was a big deal, and the win came with a large trophy and write-up in the local paper. My mother hid the trophy and news article for years, concerned that I would become vain or pompous if I were to discover my baby beauty pageant success.

My mother had some strange ideas, not inimical to the Sicilian mindset, in which superstition and evil spirits governed the same space as the infant Jesus and the rosary. When I was going through my baby album one day, I noticed a lot of articles on caring for a Down syndrome child. Apparently, my parents were told of the risks of mid-life pregnancy, and one of the risks was Down syndrome. My mother was all set to care for me as a Down syndrome child and later worked as a nurse in a state-run home for mentally disabled women who, in those days, were labeled "retarded." For a number of years, Mom would bring home "one of the girls" to clean the house, but really it was to give her a day out. She would prepare a nice lunch, and, if I was home, we would sit together at the table and have a community meal. Mom had a real sense of justice and human dignity, and I think these meal gatherings with the women of North Jersey Training School instilled in me a sense of human dignity as well. Years later I volunteered at a L'Arche community in Washington, DC, and loved it. Jean Vanier, the founder of L'Arche, felt the same way as my mother, to bring those left outside community into community and to live with them as a sister or brother because, in truth, we are all fragile and broken in some way and thus we are all one in the family of life.

Imprinting is a phenomenon described as a pattern or set of behaviors established in the first hours of life between parent and child, usually between a single parent and child. However, I think I had the rare fortune of a dual parental imprint. From my father I received a contemplative spirit coupled with a sense of humor; from my mother I received a philosophical mind with a sense of mystery. In fact, I had a sense of divine mystery very early in my life. I remember telling my mother at the age of three that I wanted to be a nun, although I am not sure why. I cannot say that it was an encounter with nuns that influenced me, since my mother's oldest sister, Teresa, became a nun and left the convent to marry a divorced man and later divorced him. I am sure she was a good woman, but every time I visited her she scared me, probably because she was a hairdresser who always had a pair of scissors in her hand. However, I do recall telling my third-grade teacher, Sister Francis, who was the principal of our Franciscan grammar school in Totowa, New Jersey, that I wanted to be a nun when I grew up. I remember standing before her desk one day while Sister Francis was immersed in a book. She looked up and gazed at me with her lively blue eyes cloistered behind her black rimmed glasses and said something like, "that is wonderful Denise. I will pray you become a nun." I am not sure what prompted me to blurt out my vocational plans but having Sister Francis's approval gave me peace of heart, and I returned to my seat and stuffed my dark blue-plaid jumper into the wood-framed desk.

Entangled with the Mystics

Modern physics has impelled me to think in new ways about the communion of the saints as transformed lives quantumly entangled with us. Quantum entanglement is that strange phenomenon of physics (which Einstein reluctantly accepted) which says that interacted particles are forever mutually and reciprocally interacting, even if separated at vast distances. Scientists call this phenomenon "spooky action at a distance." Quantum entanglement has caused me to ponder if I have been entangled with Denis the mystic (Pseudo-Dionysius) from birth. I say this because I had a real sense of God as a child, a divine presence that was so close to me that I was happy just to sit and talk to God; solitude was my delight. In fact, I talked to God on a regular basis and enjoyed being in my own inner cell. I loved being alone, and my parents worried that I would be socially awkward, maybe even turn into a sociopath. To prevent such a tragedy they allowed me to have a dog. When we moved to Totowa, New Jersey, I got a cute dog, a basset-hound with beagle ears, and named him Shakespeare because he often sat with me while I was writing poetry (which I did a lot). Shakespeare was my best buddy, and we did everything together, including sleeping in the same room, where he had his own twin bed. Besides Shakespeare, I had my spiritual friends, Saints Peter and Paul. I cannot tell you how or why Peter and Paul came in my little life, but they appeared in my mind one day and I began to consult them on every matter. This spiritual friendship lasted for several years.

I was a deeply impressionable child, and we were New Jersey cradle Catholics, attending the 9:00 a.m. Mass every Sunday and the Saint Anthony of Padua devotion every Tuesday in Patterson, New Jersey. By the age of six years old I had memorized all the Mass parts in Latin and would recite them along with the priest. For a number of years, every time the priest said "Deus ibi est" I thought he was saying "Deus CBS" and wondered why he was talking about television. The Saint Anthony devotion took place in a small, crowded chapel where women with chapel veils and rosaries faithfully knelt every Tuesday before a life-size statue of St. Anthony surrounded by a fog of smoke from the overzealous priest frenetically swinging the censor, as if to create a smoke screen between himself and the women surrounding him. I was intrigued by this mysterious gathering of devotees to Saint Anthony whose prayers rose up to God in a dark and smoke-filled room of incessant intercessory prayers—like bees wildly buzzing on a summer evening. Only later did I realize that Saint Anthony was a Franciscan priest.

Driven by Fame

Despite my love of solitude, I was ambitious to become famous and or to do something outstanding in life. Life in those days was not deluged with computer information; rather, creativity and imagination took place usually outdoors in the simplicity of nature. I remember one day digging for China with Ellen Farkash and Patty Mancuso in the backyard of Patty Mancuso's house. I recall how real and exciting that experience was because I truly believed that if we dug deep enough, we would reach China and get a ride in a Chinese cart. I can still see myself frantically running home (I was scared Ellen and Patty would reach China before I returned) and asking my father for money. He kindly gave me fifty cents. I returned to the scene with my fifty cents, but by then Ellen and Patty had struck water.

One day I got this brilliant idea to sell the children's books from the Hickory Dock Nursery School to my Totowa neighbors. I got the other "Denise" in the neighborhood, Denise DuBosh, to load the books onto my four-wheel red wagon, and we began our door-to-door sales pitch. By late afternoon we managed to sell almost all the books in the cart. When my mother discovered that her books had been sold, she was livid. A livid Sicilian mother is not a pretty sight. At that point she became a live torpedo missile, and I hid in a closet. When my father got home from work, I hid behind him. It was my Brooklyn Neapolitan father who often mitigated the severe temper of my Sicilian mother.

I dreamed of fame—winning a Nobel Prize or the Olympics or both. I was simply not satisfied with being Denise from the Italian-American suburban neighborhood of Totowa, New Jersey. I am not sure if it was due to being raised as an only child, since my brothers and sister were out of the house by the time I was five years old, or that both parents worked full-time and were already in their early fifties by the age of seven years old. My parents were always so much older than everyone else's parents (evidenced by their grey hair), and I lived with a constant fear that they would die before I was ten years old. When I was about eleven years old I mustered the courage to face my parents in truth, since every year my mother insisted she was thirty-nine. "How many times can you be thirty-nine?" I thought to myself. So one day I sat down with my mother at the kitchen table and looked her straight in the eye with my burning question: "Mom, exactly how old are you?" "Do you really want to know?" she replied. "Yes," I said. "I want to know the truth." "Well," she said, "I am fifty-five years old." When I heard the number "fifty-five" I thought she would die at that moment and that I would be orphaned by next week.

The fiery name "Denise" meant that I would always live between life and death. One day I got on a bicycle that Ellen Farkash's mom gave to me. It was an old bike that looked like it should have been in the dumpster, but I imagined myself to be a contender for the Tour de France. I got this bright idea that I would practice bike riding to win the race. This was a period of time right around the World's Fair in 1965, which was held in New York, and which I had the good fortune to attend with my parents, who took me on rides, into the pavilions, and ate cotton candy with me. When I saw something I liked or wanted, I fixed my attention on it. At the World's Fair, it was a pair of goggles. "Why do you want *those*?" my mother asked. "Because I DO," I insisted. If my mother said "no," I would rebel and not budge from my position—a recalcitrant, if not incorrigible child. The goggles were in my hand by the time we left the World's Fair and I put them on the next day, as if riding alongside Lance Armstrong. However, I did not have a helmet, since bike riding in the neighborhood was considered play and not a major sports event. I started to ride at top speed, with my goggles firmly in place and my attention firmly fixed on the road ahead. I am not sure how fast I was going, but the only thing I remember is that in a moment without notice, the bicycle split in two. Instantly, I was thrown to the curb and was unconscious. A neighbor by the name of Mrs. Gebbia saw me lying by the side of the road and quickly called my mother, who ran down the street, carried me home, and called a doctor. I awoke several hours later, groggy and confused, with a slight concussion. This was to be the first of several head injuries.

My mother often said that my head injuries made me smart because they "jostled my brain" (her words not mine). I am not sure if this is really true, but I later noticed that I had a minor form of dyslexia insofar as I did not have a good sense of spatial relationships, causing me at times to confuse right and left, up and down. The irony is that I loved relationships; I saw the world in relationships. In fact, mathematics was one of my strong suits. When our eighth-grade class took a battery of aptitude tests, I scored in the ninety-ninth percentile in mathematics and in the ninety-seventh percentile in literature and music. My lowest score was in mechanical aptitude, which is why I could take things apart, like the Mr. Machine toy I got for Christmas one year, but could not put back together. My Italian-American parents were not focused on aptitude test scores or high achievement, however; their aims were much more modified, get a college education and a good job.

The Matrix of Attention

School was fine, but I spent a lot of time in the classroom seeking attention in one way or another. In the fourth grade, I was seated in the back of the room due to the fact that I was taller than most of other girls in the class. When the teacher, Mrs. Santangelo, announced that front row seats belonged to the smaller students and those who needed glasses, I got the bright idea that needing glasses would be my ticket to the front row. I convinced my parents to take me to the eye doctor who declared that I had 20/20 vision. Disillusioned with the result (since it would mean moving to the back of the class again) I decided to steal my mother's glasses. Now my mother, like myself, had a thin, narrow face, but she wore a pair of big, ugly, black-framed glasses for reading. The glasses were large enough in diameter to engulf her cheeks. These are the glasses I took from her bag and wore in my fourth-grade class for almost a week. Mrs. Santangelo was suspect of my new glasses since they were entirely too large for my tiny face, and it looked like I was wearing two black-framed window panes on my face. Every day my mother would complain that she could not find her glasses anywhere.

About four days into my new glasses, there was a knock on our classroom door. Mrs. Santangelo opened it to see my tiny Sicilian mother standing there like an oil fire because she realized that I took her glasses. I was stunned to see my mother standing on the threshold of our classroom and thought I would melt into the wood of my seat.

I was called out of class and had to return my oversized, black-framed, window-paned glasses to my mother on the spot. I was mortified and wished that, like Samantha on *Bewitched,* I could wiggle my nose and disappear—a moment of sheer humility and embarrassment. Lesson learned.

In the fifth grade, I was smitten by the adorable, blond-hair, blue-eyed Robert O'Neil. Because Robert broke his right arm, he was forced to do his schoolwork with his left hand. I sat next to Robert in class and to win his attention, I switched hands and wrote all my notes and even did my artwork with my left hand for the entire fifth grade year. One day he noticed me writing slowly with my left hand and said something like, "I didn't know you were a lefty." I smiled and said, "Oh yes, I am a left-hander like you!" To this day I cannot believe that I forced myself to be ambidextrous to win the attention of Robert O'Neil and actually got an "A" for my artwork done with my nondominant hand. From that moment on, I realized that I could do anything if I set my mind to it.

At home my life was lived in the solitude of the lower level of our split-level home or in the backyard. My father worked hard to provide for our family and to ensure that we could live the American dream life in suburban New Jersey. He worked the evening shift for the railroad every Friday night; on Sunday morning my parents and I would get in the car and head to the 9:00 a.m. Mass. My mother had a habit of being perpetually late, almost as if to intentionally annoy my father, who hated to be late for anything. After Mass, Dad would make a delicious scrambled egg breakfast with fresh rolls from the bakery. Usually on Sunday afternoon, the relatives from Queens and Brooklyn would visit or we would go to visit them. One of the best memories of my father was the day he took me to Coney Island in New York. It was a place where he and my mother went on dates, and the good memories of Coney Island were deep within him. We boarded the train in New Jersey, and the first thing we did when we got to Coney was to eat a Nathan's hot dog, which was superb. The fast and furious rides were our main attraction, and I can still hear my father and me screaming with delight on the bobsled ride, as we rounded the corners at top speed.

My parents bought me a piano when I was ten, and I fell in love with music. I took piano lessons from a Montclair College music major by the name of Barbara Smith and dreamed of being a concert pianist one day. While I had a talent for music, my talent depended on a very good, finely-tuned ear—almost perfect pitch. I could play virtually anything by ear if I heard it a few times. I learned to play piano by sight reading sheets of music, but I would often add notes or delete them, depending on my mood and how the sounds of the keys struck me. My unwillingness to properly read music, especially the classics like Bach, Beethoven, or Mozart, caused my teacher to issue the same warnings every week: pay attention to the notes! After six years, I relinquished piano lessons but continued to play on a regular basis and would spend hours at the piano in my imaginary world of the concert auditorium. My father loved music and was a gifted singer. Usually on a Saturday afternoon, he would come to the "piano room," sit in his tan leather recliner with his feet up, smoke his favorite cigar, and listen to me play my renditions of Bach, Mozart, as well as popular music. Always a gentle soul, he would say, "That was wonderful, Denise!"

My mother, the intellectual, made sure that I read books and not squander my time in mere play. In fact, she read me stories each night up until the age of three and four. I had a very good memory, and after one or two rounds of the same book, I could repeat the passages to her. She was the one who engaged me in ideas by asking big questions, always probing and wanting to know what I was thinking. "What is God?" she would ask? Or "What is heaven?" She was an amazing woman on many levels—a poet, philosopher, writer of children's books, nurse, business manager, real estate investor, and stock analyst. Her influence was felt throughout the family like an electromagnetic field. Tiny in stature but powerful in voice, she was a feminist before the term was coined. She lobbied for equal rights and social justice; wrote letters to business managers, congressmen, and whoever held the strings of power when power was being used unjustly. Her ability to write was both a gift and a curse. She could wield words like weapons and surgically slice open a human heart with her words without ever realizing the extent of the damage she inflicted. Her power of words came from a deep, intense, unresolved inner life, being raised in poverty and neglect, having a profound need to express what could not be fully expressed. She was a brilliant woman who was frustrated in her ambitions but daunting in her intellect.

In light of my father's gentle spirit, ours was a matriarchal family, and Mom had a significant influence on the shape of the family. For one, education was a number-one priority, and she made sure that every child achieved a college education, even if it meant—in Vincent's case—to intervene with the dean or find him another school. Anne Marie went to nursing school, although it is not clear if she chose this profession or if Mom convinced her it was the best profession for a young woman; she later got a college degree in business. Richard graduated from Fairfield University and became a CPA in a large corporation. In an age when a high-school diploma was still seen as acceptable for employment, it was significant that the first three children (the "first family") all went to college; the boys went on to receive graduate degrees in their respective fields of sociology and business. The grandchildren, too, were influenced by my Sicilian, intellectual mother. All six grandchildren completed college, and five out of the six went on to graduate school. Two of the five hold doctorates in their respective fields of philosophy and theology.

And then there is me. For about the first quarter of my life, I had no real relation to my siblings. They would come to visit Mom and Dad and would sit around the table smoking cigarettes and talking about business matters, usually stocks. I remember sitting under the table with Shakespeare's head on my lap, listening to the conversations on housing, stocks, and politics and wondering if anyone was missing me. My sister Anne Marie, who was sixteen years older, was like a second mother, but Vincent and Richard were caught up in the tumult of the sixties and the emerging postmodern milieu. Vincent had his own struggles of self-doubt and self-worth, while Richard felt neglected and often recounted how he had to pay for his own college education by working on weekends and in the summers. I truly am not sure the extent of their feelings, but I do know that when they returned home to visit, my brothers complained that my parents gave me too much (and that they never received half as much!). They were probably right, but I was always happy to see them leave by Sunday afternoon so that my solitary life with Shakespeare and Bach could resume a normal pattern. Fortunately, time and distance changed the threads of resentment and turned them into bonds of love, as life unfolded with the death of my father, then Vincent's second son, and eventually my mother. We do not know as a child what will emerge as an adult, as our tree of life reaches toward the sky.

2

No Angel Am I

WE MOVED TO FAIRFIELD, New Jersey, when I entered middle school, and it was both a curse and a blessing. For one, most of the kids in middle school knew each other from grammar school, and I had a hard time making friends. After school I would return home to have a cup of tea with my mother, whose nurse's job ended at three o'clock in the afternoon. I would then retire to my bedroom, close the door, and write poetry while listening to Cat Stevens sing "Where do the children play?" or Carole King soulfully sing her "Tapestry" of rich and royal hues. I would lose myself in fields of poetic words, and when the words were spent, I would go downstairs, sit at the piano, and play popular tunes, as if I might be preparing for an upcoming concert. My dog, Shakespeare, faithfully accompanied me as a devoted companion, and it never occurred to me that most of my clothes were covered with his hair. My father complained incessantly, however, about the fur on his clothes, and eventually we had to give Shakespeare away. It was a heart-wrenching decision, but shortly after we welcomed into our home a beautiful black poodle by the name of Misty, who became my mother's faithful companion.

The Triumph of Goodness

When I wasn't writing poetry or playing music, I was involved in sports and outdoor activities. In the winter I went ice skating at the local rink around the corner, and in the summer I went swimming, usually at my Aunt Lena's pool in nearby Lincoln Park. One year, when I was in seventh grade, I joined the local pool in Fairfield, but it was here that I encountered a clique of Jersey girls that awakened me for the first time to human malice. They were tough and mean-spirited girls. Anything I tried to do to win their approval was met with increasing meanness. They wanted me to pay a price to belong to their clique, and at first I felt I had no other choice but to go along and be demeaned by their demands. One humiliating summer at the pool I was made to dress in heels and a two-piece bathing suit with a boa around my neck; the clique wanted me to parade around the pool and wave to the sunbathers. The sneers and chuckles from the clique were intolerable, and I was deeply humiliated. It was my first awakening to human cruelty and the cavity of darkness that can lurk in the human heart. I did nothing to merit their meanness other than wanting to be their friend; yet their cruelty continued unabated. It is hard to say what exactly provoked their malice, but eventually I could not tolerate it, so I stopped going to the pool.

Loneliness settled in like a blanket over my heart, and I found myself withdrawing into myself and talking more to God. It was God's nearness that gave me a feeling of protection in the face of the Jersey bullies. By eighth grade I decided I would not be bullied and would not be part of any Jersey-girl clique. I would be myself and find my own way—and so I did. My parents were concerned, however, that I did not have a lot of friends and approached me one day with the opportunity to attend an all-girls boarding school in Sloatsburg, New York, about an hour from where we lived. The idea of getting away from the Fairfield crowd was very enticing, and I jumped at the opportunity to enroll at Saint Mary's Villa Academy in Sloatsburg, New York, in the fall of 1969.

Saint Mary's Villa Academy was an all-girls boarding school run by the Sister Servants of Mary Immaculate, a Ukrainian Byzantine Rite Order with an interesting origin, founded by a young woman from Lviv, Ukraine, by the name of Michaelina Hordashevska. After the rise of communism, the sisters' homes and institutions were seized, and the Order was forced to go "underground." With the downfall of communism the sisters branched out beyond Ukraine and reestablished their homes and mission work, including their ministry of education at St. Mary's Villa in 1943.

I never heard of Ukraine before I went to high school (actually, I did not know there were other cultures besides the Italo-American culture of New Jersey and New York), but from the moment we enrolled at

St. Mary's we were inculcated in Ukrainian language and culture. I eventually learned that the Ukrainian Catholic Church is the second largest jurisdiction after the Roman Catholic Church and has followed the spread of the Ukrainian diaspora in the United States and Canada.

The Trouble with Angels

My parents learned of this school through my sisters' friends, Lois and Jean Farabough, who graduated from St. Mary's in the 1950s. From the moment I arrived at St. Mary's I felt at home. The school was a beautiful stone mansion set on a forty-acre estate that was built around the turn of the century in 1900 for William Pierson Hamilton, the great-grandson of one of the founding fathers of the United States, Alexander Hamilton. His wife was Juliet Pierpont Morgan, the daughter of the financier J. Pierpont Morgan. The home was originally part of the two-thousand-acre Table Rock estate and was known as Table Rock Villa. With fifty-two rooms lined with inlaid wood carvings, elaborate lintels, and deep reddish-brown oak paneling, the magnificent stone school was gorgeous with a large homey feel and could be used as a movie setting for an American version of the *Sound of Music* or the 1966 movie *The Trouble with Angels*, which I must admit was the film version of my life. The *Trouble with Angels* recounts the story of a rebellious teenager, Mary (played by Hayley Mills), and her friend Rachel. The young women went through their high-school years pulling pranks on the sisters and repeatedly getting into trouble. Eventually the lead culprit (Mills) was inspired by the sisters' lives and eventually joined the Order. While my story did not quite follow so smoothly, the movie made an indelible impression on me, and I am sure it was in the back of my mind as I began my four mischievous years of high school.

Most of the girls who boarded at the school came from New York City or one of the surrounding boroughs of New York; only a few of us came from New Jersey. I quickly made friends with Vicky Formica, whose first-generation Italian family lived in the Bay Ridge section of Brooklyn, not too far from my grandmother's house. Vicky was free-spirited and adventurous. She was of average height, twiggy thin, and with straight, waist-length brown hair, and her temperament was such that she always had a boyfriend on the docket. From the moment our freshmen year of high school began, I knew Vicky would be a good friend. We were both rule testers and boundary crossers, and the extent of our shenanigans knew no limits. We tried everything from leading harrowing expeditions down the mountain to Shepherd's Lake, which was about a mile away, sometimes taking food from the kitchen and (audaciously) charging our classmates for nourishment on the journey. When we were not running lake tours, we would do things like turn all the religious statues in the school backward, rearrange the card catalogue in the library, put starch in the nuns' laundry, or dress up as Sonny and Cher.

Our study halls were usually monitored by one of the nuns, and in our sophomore year we had an eccentric elderly nun by the name of Sister Lenore as our monitor. Apparently Sister Lenore was from the Midwest and sent on assignment to a school in the East. However, she took the wrong bus and wound up at our school; luckily, St. Mary's needed a teacher and hired her. Vicky and I sauntered into Sister Lenore's study hall one evening chomping on bubble gum; I was swinging a yo-yo. Vicky was dressed in a two-piece bathing suit top, jeans, and a knit vest, and I had on an army jacket, jeans, and a mustache. The students were laughing uncontrollably while Sister was completely oblivious to the scene. The cackling eventually woke her from her concentrated work, and she cleared her throat with a stern "Ahem!" She jumped out of her chair and pointed a long finger at us, showing us the way to the door and yelling, "To the principal's office—*now!*"

Despite the fact that I could form logical arguments and defend my position, I played so many pranks in high school it is a wonder I graduated. We played pranks during class (for example, putting dead beetles and worms on a student's head while taking notes), after class (short-sheeting beds and oiling doorknobs with Vaseline), and in the evening (séances, smoking rings, and the classic pillow fight). It was the smoking ring that almost got me expelled. Vicky and I hooked up with another room of girls and decided to start a séance club. It was a corner room, and the séances were a good cover-up for gathering on the fire escape and smoking cigarettes. Someone reported us, and the hammer came down hard. I was called to the principal's office on the red carpet one evening, and I knew I was in trouble. A sophomore never went on the red carpet unless the matter was critical, and certainly no one met with the principal in the evening unless it was urgent. But there I was in my sophomore year, standing before the benevolent principal, Sister David, and the stern disciplinarian, Sister Roseanne. I got a full lecture on the potential of fire with fifty-two rooms of oak-paneled walls and hand-carved lintels. I remember Sister David saying that she was going through menopause, and I was making life ever the more difficult for her. I did not know what menopause was at the time, but I assured her of my prayers and support. The sisters, in turn, did not quite know what to do with me. I happened to be in the top of my class (surprisingly), and they did not want to expel me. So they called my parents to tell them of the incident and removed me from the honor roll that semester.

Holy Terror

I loved St. Mary's Villa; it was the place where I began to develop as a person. Every morning we rose in the dormitory, dressed in silence in our knee-length blue uniforms, put on our blue socks and Oxford shoes, and lined up with our chapel veils in hand to process into the Byzantine Rite chapel for 6:00 a.m. Mass in Old Slavonic. In the warm weather, we wore a mint-green one-piece dress that looked like a prison outfit. One time a group of us went to the shopping mall in our mint-green spring dresses and frightened the public because we looked like a prison gang out for the day.

My parents claimed that they did not know St. Mary's was Eastern Rite until much later on—nor did it make a significant difference to them, or to me as well. In fact, I fell in love with the Byzantine Rite. The ancient Slavonic chants, the chapel filled with icons, the iconostasis separating the place of the Holy of Holies from the faithful, all made the liturgy mystical and transcendent. To this day, Byzantine churches are beautifully adorned with icons. Leavened bread is used for the consecration of the body of Christ in the liturgy (not called the "Mass" in Eastern rites), which is either the Liturgy of St. John Chrysostom or that of St. Basil the Great. Communion is received under both species (bread and wine) and administered by the priest from a spoon. Scripture plays a large role in Byzantine worship. The entire psalter is read each week and twice weekly during Great Lent. Traditionally, the congregation stands throughout the whole service but are very active in their worship, making frequent bows and prostrations. I think this is what I loved about the Byzantine liturgy; God was worshiped as transcendent mystery, and we were part of the mystery through the repetition of making the sign of the cross (which is right to left or east to west, rather than the Roman Rite's west to east), and bowing low throughout the liturgy, singing virtually every response according to the canons of the day. Byzantine chants are ancient in origin and are marked by tones that are foreign to the modern, Western ear. When my eldest brother once attended a Byzantine Rite liturgy he said, "That was the worst singing I have ever heard!" "Well," I said, "that's because it was not singing but liturgical chant." He remained unconvinced.

While I made a career of pranks at St. Mary's, or perhaps developing my darker, creative side, I was inwardly drawn to God. I found myself going to the chapel during the day just to sit and bask in the awesome mystery of God conveyed by the beautiful icons. Icons are divine images written out of sacred space. While the Westerner may look at an icon as a painting, it is in fact a form of sacred writing. The word *icon* derives from the Greek *eikon,* which is variously translated as "image," "likeness," or "representation," and is one of the earliest and most distinctive elements of Byzantine spirituality. Used in worship, icons are not intended as realistic portraits but rather as windows linking earthly and heavenly realities. Icons are designed for devotional purposes and to help bridge the gap between divinity and humanity. The aim of the icon painter is to create a "window into the spiritual world" rather than a "window into the material world." Perhaps it was living in an environment of icons and spiritual realities that attracted me to the mystical depths of the liturgy, where God was praised as the "Holy and Mighty One," or perhaps it was simply living in an environment where transcendence was part of the daily milieu that impelled me to linger in the chapel.

Although I was inspired and illumined by icons and participation in the Liturgy of John Chrysostom, my prankster high-school career did not single me out as a potential vocation to religious life. Quite the contrary. Though the sisters liked me, I'm sure they had no holy aspirations for my future; neither did I have such aspirations for myself. The typical question asked to a fourteen- or fifteen-year-old, "What do you want to be?" met my response of "I want to be a doctor." I did want to be a medical doctor so that I could find a cure for a rare disease, or so that I would not have to become a nurse like my mother and sister. But while I was driven to pursue a career (part of the American dream life), the truth is that I just wanted to have fun, play music, and never work too hard.

I started playing guitar in high school (thanks to the influence of Joni Mitchell) and considered a career as a coffee house singer in the East Village, where Bob Dylan played. My full-time occupation was teasing people and seeing how much I could get away with; I delighted in the fact that I could talk my way into and out of trouble. Given another set of circumstances I probably would have wound up in a gang. But the divine threads of love were deeply entangled with my heart; and while I would push the limits of the impossible, I never crossed the limits of danger. My teachers applauded me for being smart but were annoyed by my constant need to challenge the boundaries of civility in the classroom, dining hall, or dormitory.

During one of my many pranks I knocked over a wooden desk while leaning back in my chair shooting spitballs during class, causing a booming sound like a gun. The school was promptly evacuated, and I marched out with my classmates, never letting on that I was the culprit. I was a borderline delinquent and not a potential vocation to religious life.

I got to my senior year virtually unscathed by several near-expulsion experiences and enjoyed the status of class president while holding the rank of second in my class. I am not sure how I arrived at this rank since I never took a page of notes (at least as far as I can remember) in my four years of high school. One time, I actually got a zero on an English quiz that was a simple conjugation of the verb *to be*. I must have been mentally absent when the verbs were explained because my paper was returned with a big "goose egg," as our English teacher, Sister Jonathan, explained: a big, fat zero. I spent a lot of time in our geometry class trying to upset Sister Dorothy Ann, a high-strung, tense woman who looked like she could crack at any moment. One time I tested her patience to the point where she slammed the chalkboard ledger, splitting it in two, the pieces falling to the ground. I started laughing, and she proceeded to throw the chalk at me. She was prepared to give me a "C" for the course until I scored the second highest on the Regents exam in geometry. She reluctantly gave me an A- grade, and I graciously thanked her.

Mary Donworth, my compatriot from Nutley, New Jersey, was the number one student in our class, highly motivated, diligent in her work, and perfectly clear in her responses. Her class work reflected her entire demeanor: sharp, poised, and perfectly balanced. Even her long, brown, waist-length straight hair was neatly combed each day, while my black head of curls flew about my head and sometimes in a black ball that looked like a white Jersey-fro. If hair is a reflection of character, mine was a volcanic explosion while Mary's was a country road in Kansas, straight and flat. I spent a good deal of time in our honors study hall trying to mess up Mary's hair—even mess up Mary's controlled demeanor. Once I actually got into a fist fight with her over a Pysanki, a decorated Easter egg with intricate designs and colors, part of the Ukrainian culture (did I tell you the sisters were Ukrainian?) When the principal, Sister Jonathan, stormed into the library and sternly reprimanded us, Mary's face went ashen. We both got into trouble and were sent upstairs to join the rest of the class, who were diligently completing their homework.

One weekend five of us, including Mary, had to stay at school and clean the school from top to bottom, mostly on our knees. The crime was a high-spirited pillow fight that caused Vicky to scream after lights were out. Our French teacher, Sister Marion, was proctor that evening; although she was stooped and a bit deaf, she heard the screams and charged into our room, sending us immediately to Sister Superior. Because the superior was called out of her bedroom, she was livid. She stood outside the nuns' cloister area in her black veil and bathrobe. As we (gingerly) approached, I could see steam blowing out from under her veil. I started to talk, and she cut me off with a stern reprimand. "For every word you utter," she said, "you will have a closed weekend," that is, a weekend at school. We accepted our punishment for the crime and stayed that weekend to clean the entire school, top to bottom. I wound up cleaning the cracks of the wooden floors that covered the large rooms of the grand estate with a toothbrush. To lighten the burden of our punishment, the girls decided to iron my hair. However, the iron job just made my black curly globe of hair look worse, so they decided to wrap my hair in soda cans, like giant hair rollers, and I wound up with a Shirley Temple look that just wasn't me.

Training for God

The sisters who ran our school were a hard-working and no-nonsense group who embodied the Eastern European values of ruggedness, commitment, perseverance, and common sense. They were community oriented, kind, and, when not reprimanding us, fun. In my junior year, the sisters decided to open the novitiate (the boot camp for "wannabe" nuns) on the grounds of St. Mary's Villa. Part of the Hamilton estate had a large horse stable, about a third of a mile down the road from the main house. The estate was entered by a half-mile-long, tree-lined driveway that gently curved around and ascended into the open space of the Villa. The renovated horse stable was known as Cotswald, and it was the first turn off the ascending driveway. After the renovations, Cotswald became a beautiful Tudor-style home with wooden beams throughout the house and some of the original wood from the stable as supporting walls. In the early seventies it became home to the sisters-in-training, known as postulants and novices. I had no idea of what constituted a postulant or novice, but at fifteen years old, I thought it was kind of weird that these young women wanted to confine themselves to a convent for life. They looked pale faced and downcast, as they piously lined up for communion each morning in their long, blue polyester one-piece dresses, their eyes lowered and their arms folded over their chest, ready to receive the sacred Body of Christ. They were curious to me, and I was curious about them; but my curiosity went no further than the doors of my soul.

In my senior year, a new sister was sent to the school as prefect of the girls (the "rule-keeper") and home economics teacher. Sister Helena was young and charming. She took a liking to me precisely because I was a disaster in home economics, with my burnt cooking and oversized sewing disasters. One time I made an outfit for my six-month-old nephew that could fit a two-year-old toddler. Rather than reprimanding me on my mistakes, she often laughed at them in a gentle and jolly way. I grew fond of her and took up her challenge to become a Ukrainian dancer. Now mind you, I was a tall, chunky girl who liked pizza and hamburgers, so training as a Ukrainian dancer was a real effort. But I trained hard and learned to do the energetic, fast-paced folk dance and was asked to do the boys dance, which required a lot of leaps, jumps, flips, and headstands. I loved it but was exhausted after every performance, as my leg muscles would be completely taut.

It was after one of the dance practices in my senior year that Ana Maria Guerrero and I decided to try the bicycle built for two that had been sitting in the basement. Vicky was afraid to get on the bike, but Ana Maria and I were fearless. One fall afternoon we took the bike for a spin down the long Villa estate driveway. I was the first rider, and Ana Maria was the second rider—no helmets of course and no goggles! It was an exhilarating ride, with the leaves of the November trees gently falling around us. I could still see us giggling and screaming, as we flew down the driveway, as if on a roller coaster. Just as we were nearing the driveway to Cotswald, I tried to slow the speed only to realize the bike had no brakes. I was the lead driver and had to make a quick decision, either head toward the main road and get hit by a car or quickly turn off the driveway into the woods. I chose the latter, hoping that we would land in brush. Instead, I managed to crash the bike straight into a tree. We were both stunned, literally, briefly unconscious, and covered in leaves. I remember looking up and seeing Sister Helena and Vicky standing over us—Sister Helena was laughing, while Vicky yelled out in her Brooklyn accent, "O my gawd!" This was my second major head injury, and this time the entire left side of my face was swollen, along with a black eye and a crooked nose. It was unclear if my nose was broken or not, so the sisters called my father, who promptly had to leave work in Hoboken, New Jersey, drive to Sloatsburg, New York, and take me to the doctor in Lyndhurst, New Jersey. He never complained. The elderly doctor in Lyndhurst, Dr. Sims, looked in worse shape than me, so I felt much better when he declared that nothing was broken, but my nose was seriously bruised.

Senior year of high school was a mixed blessing. On the one hand, the liberation into adulthood was just around the corner, and, on the other hand, the idea of going to college was both alluring and frightening. The loss of good friends and classmates—really soul mates—was hard to think about, however. I had to make a decision as to which college I would attend, and my choices were narrowed from the beginning by my parents' insistence that I had to go to a Catholic college. Embedded in the Jersey milieu (having emigrated from Brooklyn), my worldview was limited to the tristate area. I did not want to live at home, so I immediately ruled out Seton Hall University and Caldwell College. Since my operative geography did not extend beyond the borders of Pennsylvania, considering a college in the Midwest or on the West Coast was unthinkable. For all practical purposes, I did not realize that the Midwest or West Coast actually existed, in the same way that I thought meat came in cellophane packages at the A&P supermarket. Beyond the New Jersey/New York border there was simply a blank "there-ness."

I decided to apply to the college where my roommate, Marilyn Mitchell, was attending. Marilyn was full of life, the daughter of a divorced taxi cab driver in New York City; she had a quick wit and loved basketball. Marilyn was going to Allentown College of St. Francis de Sales in Center Valley, Pennsylvania, so I decided to apply there as well. I declared a major in biology/pre-med on the application form and, given no other real interests (except perhaps, to become a concert pianist or coffee house singer), I decided that this would be my future. I graduated salutatorian in my high school class with various awards: the four-year general excellence award (amazing), as well as awards in French and history. Not too surprisingly, Mary Donworth swept through all the awards, including excellence in science. I was disappointed but not surprised. Mary simply had a quiet brilliance. I had the honor to deliver the salutatorian address in Ukrainian and English, and my flawless Ukrainian evoked a hearty congratulations from the bishop who presided over the outdoor ceremony. As I walked away from the podium, thanking him for the accolades, I tripped over the cables that connected the sound system to the podium. When Mary got up to the give the valedictorian address, no one could hear her. I could see the principal, Sister Jonathan, flustered and fuming in the back row of sisters who were seated to the left of the podium. They had to scramble to find the workman, Jose, to reconnect the cables. Of course, I was chuckling to myself because it was a perfect ending to my "trouble-with-angels" career at St. Mary's Villa Academy.

The Fire of Love

There was something lurking deep within my heart; however, it rose to the top of my mind in a moment of silence and receded with the waves of my shenanigans. It especially rose to my attention every time I passed the junior classroom and saw the stitched banner of Carl Sandburg's poem hanging on the door: "Go alone and away from all books; go with your own heart into the storm of human hearts; and see if somewhere in that storm, there are bleeding hearts." Sandburg's poem spoke deeply to me. I wanted to go into the storm of bleeding hearts, but I had no idea what this meant or what a bleeding heart might look like; however, the lure was real. But then there was also the lure of dating.

In the early seventies, at least in my world, dating was strictly heterosexual. Although lesbian relationships were somewhat evident at our all-girls' boarding school, I had no idea what a lesbian was or that there could be other types of relationships than male–female. Life in the seventies was pretty much a straight line from home to school to marriage to family. Being a cradle Catholic from New Jersey with a Sicilian mother did not leave any opportunity to explore various options for relationships. Marriage was the bread and butter of family life. Religious life (becoming a consecrated nun or priest) was considered special, above the norm, a calling from God. I resented the straight-line option of marriage and thought religious life, evidenced by the novices at Mass each morning, looked rather deadly, even though religious life secretly brewed within me.

One Saturday in 1973 changed forever the direction of my life. Usually we returned to our family homes on the weekends, but one weekend in February I was invited to attend a dance at West Point Academy, which was about a twenty-minute drive from our school in Sloatsburg. The idea of meeting a cadet was alluring, and so I accepted the invitation and had to remain at the Villa from Friday to Sunday. On Friday evening, Sister Helena and I sat before the large fireplace in the Green parlor on the main floor. It was a cold evening, and the crackling fire created a warm glow that animated the spirit of our friendship and discussion. We were talking about giving our material things away, and I said that I would be happy to do so if the occasion arose. The next morning around 9:00 a.m. the fire alarm system went off with a loud piercing sound, blaring throughout the main house. It was to alert everyone that there was a fire raging in the vicinity. Cotswald had caught on fire, and it was burning to the ground. Fire engines rushed in from the various nearby stations, and there was a flurry of activity, because it was unclear whether or not the sisters were in the burning home. I remember running back and forth with Sister Helena to find the novices and postulants. Luckily, they got out in time before the fire spread; however, in the split decision to leave, they left behind everything they owned. Sister Helena asked if I would lend them some of my clothes, and I quickly gathered up shoes, socks, and sweaters to give to the sisters. It was such a chaotic day of fire and destruction that I almost forgot about the dance at West Point that evening.

By the time 5:00 p.m. rolled around, the last thing I wanted to do was go to the dance at West Point. I found myself washing my hair under the sink in the basement, exhausted and confused, but mindful of the time. Now, in this moment, *chronos* (sequential time) turned into *kairos* (interrupted time or a critical moment). I remember lifting my head out of the sink and drying my curls with a towel, when all of a sudden, I felt the power of God's love invade me, as if swallowing me up. It was as if everything inside me no longer belonged to me but to God. My heart had burst into a fire—the fire of Cotswald now became the fire in my heart, and I felt myself grasped by a power beyond my control. In that moment I knew I belonged entirely to God, and there was no way out. All of the prophets at that moment came to life in me: Jonah, Jeremiah, Isaiah, Hosea, Micah—they were all together in a flash of divine outpouring love. I was exhausted and confused and could only repeat Mary's *fiat voluntas tua*: "May your will be done!"

It was a profoundly incarnational moment, and, ever so briefly, I felt impregnated, so to speak, by the seed of God's love. I ran to find Sister Helena, who was in the sewing room sitting underneath a framed picture of Saint Thérèse of Lisieux. I was crying and could not find the words to convey the powerful experience of God that had seized my life just a few minutes ago. She looked at me with a big smile, almost as if she knew something that I did not. All I could to say to her was, "I belong to God." And she calmly replied, "I know." I went to the dance that evening and was matched with a tall, strapping West Point cadet. We danced throughout the evening, but my head and heart were not in the rhythm of the music. I was somewhere in a fire, and the fire was God. I could not wait until the evening ended. I returned to my dormitory room in the wonder and darkness of a religious vocation, and for the first time I began to really pray: "Who are you, O Lord, and who am I?"

The Cotswald fire broke out on February 3, the Feast of Saint Blaise, and from then on, my heart was sealed with a divine imprint that read, "You belong to me." However, I wanted my normal life back and tried to live in the levity of life as much as possible. I told no one of this event, except Sister Helena, who became my confident and spiritual director. Deep within me the waters of life had shifted, and the dry bones the prophet Ezekiel spoke of began to rise with a new spirit (see Ezek 37:1–14). I wrote poetry to express this deep inner birth of divine love, and the first words I wrote after the Cotswald fire were simply: "fire burns and so does love." Fire and love took on a whole new meaning for me, and I began to reflect on my life in terms of destruction and new birth, darkness and light. I was reminded of my namesake, Denis, the Boy Scout of fire; Denis, the mystic of divine love. Little did I know that these two symbols, the flame and the heart, would mark my journey of life.

A religious vocation is not like a job application or a personal assessment. It is an unmerited, pure gift of grace. It is a "call," because the grace of God awakens within unannounced, like a high-pitched alarm clock (at least in my experience), blaring when you least expect it. It is an invasion, an interruption if not outright intrusion of grace, and it does not allow you to go back to rest in your former life without either forgetting what you heard or responding to the gift. I vacillated each day between wanting to forget the call and wondering how to respond to the gift. The thought of being a nun scared me. Who would want to wear black Oxford shoes for the rest of her life? Or a long, polyester skirt? Or a black veil for that matter? The impending threat of looking pious for the rest of my life was frightening; yet, the deep inner presence of God drew me like an exotic aroma of spices. I lived between the inner world of God's alluring love and the outer world of adolescent changes. In this wavering life, I learned my first lesson: God is irresistible and unyielding in love. God has infinite patience; God is a jealous lover. God will pursue the soul relentlessly and never gives up because there is nothing to give up: "I have loved you with an everlasting love," the prophet Jeremiah wrote (Jer 31:3). From all eternity God loves *this* particular life in *this* particular way for reasons hidden in the inscrutable heart of God.

3

The Fire in My Heart

IT WAS SENIOR YEAR and the May prom was on the horizon. To ensure a date for the prom, I organized a dance with the nearby all-boys school, Don Bosco. I thought briefly of announcing that I would bring God to the prom, but I was such a least-likely candidate for religious life, I would have been sent for therapy. About a dozen or so boys showed up for the dance at Villa Maria, and during the activities, I was approached by a charming young man by the name of Joseph Keary. Joe was about five-foot-ten, sandy blond hair and glasses, with a tire-tube midriff and a slightly bent left ear. He was talkative and rather attractive in his own way. He asked me to dance and then on a date; the date led to the prom, and the prom led to what we called then in New Jersey a "steady boyfriend."

Joe lived with his parents in Pearl River, New York, about an hour from my home in Fairfield, New Jersey. However, every week during the summers, he drove his clunker of a car, which basically had an engine and four tires, to New Jersey to take me out on a date. We had fun going to concerts (I remember especially the Cheech and Chong concert), the Jersey shore, the movies, mall shopping, and all the things young couples do. We were the ideal boy-meets-girl, and my parents were delighted that I had met "such a nice boy." Joe was affable and smart, the kind of smart kid who took standardized tests just for fun. He did much better than I on his SAT and got a scholarship to Michigan State University. He too wanted to be a doctor, and we would sit for hours speculating about our life together in medicine. We spent so much time together between senior year of high school and the first year of college that his parents and brothers had begun to incorporate me into the family. I fell in love with Joe and was not sure just where the relationship would lead.

The Ambivalence of Love

One day we were riding down Route 3 bantering about different things. Then Joe turned to me and said, "You know my idea of a wife is someone barefoot and pregnant in the kitchen." I gasped and looked at him wide-eyed: "You cannot be serious!" (Or, how do I jump out of this speeding car?) It was my first real inkling that the relationship was doomed. We dated for almost three years, however. He was extremely faithful in picking me up and driving me to wherever I wanted to go, year after year. Like my father, he doted on me, but I cannot say that I equally reciprocated. I loved the goodness of his person and his willingness to try just about anything I wanted to do, but I could not stand someone hovering over me all the time.

If he knew what was percolating in the depths of my soul, I would have been the last choice for a wife. In fact, I did not want to get married; I knew I belonged to God, but I could not quite get myself to have this conversation with him. Every time I thought I could find the words, I lost courage when I saw his face. By spring of our sophomore year of college, he asked me to marry him and proposed with a lovely ring; in the moment, I was smitten by the offer. I said "yes," but in my heart I said "no." By junior year of college, I was living between the "yes and no" of a marriage proposal. He was a good man, but I knew that I could not string him along indefinitely, so I stopped writing every week and found excuses for him not to visit. He got the point and was deeply hurt, especially when I returned the beautiful preengagement ring and the many pieces of jewelry he had bought me over the years. Interestingly, he married a woman by the name of Diane on the day I made my first vows as a Carmelite nun. (I heard later on—from his mother, of all people!—that two children were engendered, but sadly the marriage didn't last. Joe settled on a military career as a medic and did four tours of duty in Iraq.)

A Competitive Streak

Liberation from Joe did not mean being liberated from men. This was the late seventies, and relationships had entered a new era of freedom and experiment. Our particular baby-boom generation was like an extended Woodstock festival of drugs, sex, and rock and roll.

Luckily my rigorous and highly competitive pre-med track in college kept me locked up in the library with the class nerds, all competing for an "A" in our courses. I was a biology pre-med major at Allentown College with a minor in chemistry. I loved my classes and found the coursework demanding. Science was a noble discipline, and I had full confidence that science could lead me to the truth of reality. I especially liked organic chemistry (once we got past the first semester), biochemistry, and physiology. In our senior year, the organic chemistry prof offered an elective in enology (the science of wine making), and I took it for fun. Enology is a serious science, and we spent hours in the lab making wine and testing it for acidity, glycerol, tannic acid, sweetness, and other components. The final exam was a multiple-choice exam with a wine-tasting section. I had a difficult time distinguishing the various acidic contents and had to drink a few samples of wine before I could answer the questions. Though I was a bit tipsy by the end of my final exam, I managed to pass. Others were not so fortunate; four seniors in the class did not pass the final enology exam and could not graduate. I could not imagine spending the rest of my life knowing that I had failed wine making.

Allentown College (today known as DeSales University) was a small Catholic college run by the Oblates of Saint Francis de Sales. There were two seminaries on the college campus, and one of them belonged to the Oblate priests. Being at a Catholic college meant that we were required to take two theology and two philosophy courses. As a science major (and a science snob) I did not have an inkling of interest in either theology or philosophy. Every time talk of theology came up (which was rare unless it was in class), I would wave my arms dismissively at such an undertaking. "How can one study *God?*" I would quip. "That makes no sense." Such an idea seemed preposterous or, better yet, ridiculous. I would wax eloquently along these lines: "If you try to study God, are you really studying *God* or *your idea* of God?"

Father James Langelaan, a small Dutch priest who planted tulips every year along the campus sidewalks, taught us theology; and while I am sure he covered writings from Vatican II, I don't think I gave the course more than an hour of attention the entire semester. I literally memorized the notes and promptly forgot the material after the exams. The same could be said for philosophy. I liked the ancient philosophers but spent no time to learn their ideas. Rather I memorized the material, spewed it forth on the written exams, and then discarded my notes.

I was a science major, and I considered science alone as a worthwhile area of study. In fact, I disregarded most of the humanities as annoying disruptions to my otherwise serious pursuit of learning, which was defined by biology, chemistry, physics, and mathematics. I did well in my coursework overall, but I was erratic. I could be the first in the class or at the bottom of the barrel. It all depended on whether I was paying attention or not. But my game could be thrown off by too much social life (coed dorms meant late night parties) or too much stress. We were a small, competitive class, constantly keeping vigilance on one another's grades.

Luckily, I had two roommates who helped balance my academic drive with late night fun. Marie Glunz and Susan Ward were my college companions, and if we were not studying together, we were out driving in Susan's 1965 Mustang that had a hole in the floor on the driver's side. Susan and I wound up in a dormitory suite in our senior year and hung a dart board in our "living room"; hence we regularly hosted beer and darts every Friday night.

Summer Jobs

In the summers during college I held various jobs. My first job between my freshman and sophomore year opened my eyes to the wide diversity of people that inhabit the planet. I was a daytime maid at the Holiday Inn in Wayne, New Jersey. When I told my mother that I got a job as a maid, she gasped, since I never cleaned my room at home; in fact, I am not sure I knew what dust looked like, since I was never conscious of it. However, at the Holiday Inn I was assigned to clean eighteen rooms a day, and it was laborious. I cannot say that I cleaned every room thoroughly; rather I would walk in and assess the room. If it looked in better shape than my room at home, then I did a once-through rag clean and a wipe of the sink, leaving aside vacuuming the rug. Apparently, another maid was keeping an eye on me and reported me to the maid superior, who called me in one day and threatened to fire me if I did not do my job properly. Of course, I gave her a big "yes" after each round of admonishments and told her how wonderful she was in her role as maid supervisor. She was easy to please, and I knew that a healthy dose of plaudits could go a long way.

Since the hotel was on a major highway, we had a number of foreign visitors who checked in and out. One day a Frenchman was staying at the Holiday Inn and made some gestures to my maid superior. She called me into her office and asked if I spoke French. "*Mais oui*," I said. She was thrilled and told me I could keep my job as long as I wanted, on the condition that I translate what the Frenchman was saying to her. "I would love to," I said. So off we went to the Frenchman's room where he was sitting in a high-back chair reading the newspaper. He swiftly rattled off something in French, but it was too fast and with a patois incomprehensible to my high-school trained ear. However, I wasn't about to miss the opportunity of ensuring my job, so I turned and said, "Monsieur says that you are a beautiful and charming woman and delights in seeing you each day." She was ecstatic with the news, and skipped back to her office.

The following summer involved a different matrix of jobs, camp counselor in the daytime and Holiday Inn on the evening shift. The evening shift started around 4:00 p.m. and lasted to 10:00 p.m. I was the evening maid on call at the Holiday Inn when residents needed towels, soap, or extra blankets after hours. I would also finish cleaning any rooms not completed by the day shift (only if they were visibly in need, of course!). That summer a young mother and her two children were living at the Holiday Inn because their house had burned to the ground. The kids took a liking to me and would ride on my cart as I circled the floors of the Holiday Inn. I learned quite a bit about their abusive and absent father and the struggles of single motherhood.

One time I was sitting in the supply room around nine in the evening when the phone rang. A man by the name of Ed wanted me to deliver towels to his poolside room. Luckily, I brought one of the kids with me because Ed was a bikini salesman and wanted to give me two bathing suits in exchange for the towels, even asking if I wanted to try them on for size. "Thanks, but no thanks, Ed," was my reply, "it's against policy rules to accept gifts." I am not sure if this was really true, but it sounded good in the moment.

The following summer, I decided to graduate from the Holiday Inn and took a job at the mental hospital in Cedar Grove, New Jersey, where my mother worked as head nurse on one of the women's units. Over-brook Hospital was a large psychiatric hospital that began as a general hospital in 1898 and was converted to a psychiatric institution by the 1900s, serving all ages, from adolescents to the elderly. Patient numbers reached as high as three thousand between the 1930s and 1960s. Later in the twentieth century, more effective psychiatric medications led to increased outpatient care and decreased institutionalization for people suffering from mental illness. The hospital eventually closed in 2007. When I started working there in the summer of 1976, the floors were filled with mentally ill people. I was assigned to a long-term psychiatric ward of women which I could only enter each morning by first walking through the long-term psychiatric ward of men.

Every day a middle-aged man by the name of Philip would approach me as I was trying to unlock the door to my ward. Philip was delusional and schizophrenic and would sneak up from behind and ask, "Can I be your voice?" I would cringe for a moment and then quickly gather myself to respond: "No Philip, not today." It was at Overbrook that I became intrigued by the fragility of the human mind. I was assigned to a long-term psychiatric women's ward where women of all ages were placed, usually for life, by the state, the police, or their families. One woman sat in the same chair every day rocking back and forth and repeating the words "You said it, I didn't," as if something in her mind froze or snapped, never to be repaired. To liven things up on the ward, I would take the twenty or so inmates on nature walks or sit with them on the porch playing rock and roll and dancing with them. I felt my job was to bring a touch of humanity into their otherwise over-institutionalized routines.

The Price of Freedom

In my last summer of college I was assigned to work in the medical laboratory at Overbrook, which was disappointing, since I had enjoyed working on the floor. However, it was felt that my biology background could be put to better use doing urine and blood tests required by the state. In the lab, I was also asked to become a venipunctionarist—that is, someone trained to draw blood for testing. I found this job difficult, as I was often scared to draw blood from mental patients, especially if they were highly agitated or resistant to having their blood drawn. I remember one day getting a phone call from a floor indicating that five patients were being sent to the lab to have their blood drawn. I was the only one on duty that day and panicked at the sight of five mental patients standing before me. However, I quickly gathered myself together and managed to draw blood from four of the patients, while the fifth patient frantically paced back and forth shouting, "You're not going to take my blood! You're not going to take my blood!" Finally, I took control of the situation and said, "Yes, I am." I got hold of him, sat him down, sat on his arm, and drew the blood.

The Overbrook job awakened me to the mystery of life beyond our everyday experiences. It is easy to forget the mentally ill and the mentally disabled who are placed in institutions—out of sight, out of mind. Who were these people? What happened in their lives that landed them in a mental hospital? Later on I discovered the work of Jean Vanier, the Canadian philosopher who was transformed by living with two mentally disabled men and found the L'Arche community, originally in France, and later around the world. I volunteered at a L'Arche community one summer and learned that brokenness and incompleteness are what binds us as a human community. But it was at the Overbrook job that I became fascinated by the study of the brain and the way chemicals affect it.

When our college senior year began, Susan and I decided to collaborate on our final biology project. I had an interest in the drug Elavil, which was a new antidepressant on the market; however, there was work to be done on its side effects, which were still largely unknown. Our classmate, Paul Yakshe, who had joined the Oblate priests in his senior year and was a postulant at the seminary, was interested in working with us on the project. So the three of us pursued a series of experiments to investigate the side effects of Elavil. We submitted an abstract to the Pennsylvania Academy of Sciences and wound up publishing our paper in the Proceedings of the Pennsylvania Academy of Sciences. Paul became the lead author, even though I was the organizer and initiator of the project. The department was so impressed by our final project that we received an award for excellence in research at graduation. (Paul eventually left the Oblates and went on to become a successful gastroenterologist and now owns a practice outside St. Paul, Minnesota.)

I liked scientific research very much because it involved the solitary work of exploring the details of nature. I applied to medical school in my last year of college and was called to an interview at Rutgers medical school in New Brunswick, New Jersey. I was so nervous just thinking about the interview that I basically froze on the actual day of the event. I don't remember answering the questions, but I do remember staring at the interviewer and her kind dismissal of me at the conclusion of the hour. As I departed her office, I knew that I would not be attending Rutgers medical school in the fall.

I graduated college in the spring of 1977, and that summer, my parents decided to retire and move to Florida. At the ripe age of twenty-two, I was on my own, and the independence was exhilarating. Susan applied to the master's degree program in biology at Seton Hall University; and, since medical school did not look like an option, I decided to follow suit. We both received research assistantships and entered Seton Hall University in the fall of 1977. The decision was appealing since I would receive a free graduate education in biology and live with Susan in an attic apartment of a single-family home in Maplewood, New Jersey. The apartment was literally a converted attic of four rooms and had a quaint charm. The kitchen was a converted closet, and the bathroom was one of the largest rooms in the apartment. Susan and I would sit in our living room–dining room with the attic ceiling slanting over our heads and write words to songs or dream of new world orders.

My decision to go to graduate school at Seton Hall proved to be an intervening period of growth and discernment. During my four years at Allentown College I went to Mass almost every day, usually with Marie Glunz, keeping the small flame of divine love alive in my heart. But once I entered graduate school, I found a new freedom in the shifting culture of change and complexity. I controlled the tiny inner flame of divine love by putting a lid on it, making a conscious effort to ignore it, hoping it would disappear. By compartmentalizing my single-hearted love of God, I allowed myself to explore a nontheistic phase of life and became a lukewarm agnostic. Science was beginning to explode in many areas, and I was smitten by the philosophy of science and even, to some extent, scientific materialism, that is, the idea of matter as self-explanatory and its own end. I stopped going to Sunday Mass and starting reading more about socialism and communism.

Mary Donworth had started a graduate program in international studies at Columbia University in New York, and we had long discussions on the various schools of Marxism. Somehow I became enamored with the life and thought of Leon Trotsky, one of the original heroes of the Russian Revolution, before he was exiled and assassinated under orders of Stalin.

Revolution

Revolution was not exactly in the air at Seton Hall in the late seventies. But we all drank from the well of "postmodernity." Postmodernity (literally, "after" the modern) was a name for the new cultural milieu emerging from the wreckage and upheavals of the twentieth century in which the self-assured quest for certainty and objective truth that characterized the post-Enlightenment age was questioned. Postmodernity challenged the assumptions of philosophers like René Descartes and Immanuel Kant, who had constructed the modern person as a rational, autonomous self who thinks and acts independently of other selves.

The tragedies of the twentieth century, especially two world wars and the Holocaust, had exposed the weakness of such claims. Religion and the very quest for truth were suspect, but even science and technology were unmasked as narratives of power. The only real option seemed to be a plurality of truths—every supposed truth simply representing a perspective, situated in a particular context. That seemed to eliminate the authority of grand universal narratives, including the claims of Christianity and other religious stories. Various developments in science itself contributed to this erosion of modernity's claims. Discoveries in the area of quantum physics, for instance, made it clear that the world was significantly more complicated and much more difficult to understand than what the post-Enlightenment modern worldview had supposed.

Postmodernists questioned the idea of an *objective reality* out there waiting to be discovered; everything is subjective and relative. They abandoned foundationalism (the idea that we can identify a solid foundation on which to build other systems of knowledge) and were suspicious of "metanarratives" that were supposedly true for everyone. Although they did not reject the use of reason, they did not believe reason is the *only* or even the best way to know the world. Emotional responses were given equal status to logical ones. The whole surrounding world could be perceived as an extension of one's flesh giving new emphasis to the body as integral to the knowing subject.

Playing With Fire

All these ideas led me to think in more radical ways, ways that could lead me out of the lull of the Jersey Mall toward a liberation of the mind, a world of justice and equality, a new world order. Susan and I wrote revolutionary manifestos while studying genetics, developmental biology, and immunology among other courses in biology. Although we were at a Catholic university, life in the Biology Department at Seton Hall seemed to be a world unto its own, unaffected by the Catholic identity of the university (except for Father Stanley Jaki, a Benedictine priest who wrote intellectual tomes on the relationship between science and religion, and who was known around campus as an odd intellectual). Our world was science, our morals were loose, and smoking pot was typical at graduate school parties. (In this respect, at least, I differed from my cohort: I never liked inhaling or ingesting anything stronger than a vitamin or, if necessary, an aspirin.)

I was in a rebellious stage, happy that my retired parents were in Florida. I was free in many ways, and yet I lived with the Cotswald fire deeply embedded in my religious psyche. I did not want to dwell on the call of that fire but could not relinquish myself of it. I likened my predicament to Jonah and the whale. God called to Jonah one day and told him to go preach to Nineveh because the people were very wicked. Jonah hated this idea because Nineveh was one of Israel's greatest enemies and Jonah wanted nothing to do with preaching to them. Instead, he tried to run away from God in the opposite direction of Nineveh and headed by boat to Tarshish. God sent a great storm upon the ship, and the men decided Jonah was to blame so they threw him overboard. As soon as they tossed Jonah in the water, the storm stopped. God sent a big fish, some call it a whale, to swallow Jonah and to save him from drowning. While in the belly of the big fish (or whale), Jonah prayed to God for help, repented, and praised God. For three days Jonah sat in the belly of the whale. Then, God had the big whale throw up Jonah onto the shores of Nineveh. No matter what Jonah tried to do, he could not get away from God or God's desire—and, try as I might, neither could I.

I continually tried to extricate myself from entanglement with God and found it impossible to do so. Thinking that if I crossed a particularly daring threshold I might be struck from the divine list of potential lovers, I allowed myself to fall in love with a much older man, a married professor. He was one of my graduate professors at Seton Hall, a neurobiologist by training and a charming man of German origin and artistic talents. Apart from his interest in neuroscience, he was an artist and aspiring novelist who spent the summers with his wife at Wellfleet, on the tip of Cape Cod. He introduced me to the world of art in New York's SoHo and to books and ideas that expanded my mind. My small Jersey worldview began to open up to exotic flavors of international proportions, and I began to experience the world on an entirely new level of art, music, and neurobiology.

I was now a liberated child of postmodernity who frequented the art museums of New York City, slept in exotic places, and studied the work of black revolutionaries at the New School for Social Research. My innocent days of pranks at an all-girls school had turned into a free-spirited experiment in boundary crossing, pushing the limits of a young woman's independence beyond the Jersey-Italian stereotypes. My parents knew I was up to no good and suspected that I was dating a married man but never confronted me directly on the subject. I came to my senses when his wife was in a car accident and I realized the tremendous anguish I had inflicted. I was sorry for her and quickly came to my senses on the meaning of rightness and wrongness and knew that my actions were wrong.

I ended the relationship and briefly dated a medical student, and then I simply gave up dating because I knew it was to no avail. As my life unfolded, the probability of life as a random event did not seem entirely reasonable. There were underlying forces of attraction that kept the question of religion as an ever-emerging horizon of dawning light. I had a hard time admitting that I was not fully in control of life; there was a power of life that exceeded the frame of my limited worldview, a power of life that was relentless even in the face of destruction. "I am the way, the truth, and the life," Jesus said (John 11: 25). I would soon discover that life can really flourish only in truth: life and truth are one.

4

On the Path to Redemption

THE DAY I COMPLETED my master of science degree in biology was an ordinary day in the life of the universe. After picking up my diploma in the library at Seton Hall I went over to nearby Madison, New Jersey, where my Aunt Lena Jersey made a special dish of pasta to celebrate; otherwise, no one called or sent a card (except my parents who called from Florida—*and* sent a card). I was still emotionally tied to my neurobiology lover and did not want to leave the area, so I applied to the PhD program in pharmacology at New Jersey Medical School in Newark, New Jersey, which was right down the road from Seton Hall.

My real interest was neurophysiology; but the Pharmacology Department offered me a teaching assistantship, and I was told it was a better department than Physiology. I began the doctoral program in pharmacology at New Jersey Medical School in the fall of 1979. The PhD in pharmacology (like all other departments) was constructed as a hybrid of medical school courses, graduate courses, and laboratory research. The first two years of the program entailed matriculation with the medical school students in the foundational courses, including microbiology, physiology, and neuroscience, among others.

The Lab of Discovery

I started to reflect on the relationship that had ensnared my life in a web of passion, and I had to confront my capacity for duplicity and infidelity. Who was I and was the person caught up in a dishonest relationship the same person who had experienced the profound love of God several years before? What kind of God allows the beloved to stray into the wildness of passion yet still remains a faithful God? The letter to the Hebrews states: "I will put my laws in their hearts, and I will write them upon their minds. . . . Their sins and their evildoing I will remember no more" (Heb. 10:16–17). Truly something other than me was engraved on my heart because when I gained consciousness I had a profound sense of my infidelity to God in a way of deep sorrow—what the ancients called "compunction," a piercing of the heart. I started to return to Sunday Mass, and slowly an inner peace began to emerge while the pangs of conscience subsided. I felt as if I was awakening from a dream or a deep sleep—the slumber of the mind intoxicated by the passions. We humans are so mysterious, often unaware how the mind can capture an idea and spin it round and around, like a spider's web, until the captured idea holds the mind prisoner of its own captivity. Something like that happened to me when I realized I was part of an entangled web of passion and pain and prayed in earnest to a merciful God.

Nevertheless, I was a scientist, and religion was a private matter. Science fulfilled the intellectual pursuit of knowledge while religion soothed the soul. The world of the medical school was filled with atoms and molecules and the desire to solve physiological problems; God was a novel idea and at best a diversion for more light-hearted discussion. To consider religion as somehow holding a pillar of weight next to science was completely unthinkable and untenable.

My particular area of research was the spinal cord. I chose to work with Dr. Herbert Lowndes, a specialist in spinal cord physiology and neurotoxicology. Herb had risen to success early in life and achieved the level of full professor by the time he was forty. He was smart and handsome, with the ruddy looks of a Canadian Mountie. He was born and raised in Saskatchewan but attended Cornell University Medical School where he excelled in the field of neurophysiology. He landed the position at New Jersey Medical shortly after he completed his doctorate at Cornell and quickly rose through the ranks to become a leading scholar in the area of neurotoxicology. He served on several government regulatory boards and was on the neurotoxicology board at the National Institute for Health (NIH), where the big research grants were carefully sifted through and gingerly funded.

Herb had grants for a number of different projects, but one of his interests lay in the underlying neuropathological mechanisms of ALS (amyotrophic lateral sclerosis), a progressive neuromuscular disease that eventually leaves the patient completely paralyzed but with cognitive function. It is a dreadful disease, and the possibility of helping to understand the underlying causes of the disease was attractive. An experimental compound known as IDPN was found to mimic the pathology of ALS in motoneurons (the nerve cells that regulate motor function and muscle movement), and Herb wanted me to investigate the changes induced by IDPN on single motor neurons in cats.

I started in his lab in 1981 and worked alongside a hot-tempered, smart young Jew who had a fragile emotional constituency and could fly off the handle at any moment. He scared me to some extent because one never knew when the emotional bomb might explode. Herb managed to trigger it more often than not, and the two of them often did not see eye to eye. We got along, however, and he taught me the art of electrophysiology. I worked on cat spinal cords, since the anatomy and physiology of the cat were close to those of humans, and the cord could be readily accessed by surgery. I loved cats and had an adorable cat at home in my apartment by the name of Sasha, a white, long-haired, blued-eyed male charmer; yet, as with everything else, I could disassociate my personal feelings from my professional life.

I performed an elaborate three-hour operation several times a week for almost two years, gathering the data from about three hundred motor neuron recordings. The surgery had to be precise in order to limit the target pool to several thousand neurons so that I could isolate one neuron and trace its connection to the leg muscle. Keep in mind that the brain, spinal cord, and nerves represent about 300 million neurons in a cat (compared to 100 billion neurons in a human). The first time I actually recorded a single motor neuron and watched an action potential (the electrical trace) run across the oscilloscope, I was ecstatic. I ran out of the lab and down the hallway looking for someone to share my news. I was recording one single motor neuron out of a pool of 300 million neurons! It was truly an incredible moment.

In my second year of research, I worked with a wonderful neuropathologist from Milan, and we became good friends. His wife and son remained in Italy, and he missed them deeply. I am not quite sure why but he would often say, "I am monogamous," meaning that he was committed to his wife (thank God, because I was not interested). I would shake my head and chuckle. Our laborious work began to bear results, and we started presenting our research at the annual Neuroscience Meeting and published our findings in journals. It was thrilling to look under a high-powered microscope and see the intricate world of a single cell, as if peering into the hidden life of a neuron with its own tarot cards. I was stunned by the incredible visualization of nature's exquisite secret lives and wrote on the first page of my dissertation: "In a single cell of life lay the mysteries of creation."

The basis of our work involved an integral component of nerve cells called "neurofilaments," protein structures that formed like railroad ties along the nerve cell, supporting transport of nutrients down the axon. I often think of neurofilaments when I ride the Amtrak train because the protein structure of a nerve cell is like a train track. A few years ago, there was a major train wreck in Washington, DC, due to the fact that at a certain spot the railway ties became loosened and separated so that nothing held the tracks together. When the speeding train hit the spot of broken ties, the cars uncoupled, and the train derailed resulting in significant casualties. Something like that train wreck characterizes the pathology of ALS. What I proposed is that in conditions of ALS the neurofilaments exit the cell body normally, but once they start to exit they undergo some type of mutation, as if uncoupling railway ties, causing the neurofilaments to bunch up in the axon. It is as if the train cars have decoupled and are piled on top of one another blocking all further flow of activity in the axon. What we did not understand is what caused the train ties (so to speak), the neurofilaments, in the axon to unravel. My predecessor pursued this question as a postdoctoral student at Johns Hopkins Medical School under the direction of Jack Griffin, a neurologist and leader in the area, and I was eventually to follow the same trajectory.

I loved research and was fully engaged in it. The rapidly growing fields of neuroscience and neurotoxicology were exhilarating. I felt like I belonged to a secret club, a society of neuromasons who spoke a language only a few people could understand. We held keys to the inner secrets of the spinal cord and brain, and the feeling of intellectual power was seductive. I excelled in my area of research and was gaining a reputation as a top electrophysiologist in the field. I was one of a handful of women in the country doing this type of research in the early 1980s. Herb was delighted with my work, and he became both mentor and big brother. Almost every Friday we would conclude the week at the pub drinking beer (after beer), talking about the research and the people involved.

Herb had high hopes for me and saw me as his protégé. Our weekly pub talks were often lessons in how to survive and thrive in the world of academic research. He would explain to me how to talk about projects without giving away data or ideas, how to write grants, how to make influential friends, and basically how to succeed. He wanted to make sure that I would rise to the top in the highly competitive world of academic science. From Herb I learned how to navigate the treacherous waters of academia—lessons that would come in handy later on. As I was completing my degree, Herb was taking my ideas and molding them into a multiyear project that would eventually win a seven-million-dollar Jacob Javits Award. Needless to say, my budding career had a bright future ahead.

Meeting Thomas Merton

While I was intrigued by questions in neurophysiology I did not want to spend the rest of my life in laboratory research. For some reason, I had not looked into the pharmaceutical industry, where a number of my classmates landed jobs after graduation and went on to make a small fortune. I lacked ambition for my career in pharmacology, and deep down I knew that something was not quite right—or perhaps missing. The inner flame of God's love had never gone away (despite my forays) and kept vigil throughout my years of ascending to a doctorate in pharmacology.

It was toward the end of my third year of doctoral studies that I was reading the book reviews in *Time* magazine one evening and came across a new book by Monica Furlong on the monk Thomas Merton. I had never heard of Thomas Merton and was completely illiterate with regard to monastic life and the term "contemplation." The snapshot of Merton's life summarized in the review was riveting, and that evening I ran out to purchase the Furlong biography. I returned to my apartment and started reading the book. While my cat, Sasha, feeling neglected, stared reproachfully from the bookshelf, my entire attention was absorbed in the life of Thomas Merton.

Thomas Merton was born on January 31, 1915, in Prades, France, to an American mother and a father from New Zealand. He studied at Columbia University and taught English before entering a Trappist monastery in Kentucky and later becoming a priest. His life, recounted in his autobiography *The Seven Story Mountain*, tells of his quest for God that led to his conversion to Catholicism and eventually to join one of the strictest orders in the Roman Catholic Church, the reformed Cistercians, or Trappist monks. He had a powerful intellect and wrote prodigiously. His deep inner spiritual explorations that drew him to a life of radical asceticism and renunciation caught my eye and enkindled my heart. "This is what I want to do," I remember thinking to myself. "I want to give all to God and to live entirely in the heart of God."

Did you ever have an experience that "knocked you off your horse" so to speak (as described by Saint Paul)? Such was my discovery of the contemplative life, as I stayed up most of the night finishing the Furlong biography. My heart was on fire, and by morning I knew that my career in pharmacology would come to an end. I had found my "vocation" in the heart of God. Since I knew nothing of this life and did not know what to read or where to look, I called Sister Helena, my confident from high school who helped me after the Cotswald fire. She was delighted with my discovery and willing to help discern the path ahead. We agreed that I should meet some contemplative nuns so that I could get a sense of what a contemplative monastic life entailed.

Helena had been assisting a group of Discalced Carmelite nuns in Sugarloaf, Pennsylvania, with their bakery. The nuns had moved to Sugarloaf several years before and begun a new foundation of Carmelites according to the Byzantine Rite—among a handful of Byzantine Rite Carmelites in the world. Helena arranged for us to visit the nuns one weekend in September, as I was just starting the fourth year of my doctoral work and anticipating graduation within a year.

I did not quite know what to expect, as I had never been to a monastery and had never met a cloistered nun. The monastery itself was a converted farmhouse that sat atop a small hill, accessed by a curving driveway. Across the street from the monastery was a chain of low-range mountains; the one facing the monastery was called Sugarloaf because it was shaped like a loaf of bread. The first time I saw Sugarloaf Mountain I thought I saw a bit of heaven on earth.

Awakening to the Monastic Life

I knew nothing about monastic life at the time, although I would eventually learn that it is the oldest form of religious life among the various religious traditions. The term "monk," from the Greek *monachus*, meant "solitary one," the individual pursuit of God characteristic of axial consciousness. While the term "monk" could be used across genders, it typically referred to the dedication of men. The term "nun" referred to a religious woman living a cloistered life, a life separated from the world, under solemn vows of poverty, chastity, and obedience.

Arriving at the monastery on a Saturday morning, Sister Helena and I were greeted by Sister Mary, a tall woman with lily-white skin and high cheekbones. She met us on the threshold of two different worlds—the world of solitude and the world of change—and opened the door with a warm, welcoming smile. I was captivated from the moment I crossed the threshold into the cloister. It was an entirely different world than the one I had just exited off the highway or the one I knew in medical school.

The visitor's parlor was a wood-paneled room with no objects on the wall except a Byzantine Rite cross and two wooden chairs. Mother Marija Shields, the prioress of the monastery, entered the parlor like the chairwoman of a corporation about to make a major deal. She was in her early fifties, a vivacious woman of charm and intellect whose Irish heritage was inscribed in her blue eyes and pale white skin. From the moment she greeted us, she did not stop talking. I don't think I said more than five words because the gravity of Mother's presence was overwhelming. Our visit ended after an hour, and we were on the road again, back to the Jersey halls of scientific research. But something deep within me had ignited. Inwardly, I was Cotswald on fire again. Something was burning to the ground, and something was being born aloft into a new life.

From the Mind into the Heart

I continued my doctoral research on ALS and found a new energy of life in spiritual reading. I started buying books on the saints, on monasticism, relying especially on Thomas Merton's rich arsenal of spiritual writings to guide my way into an uncharted path. I also started visiting the Carmelites on a monthly basis. Returning from the Carmelites one Sunday evening, I was late getting to the lab on Monday morning, and Herb was looking for me. "Where were you?" He asked. "Oh, I spent the weekend in Pennsylvania," I replied. He gave me a big wink and a wide grin because he presumed that I had a boyfriend in Pennsylvania. I did not have the heart to tell him that my boyfriend was "God."

Religion was an odd discussion in the world of biomedical science. Mario used to tell me that he was a "deist," someone who believed in a higher power but not necessarily a personal God. I was enough of a cradle Catholic to argue for a personal God, although I had no other basis apart from my own personal experience. Our world of scientific research was literally steeped in material reality, and the notion of spirituality was marginal to the scope of the scientific mind. For this reason, I could not find either the opportunity or the words to tell my colleagues that a radical change had occurred in my life, that God had consumed my heart in a fiery way and that I would be leaving academic research after completion of my degree.

To live with a secret is extremely difficult and confusing. For one thing, the secret prevents a full transparency of life so that the breath of life cannot flow freely from one person to another. It is hard to call someone a friend with a secret buried deep within the heart. I had a few secrets buried within my heart, and the most heartbreaking of these was the reality of a religious vocation. I felt that I was deceiving the very persons who had placed so much trust and confidence in me. There was no one to talk to or confide in. Herb was confident that I would become a scientific success, and he spoke to all his colleagues about me like a proud father. I was humbled but inwardly weighed down by the accolades. I loved Herb as a friend and mentor and hated the possibility of disappointing him.

My doctoral research wrapped up in late spring of 1983, and I spent the summer and fall writing my dissertation in pharmacology. I had several postdoctoral offers (thanks to Herb) and decided to explore the option at Johns Hopkins Medical School. It was a joint offer in the departments of neurology and neuropathology. I went to visit Hopkins in October since my anticipated date of defense was in early December. To think that I had the possibility of working with some of the best researchers in the country on neurofilament diseases was too good to be true; yet, I knew that if I did not make the radical break with research science, I might forfeit the one true call of my life. So I went to visit Hopkins with a torn heart.

The faculty could not have been more congenial or welcoming. Jack Griffin and his wife, Diane, hosted me for the weekend, and I had the opportunity to visit the labs and explore the different research projects underway. The visit went so well that before I departed, Dr. Griffin appeared before me with a contract in hand. "Here it is," he said; "we would love to have you on board by early next year." My pen was on automatic pilot and I signed the contract.

"What am I going to do?" I cried to God while driving through tears up Route 95 back to New Jersey. I was truly conflicted, especially since the Carmelites had invited me to a three-month live-in to experience their way of life firsthand. I returned to New Jersey, and that December I successfully defended my dissertation on motoneuron neuropathy induced by IDPN before a committee that included Bob Taft, a neuromuscular disease expert at NIH, Jack Griffin of Johns Hopkins, Herb, and several other professors from the department, with about fifty graduate students and faculty in attendance. I was a smashing success, as the saying goes, and the sky seemed to be the only limit in sight. The doors were opening to a promising career in an area that was exploding in research possibilities. Two paths were diverging in the woods, and I had to choose one to travel on, or as the author of Deuteronomy wrote: "I have set before you life and death: choose life" (Deut 30:19).

I accepted the Carmelite offer with glee at the same time that I signed the Hopkins contract with tears. How would I resolve the fact that I was living in a black hole that separated two loves: science and religion. I decided the best way to resolve this impasse was to take a trip. I would tell my colleagues at the Medical School that I was taking a three-month trip to give myself a break before starting the next phase of life. They thought this was a good idea. In reality, I was taking a week-long trip to the Holy Land with Sister Helena and would spend the next few months as a live-in candidate with the Byzantine Discalced Carmelites.

The Beginning of a Long Trip

B eing a typical graduate student with little money, I needed to find a cheap trip to the Holy Land. I saw an advertisement for a seven-day round trip to the Holy Land that was too good to be true. The $599 ticket price covered air fare, meals, and accommodations, so I called Sister Helena and we purchased our tickets. For some reason we thought it best to tell the group that we were two Catholic sisters, so the group started calling me "Sister Denise," and I thought it sounded entirely strange, as if there might be another person in the group. Every time they called me by the title "Sister" I swallowed hard and tried not to laugh.

Once we were on board the plane I realized that we had joined a chartered flight to the Holy Land with a group of born-again Christians from South Carolina. When they asked me to lead the group in prayer, I knew I was in trouble. This was going to be a *very* long trip. One afternoon Sister Helena got sick because of something she ate, and she was confined to bed. I went on the afternoon excursion by myself with the group, and when they heard of Helena's illness they insisted on praying over her for a speedy recovery. I found myself in a room full of born-again Christians with their eyes rolling upward and arms outstretched, as if trying to grasp the Holy Spirit swirling about the room. It was my first real evangelical awakening, and it had elements of being extraterrestrial. The one real outcome of the Holy Land trip was that I was able to send all my colleagues at the Medical School a postcard to the effect, "Hi, having a great time. Wish you were here!"

After we arrived back in the States, I gathered up my belongings, packed the car, and headed off to Sugarloaf for my monastic experience. I was a cigarette smoker in those days, and the thought of being nicotine-free for several months was frightening. I smoked a cigarette on the way to the monastery and tucked one away in my suitcase, just in case I went into nicotine withdrawal while in prayer. I crossed the threshold into the cloister, as if embarking on a planetary expedition in another corner of the galaxy. The entire monastic milieu was like a reenactment of the Garden of Eden, and the dimensions of space/time took on a new psychology.

The sisters were very welcoming, and I was joining them at a propitious time in their history. Mother Marija, Sister Marie Helen, and

Sister Ann had all been part of another Carmelite monastery in Elys-
burg, Pennsylvania, when they got permission in 1973 to start a new
Byzantine Rite Carmelite monastery at Sugarloaf. Sister Mary was the
youngest of the solemnly professed nuns (solemn profession means
final commitment) and came to Sugarloaf in 1975 from the monastery in Sioux City, Iowa, to help the fledgling group, but quickly
fell in love with the Byzantine Rite and the new monastic group. She
got permission to make Sugarloaf her permanent monastic home. A
woman by the name of Martha was also temporarily living with the
nuns, and another woman by the name of Andrea would be arriving
in late spring. This would be my new temporary family for three whole
months. At the ripe age of twenty-eight, with a newly minted PhD in
hand, I was making the leap into God.

The first month of my live-in experience was like nothing I had
ever experienced in my life. We followed a rigorous monastic horarium (monastic schedule): early rising (4:00 a.m. in silence), one hour
of mental prayer, breakfast, the first hour of morning prayer (prime),
liturgy (in Old Slavonic, of course), the third hour of morning prayer
(terce), manual work (garden, kitchen, sewing), midday prayer (sext),
noon dinner, brief rest, finishing up the day's work, vespers (evening
prayer), light supper, recreation, followed by night prayer, bedtime, and
the great silence. It was an exhausting schedule, and each morning I
would have to drag myself out of bed to get to the one hour of silent
prayer before breakfast.

More often than not, I slept through the hour of silent prayer, but
there was still a deep sense of peace; God was perfectly fine with me
sleeping through our conversation together. My live-in monastic experience went quickly, and before long I had to make one of the biggest
decisions of my life: go to Hopkins or renounce a career in research
science and formally enter a traditional Discalced Carmelite monastery.
Deep within my heart, I knew the decision had already been made: I
would become a Discalced Carmelite nun. The most challenging part
was conveying the news to Herb, Mario, and all who had entrusted me
with their friendship and support.

I could not muster the courage to face my medical school colleagues
with the news of my decision to become a nun. Lack of truthfulness
can result in the sin of regret, and I regretted that I could not hon-

estly speak to them. So I wrote a long letter explaining my decision to renounce a career on pharmacology for the life of a cloistered nun. I sent a personal letter to all my friends, as well as a special letter to Herb, whose wife, Helen, had prepared an incredible spread of food upon the successful defense of my dissertation just a few months before. I had been embraced as a colleague, and I was now about to extricate myself from that embrace. New Jersey Medical School had paid for five years of my education, and I was about to close out this investment.

Even worse was confronting my parents with the decision to enter a cloistered life. I asked my brothers and sister to join me in Florida to convey the news, as I was not expecting a good outcome. I was on the brink of a successful career, the dream of every immigrant family, and I was now going to renounce this career for a life of poverty and asceticism.

My father was deeply disappointed but said little except, "Oh no, Denise," as if I had just announced that I had stage-four cancer. My Sicilian mother exploded like a cannon. She had waited the last five years for the moment when she could announce that her daughter had a doctorate. But the blow extended beyond her social card; after all, I had been living the life she herself had always dreamed of. She got in her mind that I had been brainwashed by Sister Helena and actually called Helena by phone to declare war by verbal attack. She then wrote to the pope to complain that I had been brainwashed by a nun. She made every effort to derail my decision. My siblings responded in various ways. Vincent found the family cacophony too much and quickly took the next flight home from Florida. Anne Marie kept trying to keep peace amidst the din of voices, and Richard did his best to ameliorate my parents' distress. There is nothing worse than an Italian American family in conflict.

With the grace of God, I persevered through the Florida debacle and headed back to Orange, New Jersey, to clean out my apartment, give away all my material possessions, and pack a light suitcase for the journey ahead. There was one more difficult decision to make, and that was to find a home for my faithful cat, Sasha. I loved him dearly, and he had been my companion every step of the way for the last five years. It pained me deeply to have to relinquish him. I kept repeating the words of the Gospel: "If you wish to be my disciple, you must deny yourself, take up your cross and follow me" (Matt 10:38). I was now trying to live out these words, and the emotional cost was very high. Luckily, there was a woman in the building who was willing to take Sasha into her home. The day she picked him up and carried him out the door, my world went dark. I cried inconsolably and questioned if I was making the right decision. What kind of loving God would make such harsh demands?

Leaping across the monastery wall (so to speak) from the world of academic research science was like a death for me. The words of Saint Paul kept repeating in my ears: "I have died and my new life is in Christ" (Col 3:3). I had made a choice, and now I had to follow through on this new path to wherever it would lead. My graduation ceremony to receive the doctorate took place in May 1984, but by then I was already enclosed in a Carmelite cloistered monastery. Mother Marija's sister lived in New Jersey and was kind of enough to pick up my degree at the Medical School. My PhD in pharmacology was delivered to me in a brown paper bag.

5

Crossing the Threshold

T HE DECISION TO ENTER Holy Annunciation Monastery meant that I would be leaving the world that had been home to me, the world of science, politics, movies, and social friendships. Because I thought that I would never see the world again, I thought it best to take one last memorable trip to Europe. My good friend Laura Pines, whom I knew from my Seton Hall days, was doing a residency in medicine in Winchester, England. I could get a cheap round-trip ticket on People's Express airlines before embarking on my monastic career, so with one week to enjoy my last worldly fling, off to England I went. Upon arriving in Winchester, Laura asked what I wanted to do during my week in Europe. I really wanted to go to Avila where Saint Teresa, the great reformer of the Carmelites, had lived. Since that was too far to travel in three days, we opted instead to take the ferry to France and visit the birthplace of Saint Thérèse of Lisieux. I knew almost nothing about Thérèse except that she was a great Carmelite saint. This young woman who entered the Carmelite monastery at the age of fifteen and died at the age of twenty-four from tuberculosis was not only canonized but, a hundred years after her death, proclaimed a Doctor of the Church because of her profound insight and spiritual wisdom.

A Wild Ride

T he ferry was a leisurely way to travel, and we arrived in Cherbourg in midday while the shops were still open. As we were walking to the train station, Laura saw a sign for a Peugeot bike sale. She had been looking for a good bike and was enticed by the sale. "Oh," I said, "you can take a look on our return trip since you do not want to carry a bike around." She agreed. We went to the home of St. Thérèse and then to the monastery where she lived her nine years of monastic life. We had reservations to stay overnight in the guest quarters of the monastery, and our small simple room sparsely decorated with a bed and chair gave me an insight to Thérèse's ascetic life. Laura, who was Jewish, was fascinated by the whole monastic milieu. She herself was something of a late hippie who had lived in the woods of Maine before deciding to study medicine at Ross University in the Dominican Republic.

We toured around Lisieux and collected all sorts of paraphernalia with the saint's image on it, including mugs, ashtrays, key chains, etc. Our return ferry was scheduled for Thursday evening. I had to return to the States on Friday and was scheduled to formerly enter the monastery on Saturday morning.

As soon as we arrived in Cherbourg for our return trip to England, Laura went to look for the bike store with the Peugeot sale. I went with her to the shop, but she could not make up her mind, so I left to tour the city by myself. I returned around 5:00 p.m. to collect Laura since the ferry was scheduled to depart at 6:15 p.m. She was haggling over the price, and it was taking a long time. Finally, I said, "Laura, we have to go, or we will miss the ferry." "Ok," she said. "I will buy this bike, but I don't have enough money. Can I borrow from you?" So I gave her all my French money to make her purchase. By the time the bike was tuned and adjusted for size, it was close to 6:00 p.m. I was getting frantic, and Laura said to me, "Take the bike and go to the ferry dock. I will meet you there because I have to run over to the train station and get my things out of the locker." So there I was in the middle of rush-hour Cherbourg riding a new ten-speed bike down the main street. It was the first time I had been on a ten-speed bike, and I did not know where exactly the ferry dock was located; I had to stop several times and inquire in my Jersey French accent.

By the time I saw the dock ahead, it was 6:15 p.m. I looked up and saw the boat moving, and I called out in French, *"Arrêtez! Arrêtez. On arrive!"* But my cries were to no avail. The policeman blew his whistle and called out, "The ship has departed." "What?" I screamed—and panic ensued. The ferry that would take us back to England had just left; I had no money (but a new Peugeot bicycle); no Laura; and I was about to enter the Carmelites on Saturday. I didn't know what to do, so

I starting riding the bike in circles watching all the shipyard personnel get in their cars to depart for the day. As the sun was setting I quietly panicked but also prayed to Saint Thérèse to intercede in my predicament. I was riding the bike near a fence when a Fiat sedan suddenly pulled up on the other side of the fence; a woman jumped out and yelled in English, "Are you Denise?" "Yes," I exclaimed. She said, "Your friend Laura has been waiting for you in the terminal." Apparently, Laura had gone inside the terminal while I was waiting outside. We reunited and hugged tightly, keeping the new bike close by.

Now we had the challenge of finding our way back to England. Someone suggested we could try the truckers' ferry, which would leave around 11:00 p.m., so we went to the truckers' terminal and saw many rigs lined up for the ferry. We asked one rather sleazy looking character if he could let us board with him, and he replied, "No, I cannot. I have flammable materials." An agent at the counter overheard us and called us over. "Look," he said. "What you are doing here is really dangerous. Besides, it is illegal for passengers to ride the truck ferry. If you attempt to do so, you will be arrested in England." *Arrested* in England? What? I am about to become a Carmelite, I thought. I can't be arrested! We were at a loss as to what to do next and we had no French money.

Miracle in a Diner

For some odd reason, we decided to venture over to the dimly lit diner where the truckers went to eat. We walked in with our bike and stood before the counter. Within a minute or two, a man appeared, wearing a black leather jacket. Beckoning me to approach, he said to me in a very distinct British accent, "I heard about your situation and I would like to help." My heart was pounding so hard I thought I would go into tachycardia. We were either on the brink of a sexual assault or perhaps being sold into a gang ring.

"Mr. Leather" invited us to his table of four men, all of whom guffawed and asked us our names and where we were from. We tried to keep things as vague as possible, and I wanted to blurt out that I was becoming a nun on Saturday, but did not dare to venture in this direction. We ordered a full breakfast at midnight, and just as we were finishing up, Mr. Leather asked us, "What monies do you have?" We both had British Sterling, and he asked us to give him everything so that he could exchange our British pounds for French francs. I was very leery at this point, but since we had no other options, we agreed to do so. I saw a waitress whispering to Mr. Leather and running back and forth with the money. By 1:00 a.m. our dinner partners had departed, and Mr. Leather said to us, "I have arranged for you to stay in a nearby hotel, and I will take you there myself. The hotel is in walking distance to the ferry dock," he added.

I thought to myself, "Here we go; we are now coming to the end of our lives, and I will not be a Carmelite after all." Mr. Leather took us to his truck and loaded the bike on the back of the truck. We got in, and a short time later we were pulling up before a dimly lit pub with half the letters in its neon sign burnt out. We got out of the truck and literally walked through the crowded pub with our Peugeot bike in hand. He walked us to the bottom of a long stairway and then said to us in his British accent, "Well, girls, this is the best I can do for you. You have a room to stay here, and it is paid for. Make sure you get to the ferry early tomorrow, and if you need anything else, here is my card."

I stuffed the card in my jacket and never looked at the name until two weeks later when I was recounting the story to the Carmelites. "What was his name?" Mother Marija asked. "I don't know" I said, "but I will get the card and see." Now here is the miraculous part: the man who helped us—Mr. Leather—had the same last name as Saint Thérèse—*Martin*. His name was Peter Martin. It was as if Saint Thérèse took care of us through the personal assistance of this man in a leather jacket. I was stunned by the event, and the Carmelites saw in it the hand of God. I had to repeat the story for an entire year to all who visited the monastery.

Crossing the Threshold

It was 1984 when I drove my Subaru hatchback to the cloistered Holy Annunciation Monastery. I had no idea what the future would hold for me, but I did believe that God was truly with me and would show me the way. I had made a decision to "leave the world" at a time when many religious men and women, following the call of Vatican II, were rediscovering the world. It would take a number of years before I would learn the significance of Vatican II. In fact, I knew almost nothing about religious life except for the dowdy novices at St. Mary's Villa and movies like *The Nun's Story*, *The Trouble with Angels*, and *The Sound of Music*. Hence, my idea of what a nun looked like consisted of a long habit, long black veil, and black Oxford shoes. Nor did I have any idea that a "nun" meant a cloistered (enclosed) way of life compared to a "sister," which denoted a woman in active ministry or apostolic life. I am not sure I even knew who the pope was in 1984, but I did hear that there were sisters living alone in apartments and partaking in acts of civil disobedience. Moreover, there were religious sisters who no longer wore a habit but doffed it for secular clothes, including blue jeans and tee shirts. These reports seemed scandalous to me. My romantic image of a nun was the dewomanized spiritual life totally turned toward God. Like Merton, I was intoxicated by the lure of the desert, where God speaks intimately to the heart: "Therefore I am now going to allure her; I will lead her into the wilderness and speak tenderly to her" (Hos 2:14).

When I made the break from academia to cross the threshold of a monastery, something radically changed in me. I had died to my worldly self, and now my only desire was to live for Christ. The year was 1984, the year in which George Orwell's novel had envisioned the rule of Big Brother. Even though I was coming from the vast changing world of science and technology, I was not going forward into Orwell's imaginative future but backward in time, to the third and fourth centuries of desert spirituality, from which Western monasticism was born.

My decision to enter religious life was not a job decision or one possibility among other options. I did not visit different monasteries or investigate different types of religious life (although this may not have been a bad idea in retrospect). Rather, I simply went where God was leading me. I was a child of the Spirit, and the only guide I had was the fire in my heart, the deep desire to live for God alone. I had spent the last twelve years of my life immersed in the study of science, and once I crossed the threshold of the monastery, everything I learned seemed to be irrelevant. I was confronted by a whole different set of questions that had nothing to do with empirical data but with intangible realities that included questions of the soul, salvation, heaven, and God. Now enclosed in a way of life in which I could not step outside without permission, I was impelled to confront the mystery of God in an entirely new way—the way of self-knowledge. The Franciscan theologian Bonaventure thought that lack of self-knowledge makes for faulty knowledge in all other matters. I could not have agreed more.

What is monasticism? There are lots of books written about the history of monasticism, none of which I read, of course, before entering the world of Carmel. I had no idea that monasticism had its roots in the ascetic life of the early church. The ascetic life meant a liberation and awakening of a consciousness of self in the attempt to become truly human and Christian. This meant a recasting of the whole of existence in accord with a renewed consciousness of self. This renewed existence was also framed by an apocalyptic sense: the end of the world was just around the corner. In the early church, the apocalyptic feeling bore with it a sense of antagonism to society and skepticism about the possibility of truly serving the Lord in a secular vocation.

The early Christian ascetics were men and women who lived in continence, distributed goods for the benefit of the church and the poor, and kept particular hours of prayer. They did not live in community or share a common purse and wore no special garb. Ascetics joined in prayer at the third, sixth, and ninth hours of the day when the normal working person could be expected to join in prayer.[1]

By the second century, virginity appeared to be an act of asceticism par excellence, and for women this was an act of liberation in an otherwise patriarchal culture. Thus, it is not surprising that women formed religious communities whereby they could withdraw from the world, live an ascetic life, and direct their attention to divine matters in a concentrated way. Virginity became the distinguishing feature of a lifestyle described as "religious life" that had radical social implications. For women, procreation was no longer the highest ideal; rather, there was a higher calling in spiritual preparedness, opening up a new female role outside the structure and needs of the family. Celibate identification liberated women for more creative, active lives that included intercessory prayer and the works of God.

Some scholars claim that the Christian ascetic sought to recover the old martyr spirit that was prevalent in the pre-Constantinian era

---

1. Paul F. Bradshaw, *Daily Prayer in the Early Church: A Study of the Origin and Early Development of the Divine Office* (Eugene, OR: Wipf & Stock, 2008), 72–91.

of persecution.[2] It is interesting that the stories of the martyrs circulated widely among the ascetic communities and may have influenced the shape of their lives. The Alexandrian theologian Origen spoke of monastic life as a "second baptism" and a new martyrdom.[3]

For a number of historical reasons, monasticism emerged in two forms: the eremitical life and the cenobitic life. Saint Anthony of the desert was the prototype of the eremitical, or hermit, way of life, a solitary life lived independent of other like-minded individuals. In contrast, the monk Pachomius was identified with the cenobitic, or communal, way of monastic life. Interestingly, Pachomius had been conscripted in the army before converting to Christian life and forming a monastic way of life based on community.[4] His time in the army may have influenced the shape of the life, including a uniform or habit. Monastic life followed Saint Paul's injunction: "Do not model yourselves on the behavior of the world around you but let your behavior change modeled by your new mind" (Rom 12:2 NEW JERUSALEM BIBLE).

The motives for early monasticism are unclear. Were monks puritans of the church, successors of the primitive Christian spirit that was lost following the legalization of the church under the emperor Constantine? As the church became established under Constantine (ca. AD 311/313), a certain worldliness set in; and ascetics, both male and female, may have started to retreat deep into the desert in order to pursue a more challenging life of holiness. Was the monastic life a form of protest against a church that had too easily accommodated itself to the world, or was it simply the most liberating path of the human person in relation to God?

I leave it to the historians to sort out the reasons for early monasticism. I do agree with Jean Gribmont, who wrote, "The spiritual life of monasticism is essentially hidden in the depth of human consciousness."[5] In other words, the monk is first an inner reality before belonging to a

---

2. Henry Chadwick, *The Early Church* (London: Penguin, 1967), 25–26.

3. Chadwick, *Early Church*, 177; *Origen: An Exhortation to Martyrdom, Prayer, and Selected Works*, trans. and intro. Rowan A. Greer (Mahwah, NJ: Paulist Press, 1979), 41–80.

4. Phillip Rousseau, *Pachomius: The Making of a Community in Fourth Century Egypt* (Berkeley: University of California Press, 1999), 57–75.

5. Jean Gribmont, "Eastern Christianity," in *Christian Spirituality I: Origins to the Twelfth Century*, ed. Bernard McGinn and John Meyendorff; World Spirituality:

structured way of life. Or to put it another way, the desert does not have to be a geographical reality; it must, however, be a spiritual reality. The early monks went to the desert not to escape the world or the illusory Christian identity proposed by the world; the purpose of the life was to confront the roots of illusion in oneself, which, in turn, meant a ceaseless battle of the will. It would take a long time and some harsh lessons before I could really comprehend this profound truth.

A Dramatic Beginning

I entered the monastery on January 14, 1984, exactly twenty-four hours after returning from a harrowing trip abroad. After surviving our episode with the missed ferry and overnight stay in Cherbourg, Laura and I had caught a ferry back to England the next day. When I landed in Newark I looked like such a wreck that I was searched for drugs at the airport. How could I possibly convince anyone that I was about to enter a traditional Carmelite monastery in the next twenty-four hours? God certainly works in the most obscure ways, and this was quite a dramatic beginning to a new way of life.

But when I crossed the threshold into the cloister, embraced by each of the sisters who welcomed me, something changed. I knew I was on an irreversible path into the heart of God, but the way forward was vague, as if walking into a large dark forest.

I entered with two other women, Martha (whom I had met during my previous live-in) and Andrea, from Winnipeg, Canada. Martha was the eldest in a large family and the surrogate parent, since both her parents had died when she was young. Her decision to enter the monastery was a significant one. Andrea was a social worker and had been married to a hippy. Apparently a year into their marriage, her husband fell asleep on the couch one evening with a burning cigarette in hand. The couch caught fire, and he burned to death. It was a tragic story. Andrea was a beautiful young woman with a powerful alto voice. She told me that to supplement her income (prior to coming to the monastery) she sang a few evenings in a local nightclub and once dated the singer Gordon Lightfoot for a few months. Martha, Andrea, and I were

---

An Encyclopedic History of the Religious Quest 1; Ewert H. Cousins, gen. ed. (New York: Crossroad, 1987), 89.

soon joined by a twenty-two-year-old, also from Winnipeg. Joan was a very intelligent young woman who had considered Byzantine studies at Harvard but felt a call to enter the Carmelite monastery. I remember the day Andrea and I were sent to pick Joan up at the Philadelphia airport. It was our first time out of the monastery in several months, and we got in the car with our long, brown, ankle-length jumpers, white blouses, and short white veils and took off for the airport. I happened to bring along the last cigarette I had stored in my suitcase, and there we were, passing the cigarette back and forth on Route 76 with our white veils flying through the half-opened car windows.

In the Carmelite monastery, the superior is known as the "prioress" (the "head") of the community. Mother Marija was prioress from the beginning of the foundation, since the idea for this new monastery originated with her. Of Irish descent, Maria (née Dorothy Shields) changed the spelling of her name to "Marija" to identify with the Slavonic roots of the Byzantine Rite she had adopted. She was a staunch Catholic with definite ideas about monastic life and Carmelite life in particular. Although she had been in the monastery since she was seventeen, she was an extrovert, who loved to talk. Our monastery followed the rules of strict silence, which meant we could talk only when given a signal either by the prioress or the subprioress (Sister Marie Helen). Mother Marija would usually give the signal to talk—"Praise be Jesus Christ"—and we would respond, "Now and forever"; however, she often would proceed to talk for the entire hour.

By and large, it was enjoyable to listen to Mother regale us with amazing stories of her Carmelite life. She recounted how in the early days the sisters would keep a skull in their rooms to remind them of death or would eat from a dish on the floor on Good Friday in memory of Christ's humility. She had absolutely no use for Vatican II or the radical changes in religious life that followed the council. She spent her first twenty years or so in a rigorous, ascetic life in Morristown, New Jersey, and associated radical severity with the reformed discalced Carmelite life, as if we should still live like Saint John of the Cross, held hostage in a dungeon.

Our asceticism was based on radical poverty and humility, which meant we were required to ask for everything we needed, from a toothbrush or bar of soap to a pair of sandals. Poverty and humility were twin virtues so that living dependent on God meant knowing oneself before God. If a harsh criticism was made in community, such as, "How could you *burn* that pie!" humility obliged one step up to the plate (so to speak) and accept the criticism as a practice in virtue. Chastity simply meant keeping the mind free of thoughts of the flesh. The subject of sex was a pathway to sin and to be avoided at all costs. We were told that eating meat could arouse the passions; hence the community was vegetarian.

A Carmelite's life had to be focused on God alone, and Mother Marija was firmly convinced that the long brown habit—covering the body like a twin bedspread, billowed at the waist by a leather belt, and the long brown scapular on the outside, like two seamless envelope flaps—would keep the mind free of sensual desire. By covering the body with yards of cloth, we could live like the angels, pure in mind and spirit and free of the body's shape, form, and attraction. When Vatican II called religious to open their windows to history and adapt their religious customs to contemporary culture, many religious took off their habits and put on secular clothes. Mother recounted how, at the Morristown monastery, she went into the breakfast room one day and saw her prioress in a leather jacket and knee-high leather boots, telling the sisters that she was going out to get her hair done. When I heard this story, I was shocked. "What is happening to the Catholic Church," I thought to myself! I vowed that I would live my religious life as faithfully as Mother Marija.

Encountering a Saint

Discerning God's will is never easy, since the will of God is inter-twined with human desires, emotions, and environmental factors that shape the human will. Hence, the best way to discern the will of God is in conversation with a spiritual master. This is the role of spiritual direction. Mother had several Jesuit spiritual mentors (since Saint Teresa of Avila was fond of the Jesuits), and one of these mentors became influential in the foundation of Holy Annunciation Monastery. When I met Father Walter Ciszek, SJ, in 1984, he was an elderly Jesuit living at Fordham University in the Bronx. Mother insisted that we all take Father Walter as our spiritual director at the start of our monastic life. To introduce us to this holy man, we were required to read his two classic books: *With God in Russia* and *He Leadeth Me.* I was absolutely stunned by his life story.

Father Walter was born to Polish immigrants in the town of Shenandoah, Pennsylvania. At the age of eighteen he entered the Jesuits and was sent to Rome for studies in theology and Russian language, history, and liturgy at the Pontifical Russian College (or "Russicum"). In 1937, he was ordained a priest in the Byzantine Rite. The next year Father Walter was sent to a Jesuit mission in eastern Poland. But with the outbreak of World War II in 1939, this area was occupied by Soviet troops, and Ciszek was forced to close his mission. Realizing it would be very easy for a priest to enter the Soviet Union among the streams of exiles going east, he crossed the border in 1940 under an assumed Polish name. For a year he worked as an unskilled logger in the Ural Mountains, while discreetly carrying on a religious ministry. He was arrested in 1941, charged with espionage, and imprisoned in the Lubyanka prison in Moscow. There he spent a total of five years, most of it in solitary confinement. The stories of his confinement—the darkness, depression, and despair—are heartbreaking. And yet he eventually broke through the veil of darkness into a radical trust in the will of God and a confident trust God would lead him through his ordeal.[6]

After five years in Lubyanka, he was compelled to begin a term of hard labor in Siberia. He was forced to shovel coal onto freighters, to work in coal mines, to labor in construction at an ore-processing plant. Throughout his lengthy imprisonment, he continued to pray, to celebrate Divine Liturgy, hear confessions, conduct retreats, and perform parish ministry. All this time he was presumed dead by both his family and the Jesuit Order. Finally, having served his entire sentence of hard labor, he was released with restrictions to a series of towns in Siberia. At last he was able to write his family and reveal the astonishing news of his survival. His ordeal ended in 1963 when he was returned to the United States in exchange for a couple of Soviet spies. After his return, he was quoted as stating, "I am an American, happy to be home; but

---

6. Walter Ciszek, SJ, *With God in Russia* (San Francisco: Ignatius Press, 1997). For a good biography of Father Walter see Seamus Dockery, *Surrender: Father Walter Ciszek: Jesuit Priest, Soviet Prisoner* (Bloomington, IN: Xlibris, 2012).

in many ways I am almost a stranger."[7] In 1965, he began working and lecturing at the John XXIII Center at Fordham University (now the Center for Eastern Christian Studies at the University of Scranton in Scranton, Pennsylvania), counseling and offering spiritual direction to those who visited him, until his death.

The first time I met Father Walter, I imagined a large, tall strapping fellow who had endured years of hardship and labor in prison camps. I rang the door of the red brick building at Fordham and waited several minutes before the door opened. I did not see anyone in my visual field, and it seemed that the door had opened on its own, that is, until I looked down and there before me was an elderly man stooped over, as if in tremendous stomach pain, but with a warm smile and a twinkle in his eye. "Hello Denise," he said. "Welcome, come on in." He hobbled before me and planted himself in a simple steel-rimmed chair while I placed my large basket of fruits and cheese on his table. After reading his story and his endless pangs of hunger, the only thing I could consider bringing was food. Luckily many other people had the same idea, and his tiny kitchen was stacked with all sorts of food gifts.

This was one of a handful of times I would meet with Father Walter. He would speak from the Scriptures, and when he opened the Word of God, his mind ascended to an entirely different space, as if he could see God face to face. His eyes would glisten with a radiant light, and his whole being was light filled. I knew that I was in the presence of a very holy man. His years of torture and darkness and his complete trust and surrender to God made a significant impression on me; it was from Father Walter that I learned the value of perseverance throughout life's struggles. His words became my words and the shape of my life.

> There was but a single vision, God, who was all in all; there was but one will that directed all things, God's will. I had only to see it, to discern it in every circumstance in which I found myself and let myself be ruled by it. God is in all things, sustains all things, directs all things. To discern this in every situation and circumstance, to see His will in all things, was to accept each circumstance and situation and let oneself be borne

---

7. Walter Ciszek, SJ, and John M. DeJak, *With God in America: The Spiritual Legacy of an Unlikely Jesuit* (Chicago: Loyola Press, 2016), 22.

along in perfect confidence and trust. Nothing could separate me from Him, because He was in all things. No danger could threaten me, no fear could shake me, except the fear of losing sight of Him. The future, hidden as it was, was hidden in His will and therefore acceptable to me no matter what it might bring. The past, with all its failures, was not forgotten; it remained to remind me of the weakness of human nature and the folly of putting any faith in self. But it no longer depressed me. I looked no longer to self to guide me, relied on it no longer in any way, so it could not again fail me. By renouncing, finally and completely, all control of my life and future destiny, I was relieved as a consequence of all responsibility. I was freed thereby from anxiety and worry, from every tension, and could float serenely upon the tide of God's sustaining providence in perfect peace of soul.[8]

My opportunities for spiritual direction with Father Walter were limited, however. He died later that very year on December 8.

I finished my year of postulancy grateful to God that I made it through the year in one piece, literally, without chopping off my fingers in the bakery or blowing up the kitchen. Life in the monastery was not for the faint of heart. Not only was the monastic schedule rigorous but so too was the work. I had spent the last twenty-eight years essentially pushing a pen on paper; now I was pushing fifty-pound sacks of flour across a bakery floor and rolling out three hundred dough balls for bread. Periodically, I was assigned to cook for the community, and one time I had to cook for a bishop! I was constantly checking my pulse to see if I was suffering from a rare heart disease or a lack of oxygen to the brain, which had caused me to undertake such an abnormal way of life.

We did have recreation periods, but these too entailed work. Since I was a disaster with thread and needle, my job was to paste labels on bread bags so that freshly baked loaves could be properly bagged the next day. It was monotonous work but rote enough that I could participate in conversation, that is, if Mother Marija was not in one of her talkative moods. There was no internet in the monastery—or even a television or radio. Aside from sacred books, our reading materials

---

8. Walter Ciszek, SJ, *He Leadeth Me* (Garden City, NY: Doubleday, 1973), 91.

were limited to the Byzantine diocesan paper and Carmelite News. In other words, our world was narrowly defined by the dictates of Mother Marija. Even the videos we watched were her choices. Sometimes we saw the same movie three or four times, to the point where we could recite the lines out loud. Any movie scenes that featured scantily clad bodies, excessive kissing, or suggested a sexual scene were censored. Mother Marija would call out, "Marie Helen, fast forward!" Marie Helen would jump up and quickly fast forward the clips until we got to some idyllic, pastoral, or religious scenes. Andrea and I would look at each other and chuckle or simply roll our eyes.

One time the doorbell rang around noon dinner, and Mother went to answer the door. She returned with a video in hand and said, "This was just given to us, and I am told it is an excellent movie." The title of the film was *Agnes of God*. Mother apparently did not wait long enough for our kind donor to really explain the gist of the movie. Mother heard "convent," and that was enough to accept the gift. So that evening we finished our supper early, cleaned up, and gathered in the recreation room to watch *Agnes of God*, anticipating an uplifting story about a young woman who enters a convent. We started to watch the movie and in no time we were horrified. *Agnes of God* is about a novice who gives birth in the convent and insists that the stillborn child was the result of a virginal conception. A psychiatrist (Jane Fonda) and the mother superior of the convent (Anne Bancroft) clash during the resulting investigation. It is a deeply disturbing movie, and in a closed environment where the psyche is already being squeezed into an authoritarian vice, it was sheer agony to watch. I don't think I slept well for the next week.

Sleep was essential, however, because the work was manual and physical. In the summertime, we worked from sunrise to sundown. After starting the day with liturgy and prayer, we proceeded to the bakery to bake several hundred loaves of bread for sale (we were a self-supporting monastery) or prepare a thousand jars of jelly. In the summer, we went out to the large monastery garden after supper and tended the garden until sunset. Garden work included tilling the soil and planting all types of vegetables and, in late summer and early fall, harvesting the fruits of the earth. One summer Mother Marija discovered an organic compound that could double the size of vegetable growth.

Since we were growing eggplants to sell to an Italian food company, bigger eggplants meant more profit. We used the spray religiously on the vegetable plants every day that summer and harvested the largest eggplants, squash, tomatoes, lettuce, and other produce ever picked in the state of Pennsylvania. This was a significant achievement for such as me, who, before the monastery, had never handled produce that didn't come wrapped in cellophane at the A&P supermarket.

The Rhythm of Life

There was a beauty to the rhythm of monastic life: Arise, awaken to the presence of God, give God thanks, work for your food, nourish the body, rest, complete the work of the day, give praise to God, feed the body in silence, keeping your mind and heart focused on God alone, give way to sleep to begin the journey anew. When I later learned of the Greek philosopher Plotinus and his "flight of the alone to the Alone," I recognized the shape of our monastic life at Sugarloaf. We were on a solitary flight to the great "Alone."

Not that God was alone, since God is Trinity, but that God is higher than any other created being. The beautiful Byzantine liturgy kept us attuned to divine transcendence every morning, as we sang the Trisagion at the beginning of the Divine Liturgy: "Holy God, Holy and Mighty, Holy and Immortal, have mercy on us"! We would recite this prayer three times, each time prostrating low before the great God of Sugarloaf, and, as time went on, I found myself stressing the word "mercy."

Time and space took on new qualities in the monastery. We could just as easily have marked passage of time by the location of the sun as with a watch. Space and time were a single movement between outdoors and indoors. The sun, sky, and earth were joined by the work of our hands to prayer, food, and rest—all folded in one act of the mind and heart constantly raised to God. The monastery was like a greenhouse in which the seeds of our spiritual lives could be nurtured and developed into the truth of our identity in God. "The secret of my identity lies in the love and mercy of God," Merton wrote.[9]

I basked in the rhythm and spiritual beauty of the monastic life, but

---

9. Thomas Merton, *New Seeds of Contemplation* (New York: New Directions, 1961), 35.

I loathed the constant physical labor. Mother Marija was ambitious to grow the monastery into a significant place on the Byzantine map, and we were the human workhorses who would help realize her dream. We had no say as to what work we would assume for the day; rather we were lined up each morning after prayer and given our assignments.

One day I was assigned to panel an eleven-by-twelve room on the second floor of the main house. I refused the assignment on the spot, indicating that I was spatially challenged and knew nothing about carpentry. Mother would accept no complaints or disagreements (and I was sharply told so before the gathered community). I got my hammer and nails and proceeded to the second floor, stopping by the chapel along the way and praying that God preserve my ten fingers from self-amputation. Luckily Mother sent another sister, who was a seamstress, to help me with the project.

I was reprimanded in the community from time to time for small matters. One time a jelly jar cracked, and I quipped it was "cheap glass." The sister I was working with reported me, and I was admonished for lacking a spirit of poverty. When I burned an apple pie I baked for the community dinner one Sunday, I was reprimanded before the community to the effect, "Some people may have a doctorate but *no* common sense." For the most part, I accepted the criticism in the spirit of humility, but after a while, I resented it. There was little room for error, and it seemed that the education I had acquired got in the way of monastic life. In Mother's view, a college graduate (no less a PhD) should know how to do just about everything. Humanity was an obstacle to holiness, not the way to it, and the flesh had to be tempered day in and day out through humility, silence, work, and prayer.

Recreation time was usually on Sunday, the day of rest. Sometimes we would listen to opera in the refectory (dining room) or have open talk-time, which was a break from our normal routine of eating in silence while one sister read aloud from a book. A Sunday treat was having an ice cream cone or pizza that someone would bring to the monastery. One time a local farmer donated twenty-two bushels of elderberry, and I was assigned the task of making elderberry wine. I could not figure out correctly the sugar and glycerol content and wound up making a batch of wine that was about 120 proof. The nuns decided to sample the wine at dinner time, and this probably contributed to one of our best evenings together, a happy, tipsy monastic community. Later on, needing an outlet, I regretted not having stowed away a few bottles.

There was a piano in the annex of the bakery that someone had donated to the community. It was an old, upright piano, but the keys worked and were almost all in tune. I began to play piano when I could catch a break and found solace in composing tunes. I also played guitar, having taught myself in high school; and when Mother discovered that I had musical talent, she brought me to the nearest music store where I picked out a Fender nylon six-string guitar. I loved the Fender, and between piano and guitar, I started composing songs based on the writings of Saint Teresa of Avila and Saint John of the Cross. Sister Andreja Vladia and I harmonized nicely together (she had a fabulous voice), and before long we had a whole repertoire of songs, including some of Adreja's compositions.

Mother Marija did not waste time seeing the potential of making our music into a profitable enterprise. She got the idea of recording an album, and within the year we recorded "Life in the Monastery," which included five original songs by me, two songs by Andreja Vladia, several songs by the community, and the sung Mass parts of the Liturgy of John Chrysostom. One of the best moments was recording a version of "Immaculate Mary" in Slavonic in which I simultaneously played harmonica, guitar, and xylophone, a monastic version of Bob Dylan!

The album achieved what Mother had envisioned, notoriety and financial success. Several local television stations came to the monastery to film us, and the *Wilkes Barre Time Leader* newspaper ran a feature-length article on "Baking Nuns Discover New Harmony." We became an overnight sensation, "The Singing Nuns of Sugarloarf," and for a brief moment contact with the world provided a healthy dose of oxygen. However, composing music in between baking bread did not appeal to me as a lifelong commitment. I did learn a lesson, however, that would carry me through life: whatever doors I would enter in the future, I would make sure they were revolving doors. At Sugarloaf, my energies became focused on finding a door that would swing open to the world.

6

Becoming a Prophet

THE STRICT ENCLOSURE of the monastery and the ceaseless rigor of the life created doubts as to whether or not I had chosen the right path of religious life. On one hand, I grew in love with God in a way that I could not have imagined, and, on the other hand, I felt tested in love. Was my past life now catching up to me? The words of the prophet Hosea spoke deeply and personally to me:

> When Israel was a child, I loved him,
>   and out of Egypt I called my son.
> The more they were called,
>   the more they went away;
> they kept sacrificing to the Baals
>   and burning offerings to idols.
> Yet it was I who taught Ephraim to walk;
>   I took them up by their arms,
>   but they did not know that I healed them.
> I led them with cords of kindness,
>   with the bands of love,
> and I became to them as one who eases the yoke on their jaws,
>   and I bent down to them and fed them. (Hos 11:1-4)

I was the Israel of God's love; I was the daughter of a God who stooped low in love to embrace me, despite my blindness and self-centeredness. It was God who taught me to walk the way of the spirit and God who lifted me up from the netherworld of a fallen relationship. I was smitten by this God of tender love and yet could not bear the cost of love, the suffering that love must endure to be purified in itself. I complained a lot to God while in the monastery. I was constantly freezing, constantly tired, and constantly in need of positive affirmation that might reflect something of my talents rather than domestic disasters.

One time Mother asked if I would write an article for the diocesan newspaper on the recently beatified (1987) Carmelite philosopher Edith Stein. I wrote the article and was quite pleased with it. However, I was chagrined that I could not sign the article with my name; rather, I had to sign it as written by a Carmelite nun. Every measure was taken to flatten out my education so that there would be a seamless line between the nun with the high school degree and the nun with the doctorate.

Name and Identity

I found solace in the religious name that I agreed upon with Mother Marija as I prepared to enter the novitiate, the formal training period, or what I lightly called "nun boot camp." I chose the name "Teresa Ilia of the Trinity" as my religious name, and it seemed I was calling on every heavy hitter in heaven. The title "Trinity" served as the operative spiritual guide of my religious life, and it was fitting for those who had gone before me in this great order. The Order of Carmelites had its origins on Mount Carmel, in Palestine, where the great prophet Elijah defended the true faith in the God of Israel when he won the challenge against the priests of Baal. It was also on Mount Carmel that the same prophet, praying in solitude, saw the small cloud that brought life-giving rain after the long drought. From time immemorial, this mountain has been considered the lush garden of Palestine ("Carmel" means "garden") and the symbol of fertility and beauty.

Of all the movements in the Carmelite order, by far the most important and far-reaching in its results was the reform initiated by Spanish mystic Saint Teresa of Ávila, a woman of great intellect and spirit. Teresa entered the Carmelite Monastery of the Incarnation in Ávila on November 2, 1535. She found herself increasingly in disharmony with the spiritual malaise prevailing at the monastery (I understood her predicament clearly). Among the 150 nuns living in her monastery, the observance of cloister—designed to protect and strengthen the spirit and practice of prayer—became so lax that it actually lost its very purpose. The daily invasion of visitors, many of high social and political rank, spoiled the atmosphere with frivolous concerns and vain conversations (though, truth be told, I sometimes found myself envying a little of that laxity). Since solitude was essential to the life of contemplative prayer, Teresa found herself in inner conflict to the extent that she longed to do something new.[1] The Franciscan priest Peter of Alcantara became her spiritual guide and counselor, and under his direction, she resolved to form (or reform) a new Carmelite convent, correcting the laxity that she had found in her monastery.

The stories of Teresa's life and her spiritual determination were deeply impressed on me. I identified with her strong will and her resolve to follow God's will, despite the hardships she endured. One story passed around tells how Teresa made her way to her convent during a fierce rainstorm, slipped down an embankment and fell squarely into the mud. The irrepressible nun looked up to heaven and admonished God: "If this is how you treat your friends, it is not surprising that you have so few of them!"[2]

She was human to the core and yet someone who had attained the highest level of union with God. Her *Interior Castle,* probably inspired by the words of Jesus "there are many rooms in my Father's house" (John 14:2), was a profound exploration of the stages of consciousness in the journey to God. Though she was uneducated and did not trust her own ability to write, she was the author of brilliant works on the spiritual life. She described the subject of her writing as such: "It is that we consider our soul to be like a castle made entirely out of a diamond or of very clear crystal, in which there are many rooms, just as in heaven there are many dwelling places."[3] She used the metaphor to explain the soul's progress from the first mansion of the castle to the seventh, and the transformation from a creature of sin to the bride of

---

1. For an good introduction to Teresa's life see Kieran Kavanaugh, OCD, introduction to *Teresa of Avila: The Interior Castle,* trans. Kieran Kavanaugh, OCD, and Otilio Rodriguez, OCD (New York: Paulist Press, 1979), 1–29.

2. Teresa of Ávila, *The Interior Castle,* trans. E. Allison Peers (New York: Doubleday, 1961), 15.

3. Teresa of Avila, *Teresa of Avila: The Interior Castle,* 35.

Christ. She then went on to describe how it was by prayer and meditation that the door to the first castle could be entered. A key virtue that was brought up again and again was humility. She also stressed the importance of self-knowledge. The journey was to begin by "entering the room where humility is acquired rather than by flying off to the other rooms. For that is the way to progress."[4]

I talked to Saint Teresa a lot in the monastery and confided in her as if she were my best friend. Her words never failed to illuminate my mind and enkindle my heart, and I found comfort knowing that she struggled throughout her life, yet remained steadfast in her confidence in God: "Let nothing disturb you, nothing trouble you. All things are passing, God never changes."[5] Or as she wrote in her *Interior Castle*: "If, then, you sometimes fall, do not lose heart, or cease striving to make progress, for even out of your fall God will bring good, just as a man selling an antidote will drink poison before he takes it in order to prove its power."[6] There was no doubt, Teresa of Avila was my heroine, and I desired to be a daughter of her spirit: I would bear her name.

Becoming a Prophet

But there was another figure of Carmel who spoke equally powerfully to me but in a different way: the prophet Elijah. The name Elijah appears several times in the Gospels. The author of Matthew 11:7–14 recounts the words of Jesus identifying John the Baptist as the new Elijah:

> What did you go out into the wilderness to see? A reed shaken by the wind? What then did you go out to see? A man dressed in soft clothing? Behold, those who wear soft clothing are in kings' houses. What then did you go out to see? A prophet? Yes, I tell you, and more than a prophet. This is he of whom it is written,

---

4. Teresa of Ávila, *The Interior Castle*, trans. Peers, xiii.

5. This prayer, known as the bookmark of St. Teresa, is probably not authentic. See T. Baker, *Minor Works of St. Teresa: Conceptions of the Love of God, Exclamations, Maxims and Poems of Saint Teresa of Jesus (1913)* (New York: Cornell University Press, 2009), 74.

6. *The Interior Castle*, trans. Peers, 32.

"Behold, I send my messenger before your face,
    who will prepare your way before you.
Truly, I say to you, among those born of women there has
arisen no one greater than John the Baptist. Yet the one who
is least in the kingdom of heaven is greater than he. From the
days of John the Baptist until now the kingdom of heaven has
suffered violence, and the violent take it by force. For all the
Prophets and the Law prophesied until John, and if you are
willing to accept it, he is Elijah who is to come.

The Gospel of Luke and the Acts of the Apostles draw an especially
close association between Jesus and the prophet Elijah. Jesus was Jewish and knew the Bible well enough to know that only two prophets
in Scripture were said to be anointed: Elijah and Elisha. Thus, as Luke
recounts, Jesus entered the Temple and declared: "The Spirit of the
Lord is upon me because he has anointed me to preach good news to
the poor. He has sent me to proclaim release to the captives and recov-
ering of sight to the blind, to set at liberty those who are oppressed,
to proclaim the acceptable year of the Lord" (Luke 4:18). The attending Jews, who had an impending sense of the messianic age, likely
associated him with the appearance of Elijah. Elijah also makes his
appearance explicitly in Luke's Gospel at the transfiguration of Jesus,
the moment when both Moses and Elijah appeared with the glorified
Christ on the mountain, and it seems the Gospel writer wanted to see
and portray Jesus as the new and greater Elijah.

Although the Gospel passages of Jesus and Elijah are of interest,
what captured my imagination in choosing the name "Elijah" as my
religious name was picturing this solitary prophet on Mount Carmel,
deeply attentive to the voice of God:[7] "Go east and hide by the Brook,
Elijah" (1 Kgs 17:3); eat what the ravens bring you, Elijah. Go to the
widow of Zarephath, Elijah, and ask her for food and heal her son.
Elijah became exhausted by the demands of his vocation, and after
walking miles on end sat down under the shade of a tree and wished he
could die. "It's too much Lord," he prayed. "Take away my life; I might
as well be dead" (1 Kgs 19:4). These words became my words quite

---

7. Passages from 1 Kings about Elijah are here paraphrased by the author.

often in the monastery! But the real lure of Elijah was his confrontation with King Ahab and the idols of Baal. It was the way Elijah confronted the prophets of Baal, his profound trust in the one true God, and his willingness to challenge idolatry. In the First Book of Kings we read:

> Elijah went before the people and said, "How long will you waver between two opinions? If the LORD is God, follow him; but if Baal is God, follow him."
>
> But the people said nothing.
>
> Then Elijah said to them, "I am the only one of the LORD's prophets left, but Baal has four hundred and fifty prophets. Get two bulls for us. Let Baal's prophets choose one for themselves and let them cut it into pieces and put it on the wood but not set fire to it. I will prepare the other bull and put it on the wood but not set fire to it. Then you call on the name of your god, and I will call on the name of the LORD. The god who answers by fire—he is God."
>
> Then all the people said, "What you say is good."
>
> Elijah said to the prophets of Baal, "Choose one of the bulls and prepare it first, since there are so many of you. Call on the name of your god, but do not light the fire." So they took the bull given them and prepared it.
>
> Then they called on the name of Baal from morning till noon. "Baal, answer us!" they shouted. But there was no response; no one answered. And they danced around the altar they had made.
>
> At noon Elijah began to taunt them. "Shout louder!" he said. "Surely he is a god! Perhaps he is deep in thought, or busy, or traveling. Maybe he is sleeping and must be awakened." So they shouted louder and slashed themselves with swords and spears, as was their custom, until their blood flowed. Midday passed, and they continued their frantic prophesying until the time for the evening sacrifice. But there was no response, no one answered, no one paid attention.
>
> Then Elijah said to all the people, "Come here to me." They came to him, and he repaired the altar of the LORD, which had been torn down. Elijah took twelve stones, one for each of the

tribes descended from Jacob, to whom the word of the LORD had come, saying, "Your name shall be Israel." With the stones he built an altar in the name of the LORD, and he dug a trench around it large enough to hold two seahs of seed. He arranged the wood, cut the bull into pieces and laid it on the wood. Then he said to them, "Fill four large jars with water and pour it on the offering and on the wood."

"Do it again," he said, and they did it again.

"Do it a third time," he ordered, and they did it the third time. The water ran down around the altar and even filled the trench.

At the time of sacrifice, the prophet Elijah stepped forward and prayed: "LORD, the God of Abraham, Isaac, and Israel, let it be known today that you are God in Israel and that I am your servant and have done all these things at your command. Answer me, LORD, answer me, so these people will know that you, LORD, are God, and that you are turning their hearts back again."

Then the *fire of the LORD* fell and burned up the sacrifice, the wood, the stones and the soil, and also licked up the water in the trench. (1 Kgs 18:21-38 NEW INTERNATIONAL VERSION)

Fire! God was in the fire, and this fire bore witness to the one true God. Elijah, the prophet of fire who confronted the pagan gods with fire as testimony to the true God of Israel; the prophet who listened in the gentle breeze to the voice of God; the prophet who would never die but ascend to heaven in a fiery chariot. In a mysterious way, I deeply resonated with the prophet Elijah and opted for the Greek feminine of the prophet's name, "Ilia," meaning, "the Lord Yahweh (*El*) is my strength," or as I translated it, "Watch out; God is on *my* side!"

Learning to Leave

One day I was walking outside alone, which was unusual since we were required to walk in threes (twos were considered signs of particular friendships and were to be avoided at all costs); but it was a retreat day, and I had the privilege of walking alone. I remember enjoying the quiet and peace of the day when all of a sudden in my mind the words of the *Benedictus* appeared: "And you, my child, you shall be called the prophet of the Most High. For you will go before the Lord and prepare his way."

The words "you my child shall be called the prophet of the Most High" struck me in a deep and personal way. God was saying to me, "*You*, my child, are now the prophet of the Most High." I quickly went inside the monastery to find Mother so that I could share with her this startling experience, but she did not seem too impressed.

"Oh, the Lord speaks to us in many ways," she said. But deep in my heart I knew something was stirring; indeed, I knew I would leave Carmel in the near future.

Life in the monastery was an emotional roller coaster. The harmonious rhythm of the life was punctuated by the human ego. "These women are ridiculous," I thought to myself one day while rolling my bread dough, "passive-aggressive and temperamental piety, as if seeking brownie points." The monastery brings out all the dirty laundry of the human heart and hangs it out to dry. I longed for my male colleagues at the Medical School and wondered if I could escape by building an underground tunnel through the vegetable garden so I could crawl underground to the other side of the cloister fence (like the prisoner Andy DuFresne in *The Shawshank Redemption*). Sometimes I prayed that the inactive volcano, Sugarloaf, would erupt and spew lava over the monastery. I suffered from "cloisterphobia" and felt closed-in and mentally suffocating from lack of intellectual stimulation. I looked to Saint Thérèse of Lisieux, who managed to love even her worst enemy in the monastery with great compassion and wondered how in the world she found strength to do so. She had an indomitable iron will focused on God alone—a trained athlete in single-heartedness. The Saints see everything we see, but they see out of a different center.[8] This was certainly true of Saint Thérèse. She saw everything through the inner eye of love. I prayed to Thérèse to find the right way to see through the eyes of love and was inspired to follow

---

8. Michael Himes and Kenneth Himes, "The Sacrament of Creation: Toward an Environmental Theology," *Commonweal* (January 26, 1990), https://www.commonwealmagazine.org.

her little way of self-oblation, which we recited every morning in the monastery:

> That my life may be an act of perfect love I offer myself as victim of holocaust to thy merciful love, imploring Thee to consume me unceasingly, letting the floodtide of infinite tenderness pent up in Thee flow into my soul, so that I may become a very martyr to Thy love, O my God. May this martyrdom having prepared me to appear before Thee break life's thread at last and may my soul take its flight unhindered to the embrace of Thy merciful love. I desire O my Beloved at each heartbeat to renew this oblation, an infinite number of times till the shadows fade away and I can tell Thee my love eternally face to face.[9]

I decided to bury all my degrees under the altar as my act of perfect oblation. I thought perhaps if I made a whole-hearted surrender, giving all that I have to God, I could learn to love more purely and perfectly like Thérèse.

Mother Marija was delighted with my decision and arranged with Father John Levko, a Jesuit from the University of Scranton, to have a small ceremony in the chapel. So I brought out my bachelor's, master's, and doctoral degrees and placed them in a box. After an introductory prayer and some laudatory remarks by Father John, we slid the altar to one side, and placed the box under the altar. (Luckily it was a movable altar, because later on I would need to retrieve my degrees in order to continue the journey. God is never to be outdone in generosity.)

Although burying the degrees under the altar was a sign of my willingness to give my all to God, I still suffered from a lack of self-worth. All that I had achieved seemed to vanish, and I was left with the raw materials of my life. "I have died, and my life now is hidden in Christ," I reminded myself. I was dying to self, but the question remained: What was I becoming? Merton had it right: The self is something of God, but if you lose a sense of self, you lose God as well.[10] I

---

9. Thérèse of Lisieux, *The Story of the Soul: The Autobiography of Saint Thérèse of Lisieux*, trans. Thomas N. Taylor (New York: Cosimo Classics, 2007), 278.

10. Merton, *New Seeds of Contemplation*.

was not sure if I was finding God or losing God. I did not have the language or concepts to explain this attraction of divinity at the core of my life, but I deeply experienced it, like entering into a dark cave of infinite proportions, with no road map or signs, just the burning *desire* to be drawn into God's infinite love, as if being drawn by an irresistible force. Sometimes the darkness of the cave was overwhelming; in fact, the more I sought the light the darker my life became, and I took shelter in the words of Saint John of the Cross: "Where have you hidden, Beloved, and left me moaning? You fled like the stag after wounding me; I went out calling you, but you were gone."[11] I was born aloft on the eagle's wings of divine love and yet felt abandoned in the desert of that same love. It was an unfathomable mystery that permeated every aspect of my being. The love of God filled me to overflowing, and yet I could not find peace in it and settle my weary head on God's heart. The monastery was not a healthy life for me.

Tasting the World Again

I had finished my second year of vows, attuned to the rhythm of the monastery, when I received a frantic phone call one evening from my mother. Of course we did not receive phone calls directly, but through the sister portress or whoever was on extern duty. My mother was tearful because my father had collapsed that afternoon at the mall where they had just finished lunch. He was rushed to the hospital and—as we spoke—was undergoing open heart surgery. "Can you come down to see him," she asked?

I had not been outside the monastery in more than two years, but the thought of my father near death gave me courage to confront Mother Marija with the question: Can I visit my parents in Florida? She was most obliging and saw to it that I was on the plane to Tampa by the next morning. It was a very strange experience for me and a bit overwhelming to be thrust into the midst of a busy world without reentry preparations. I sat next to a woman on the plane, and when she

---

11. John of the Cross, "The Spiritual Canticle," Stanza 1 in *The Collected Works of St. John of the Cross,* trans. Kieran Kavanaugh, OCD, and Otilio Rodriguez, OCD (3rd ed., Washington, DC: ICS Publications, 2017), 278.

saw me in my full Carmelite habit, she blurted out, "Thank God! Now I know we won't go down!" What a responsibility I had, keeping the pilot focused on his job from seat 22A in the rear!

When I got to Florida, my mother and sister picked me up at the airport, but my mother was a nervous wreck. The whole family had gathered in the moment because the prognosis of my father's condition was uncertain. Since my father was in the ICU with limited visitation, my sister Anne Marie and I thought it might be a good idea to go with Mom to the beach. Since she liked being by the water, we thought a change of scenery would do her good. Neither Anne Marie nor I knew the roads in Clearwater, so we let Mom do the driving. This was not a good decision. Mom was barely five feet tall, and her visual field was the dashboard; only her wisps of grey hair made it over the steering wheel.

Before long we were in rush hour traffic in downtown Clearwater with Mom crouched behind the wheel. Anne Marie was in the passenger's seat, and I was in the back seat. Mom was making a left-hand turn into the Clearwater Hotel but did not realize there was a blind right lane next to the turning lane opposite her. Within seconds of making a turn we were struck on the front right side by a long-haired, mirror-sunglassed fellow who stepped out of his vehicle in a bathing suit not much larger than a Band-Aid®. Two young women got out of the car as well, both in scant bikinis. My sister was trying to calm down my mother in the front seat, so I stepped out of the car in my long brown Carmelite habit and, for a moment, forgot that I was a Carmelite nun. "Where the hell were you going?" I yelled out. "You were speeding in a twenty-five-mile-an-hour zone." The sun-glassed hippie guy walked up to me, and there we were, face to face: a man in a tiny bathing suit and a nun in a long Carmelite habit, verbally duking it out. "Hey lady," he said. "It wasn't my fault; she (pointing to my mother) should have waited." An audience quickly gathered around us and were amazed by this rather bizarre scene. Someone was videotaping the event, and, in that moment, we were prime material for a TV sitcom that could have been called *Life in the Fast Lane*. The police sided with the man in the tiny bathing suit and gave my mother a ticket with points. It was a terrible day.

Time to Move On

My father survived his heart operation, and I returned to Carmel at the end of the week. Surprisingly, I was glad to be "home" in the quiet of the cloister and the rhythm of prayer. But after settling back in, I was once again on the alert for opportunities to jump over the monastery wall. Perhaps the greatest contribution to my angst was the lack of human relationships or friendships. I began to suffocate mentally and spiritually because I saw no way out of what had become an imprisonment rather than a liberation of the spirit. The lack of relationality also caused me to wonder about the core doctrine of Christianity, the Incarnation. If God had become human, then was not the flesh good enough for God? If God had become one of us, should we not take the human person as the starting point for finding God?

The life at Holy Annunciation Monastery had a deep Platonism running through it, with an emphasis on spiritual over material realities and a denial of the body as the place of holiness. Yet, the Gospels all spoke of Jesus as one who was immersed in physicality, tending to the poor, the lepers, and women and tax collectors. We avoided all people in Carmel by a radical separation from the world and from one another, and yet the world was the place where God decided to pitch a tent: "God so loved the world that God sent his only Son not to condemn the world but so the world might be saved through him" (John 3:17). Friendships were prohibited in Carmel, and I was left with little comfort other than the garden and the monastery dog, a beautiful golden retriever whom I hugged tightly at times. Something was not right.

Yet, to leave the monastery was a difficult decision because I had already made one enormous decision four years ago when I left academic research and crossed the threshold into the cloister. Now I had to face the fact that the decision I made to enter a monastery was not a final one. This was my first real lesson in how God is completely unpredictable and perfectly at home with chaos. God gives us the freedom to shape our lives, and the most authentic life can only be found in the freedom of letting go, over and over again. Only in this way can God's love grow. "To live with an evolutionary spirit," Eric Jantsch wrote, "is to let go when the right time comes and to engage new structures of relationship."[12] I had no notion of evolution at that point, but I would eventually learn that letting go is the most apt sign of being human, for our bounded existence can only grow in freedom.

I was on the search for freedom because I was not at home with myself, and my bones knew it. I had to make a decision: leave the monastery or accept suffering as a way of life until death. One evening I was walking outside, one of the rare times alone; and my gaze was caught up in the sun setting over the mountains. I was inspired in that moment to relinquish all my worries and anxieties into the hands of God; to trust that God would lead me and would not abandon me.

As I was praying for direction that evening, I was inspired to ask Mother Marija for a year's leave of absence. I thought if I could just get some breathing space, I might be better able to discern whether or not I should commit myself to solemn vows (equivalent to "until death do us part") or find a new way of religious life. The next day I went to her office and asked to speak with her. She was kind enough to listen; somehow, she knew things were not right. I explained to her my spiritual stress and the fact that I felt confined in the monastery and that a year's leave of absence would benefit my discernment.

She had to get the approval of the other solemnly professed nuns before she could give me a reply. I waited a few days, and after the fourth day she called me into her office and said that the sisters agreed to a leave of absence. I was so overjoyed I practically threw a party, but instead I went to the oratory in the cloister, and in the silence of the sunlit room, I gave thanks to God.

---

12. Eric Jantsch, *The Self-Organizing Universe* (Oxford: Pergamon Press, 1980), 40.

7

The Roads We Travel

T HE DECISION TO LEAVE the monastery was like opening the window of a dark and musty room. Light, air, sunshine, and wind all began to flow back into me, like someone drawn out from the deep waters of the ocean and resuscitated. I understood the words of the prophet Isaiah: "When you pass through the waters, I will be with you; and when you pass through the rivers, they will not sweep over you. When you walk through the fire, you will not be burned; the flames will not set you ablaze" (Isa 43:2).

Since I would now be outside the monastery, I had to have some income and a place to live. Herb had moved his labs to the main campus of Rutgers University and had brought in a top-notch neuropathologist by the name of Ken Reuhl. Herb and Ken established a new unit of neurotoxicology on the campus of Douglass College. I called Herb and explained my predicament, and he welcomed me back with open arms, offering me a full-time research associate position. The thought of being a research associate scared me, as I had been out of the research loop for four years. Nevertheless, I agreed to a postdoctoral position in the neurotoxicology labs at Rutgers.

Entering a New World

I needed a place to live near Rutgers, and Mother explained that, since I was still in simple vows, I should reside in a convent. She was kind enough to make the connections for me. Her aunt had lived in a nursing home in North Plainfield, New Jersey, run by a community of German Franciscan Sisters, so Mother called the superior of the community and asked if I could live with them for a year. When I told my parents of my decision to leave the monastery they were overjoyed, as if their daughter had just been released from prison. For the first time in four years we could go out together to a restaurant and share a meal, something that was not possible in the monastery. My mother had the idea that, since I was now liberated and back in the world, I would need a new wardrobe. She went and bought all types of clothes, including a yellow-and-white, polka-dot dress. But the fact was, I had left the monastery but the monastery had not left me. I had no desire for secular clothes (and certainly not for a polka-dot dress) and opted instead to dress in a modified religious habit.

Leaving the monastery was, psychologically, a very strange experience. I had become so accustomed to the silence of the cloister and the rhythm of work and prayer that I found the world to be frenetic and chaotic. For one thing, I had not handled money during my four years in the monastery. I don't think I saw a single quarter or dollar bill the entire time I was cloistered. I had to relearn the art of monetary exchange. I remember walking into a Ross department store and being overwhelmed by the amount of stuff spread across the aisles and wondering how to navigate the myriad clothes and people. Moreover, the car traffic on the road was frightening, what with road racers, tailgaters, and other drivers weaving in and out like at an Olympic slalom event. Everyone moved at such a fast pace that it was hard to make sense of where everyone was going. I missed the idyllic setting of the monastery where sunrise and sunset embraced the garden like bookends, and where the seeds planted in spring, and the fruit of our work harvested in the fall, provided food for the journey of life.

On the other hand, I was so giddy with my new found freedom that I said inappropriate things, like the time I had dinner with a former classmate from the Medical School who told me her daughter was in drug rehab. I said something like, "So what kind of drugs is she is using?" as if she had a cold, when in fact she was addicted to heroin. My dismissal of the seriousness of the situation resulted in my well-trained religious response: "Oh so sorry to hear. I will pray for her." She was miffed by my response, and I never heard from her again.

The world was a difficult place to navigate, and I was not sure how I would manage in such a feverish world of activity; but I trusted that

God would show me the way. The first thing I had to do was to buy a used car, and luckily my parents were able to help in this respect. I went back to my old Subaru dealer and found a cheap car with a paint-peeled, rusted roof. It had four wheels and an engine, and that was good enough for me. I drove my Subaru onto the long driveway of Villa Maria in North Plainfield, New Jersey, in early January 1988, ready to begin a new life of freedom.

Villa Maria was an old sanitarium that was purchased by a German group of Franciscan nuns back in the 1920s. The sisters were from Wurzburg, Germany, the community having been founded on the Feast of Pentecost, May 27, 1855, by a woman of great faith, Antonia Werr (d. 1868). Her burning desire was to minister to "women in need"; and along with four others, she welcomed women who had been released from prison. They eventually joined the Third Order Regular of St. Francis, and their community was finally approved by Rome in 1936. In 1929, in response to a request from the Franciscan friars in Rensselaer, New York, a group of these German sisters arrived in the United States. Thus, the community of the Holy Child Jesus was founded in North Plainfield, New Jersey, in 1929. Originally, the sisters cooked for the priests, darned their socks, folded their laundry, and essentially served as their servants and surrogate mothers (while the seminarians were in school learning theology, philosophy, and Latin). Like many other apostolic communities of its time, the community swelled in numbers. By 1962, the Franciscan Servants of the Holy Child Jesus had 1,175 members spread out between Germany, the United States, and South Africa.

Living among Franciscans

When I pulled up to the entrance of Villa Maria, I had neither a clue nor a desire to know about the Franciscan Servants of the Holy Child Jesus. I was simply grateful that they had a room available for me in their convent. I was a Carmelite who carried the monastery within me. I arose each morning for an hour of mental prayer, from 5:00 a.m. to 6:00 a.m., and prayed matins (morning prayer) and vespers (evening prayer) each day with the sisters. I tried to maintain silence interiorly and exteriorly, when possible. My task was simply to discern God's will and to try to get a sense of a normal life again. Despite the fact that I could now get in a car and drive to McDonald's or visit an old friend, I deeply missed the monastery. The words of the prophet Hosea were still etched on my heart: "I will lure her and lead her out to the desert and there I will speak to her heart" (Hos 2:14). Mother Marija called faithfully each week to see how I was doing, but I knew I could not return to Sugarloaf. I lived between the cloister and the world.

The sisters at Villa Maria were pleasant and charming in their own way. Sister Gregoria was the superior of the community, a tall large-boned woman, who walked with a royal swagger and had a thick German accent. She was very accommodating to my needs, which made my transition a smooth one. There were about sixty sisters living in community when I arrived in 1988. Many of them were German sisters who had staffed the seminaries and helped build the nursing home at Villa Maria. They were simple women who persisted through years of hard physical labor and radical poverty with little remuneration except the gift of saying their prayers together in chapel.

I especially like the old German sisters because they exemplified the counsels of poverty, chastity, and obedience in a way that was visible. In its structure and form, the community was not too different from the monastic community at Sugarloaf. Despite the fact that many religious women had replaced the religious habit with secular clothes and were accepting jobs in the public sphere, the sisters at Villa Maria retained a modified religious habit and worked together in the nursing home, which was annexed to the convent. Although they were an "apostolic" community (a form of life that arose after the Middle Ages to perform works of charity), they followed a monastic routine. In a short amount of time, I found myself attracted to the community. I was thirty-two and had arrived during a growth phase in the community. There were several novices and some junior professed sisters (temporary vows) in formation, and the anticipation of some new members made the community even more attractive.

I started my postdoc at Rutgers within a few weeks of settling into Villa Maria. Herb and Ken were most welcoming and delighted to tell me that a new postdoc by the name of Martin Philbert would be arriving shortly from Europe. Herb spoke highly of this young brilliant neuropathologist from the University of London, and I was eager to meet him. It was strange being back in the lab, after being plunged into the monastic greenhouse of God. I loved being back in research, but it was not quite the right fit for my spirit. Bruce Gold was now a research partner in the neurotoxicology group, and his relationship with Herb had not improved during my years of absence. Since Herb did not realize that I would return to research he had asked Bruce to write up my data for journal publication. My return complicated matters and led to a vitriolic showdown between Herb and Bruce.

Thankfully, Martin Philbert's arrival was a breath of fresh air. He was a tall, thin, dark-skinned Brit with a styled Afro; his parents had migrated from Granada to England years before. He was absolutely charming, and his impeccable British accent (which he maintains to this day) gave him a noble character. Martin was smart and talented and could play organ and piano with the ease of a concert musician. Although he was a Seventh-day Adventist by confession, he was open to talking about religious matters, and we had a number of good discussions on God, salvation, and the second coming of Christ. True to his religious beliefs, Martin neither smoked nor drank alcohol, and, in this respect, I was grateful.

My project for the year was studying the effects of methyl mercury poisoning on motoneurons. An outbreak of methyl mercury poisoning occurred in the 1950s in Minamata Bay, Japan, due to contamination of the water by surrounding industries. The people were eating fish caught from the methyl-mercury-contaminated water and developing symptoms that resembled cerebral palsy or spastic paralysis. It was speculated that methyl mercury or other heavy metals could be involved in the onset of cerebral palsy, especially since metals such as lead and aluminum, found in cooking utensils, were also associated with neurological disease; however, the underlying causes of these diseases were still unknown. My job was to investigate the electrophysiological changes induced by high doses of methyl mercury poisoning in rats (from cats to rats!).

I would return each day from the lab to the dining table where I sat with three older sisters, Regina, Annunciata, and Anthony, who always asked: "So how was your day? What did you do?" I inevitably answered each time: "The day was pretty good, but my rat died [again!]." They were very dear women who were genuinely interested in my work, but it was difficult to explain exactly what the work entailed.

Life at Villa Maria quickly settled into a routine, as the sisters were delighted to have a younger sister among them. I wore the Carmelite habit on Sundays and feast days; the rest of the time, I wore a simple black skirt and white blouse in the convent, and jeans to the lab or to visit a friend.

While my monastic life was deeply planted in my soul, like the roots of an old tree, the tree was sprouting in new directions. I wanted to be in religious life, but the cloister did not seem suitable to me; however, life with the German sisters appealed to me much more because the community was open to the world. I also appreciated the fact that the sisters drank beer on Sundays (part of the German culture) and had community parties to celebrate a sister's birthday or feast day. The strong emphasis on community life and the breadth of social life in general, especially since the convent was annexed to a vibrant nursing home, opened my eyes to a new way of living religious life. At Villa Maria, the habit and the daily schedule of prayer and life distinguished the Franciscan life from the secular realm; yet there was a wide range of human contact that was lacking in the cloister.

By the time my year's leave of absence was drawing to a close, I knew my monastic life had come to an end and that a new way of life, more conducive to my spiritual temperament, was on the horizon. At the same time that I was writing my letter of termination to Mother Marija, I was filling out an application to the Franciscan Servants of the Holy Child Jesus. It was an almost seamless move from one religious order to another with one small glitch: the German sisters were "Franciscan" and I had been a "Carmelite," which meant I had to undergo another novitiate, or "nun boot camp," as a Franciscan. I really had no idea what constituted a "Franciscan," so a period of time to learn this new charism was not a bad idea; however, I had almost five years seniority in religious life, which I hoped could merit some credit. Luckily, the mother general in Germany gave permission to exempt me from doing the postulancy year, which meant I could move directly into the first year of the novitiate. I was joined in formation by a young woman from North Carolina by the name of Michelle Schmidt, who was eleven years my junior. Michelle joined the Franciscan Servants as a postulant, and I became a first-year novice. From the moment we met we were an inseparable duo.

Starting Over

The novitiate is a testing ground for the religious spirit and a weeding place for those discerning religious life. As a "community within the larger community," the novitiate did not exactly follow the schedule of the professed sisters (those living vowed life) but had different activities that comprised "formation," including structures and activities that hone the virtuous life and educate the candidate in the charism of the life. Our novitiate community was called the Portiuncula ("Little Portion") after the small church where Saint Francis of Assisi began his movement in 1202. The Portiuncula community was housed above the nursing home laundry and across the driveway from the main residence. The sisters had renovated the second-floor structure with knotty-pine wood-paneled rooms and a small chapel. By the time Michelle and I were on board, the two previous novices, Patricia and Gabrielle, had moved on to first vows, so it was just the two of us in formation. We had a novitiate "team" consisting of the novice director, her assistant, and several professed sisters who comprised the novitiate community. The novice director assigned to us was a young, attractive American woman of German descent who entered the Franciscan Servants at the age of seventeen. She was warm and charming with a soft-spoken voice controlled by a powerful inner emotional engine, which could backfire without warning.

I concluded my postdoctoral position at Rutgers in early December and prepared to enter the novitiate in January. The sisters suggested that I could finish out my time in the lab as a novice but would have to terminate my work by summer so that I could begin the canonical year of novitiate. There I was in 1989 becoming a novice once again, and this time I put on a mid-calf grey habit, which included a one-piece dress, scapular, cloth belt, and black veil. As in Carmel, entering the novitiate entailed a new name for a new identity (a "second baptism") in the community (a "second family"). Sister Gregoria indicated I could keep the name "Ilia" given to me in Carmel but asked if I could drop the name "Teresa" since there was a "Sister Theresa" already in the community. I agreed to do so, especially since I like the way the German sisters pronounced my name. "Eel e-*jah*" with the emphasis on the "jah." Since I would now be named for the prophet alone, I really hoped that God would live up to his side of the bargain as my protector and strength (I needed a divine bodyguard!). The garden of Carmel would now become an interior source of life for a prophetic spirit. I would be the prophet of the Most High in the midst of a changing world.

Shortly after I was received into the novitiate, Michelle and I were sent to a retreat house in Connecticut for a weekend. One night I had a dream in which I was sitting next to a nun in a long black veil. We were sitting shoulder to shoulder, both facing Mother Marija, and Mother was talking directly to the nun: "I really think Sister Teresa Ilia should return to the monastery," she said, and the black-veiled nun insisted, "No, she has something to do in the world." This back-and-forth exchange occurred three times before I knew (intuitively) that the black-veiled nun was Saint Teresa of Avila. After that dream, I knew I was on the right track of following God's will in the world.

I put on the habit as "Sister Mary Ilia" (everyone took the name "Mary" as model of the Christian life) and returned to the lab the next week. There was something right and wrong about returning to the lab. Something within me had deeply changed over the intervening years. When I entered the monastery in 1984 and crossed the threshold into a new way of life, something had died; my life now was hidden in Christ. The ancient saying attributed to the philosopher Heraclitus, "You cannot step twice into the same river,"[1] was indeed true. I had entered into the cave of the divine mystery, and science seemed to have lost its luster, as if the glitter had worn off and what remained were simply a bunch of problems and solutions.

As "doctor-novice" I was hired by Fidia Pharmaceutical Company from Italy (thanks to Mario) to work on a project studying the effects of gangliosides on sensory neurons. Fidia was interested in developing

---

1. Plato incorrectly quoted Heraclitus in his book *Cratylus*, where he wrote: "Heraclitus, I believe, says that all things go and nothing stays, and comparing existents to the flow of a river, he says you could not step twice into the same river." See https://plato.stanford.edu/entries/heraclitus/.

a new drug for Type II diabetes that would involve complex lipid compounds, and my job was to assess their effects on sensory nerves.

Having become a Franciscan novice in a grey habit, I felt odd walking around the laboratory with a black veil and white lab coat. Herb and Ken made no real issue of it, but I could not readily join them at the pub anymore and the habit impelled them to closely monitor their curse words, as they did not want to offend me. Martin took it in stride and called me "Sister Ilia of the Five Pizzerias," since I loved pizza. I knew that being a "sister-scientist" was awkward when one day, a delivery was made to the lab and the delivery man looked at me with a startled look (almost as if he just encountered "ET") and said, "Please give this package to Dr. Delio." "I will be happy to do so," I said.

But it was not the habit alone that rendered my time in the lab awkward. I loved science, and yet I had discovered a whole other realm of reality, one that could not be accessed by formulas or equations but by stripping oneself of "self" and entering the dark, cavernous mystery of the human heart. The laboratory of knowledge was now not only in the world of science but in the world of the soul. To find God without, one must find God within. In Carmel I discovered the laboratory of the soul, and this pursuit of knowledge was attractive. As much as I tried to talk to my colleagues about God, my words fell flat on the floor, and they would often counter my points with deist or agnostic arguments. They engaged by using the logic of their intellects, while I engaged from a logic of the heart born from the field of experience. When it came to understanding reality beyond the limits of science, we were not on the same page. However, my colleagues never tried to convince me otherwise but accepted my new way of life and respected my religious beliefs. God works in the strangest ways, and I knew that, in these men, I had found true and lasting friends.

A Staunch Traditionalist

I was looking forward to my "canonical year," which was a year away from the normal routine of the larger community and without any outside ministry or work in order to focus on Franciscan life and the church. I liked the routine of the novitiate because it provided a lot of time for reading, reflection, and prayer. Through my readings I rec-

ognized that I had a deeply Platonic spirit and valued spiritual ideals
over material reality. I longed for union with God as a deep, other-
worldly union. The monastery and the piety of the Carmelite saints
provided fuel for this other-worldly spirit, and I placed a great emphasis
on love and suffering as the way into God's heart, following the crucified Christ.

In one retreat notebook I wrote, "Love and Suffering are intertwined. There is no other real path to love than through the cross."
In a way I felt that God was preparing me for a new path, as I wrote:
"Though this is a difficult time for me, going back to the beginning
of the novitiate and starting over, the Lord is calling me to something
deeper; I feel strongly that this call will eventually be integral to the
Church itself."

Yet, I was staunchly conservative in my religious views. I maintained
that Vatican II had sold out on the true meaning of Christian life and,
more so, on religious life. My mantra was, "The Christian is one who
stands in the world but not of the world, as a witness to the Risen
Christ." Hence, Christian life demands discipline and vigilance; it
requires the totality of one's life and one's commitment. The only true
Christian life is that of the martyr, the person who is willing to risk
one's entire life for the sake of the gospel. Vatican II seemed to flatten
out this rigor by diluting it with worldliness and secularism. Religious
men and women were abandoning the discipline of committed Christian life and experimenting with different forms that relied on pop psychology and feelings, rather than the crucified Christ. Since the 1970s
many religious had left their congregations to get married or simply
live in the world; others experimented sexually while living a vowed
life. Vatican II seemed to deconstruct the monastic form of religious
life, and it was like letting lions and tigers out of their pent-up cages.

I was deeply suspect, if not outright critical, of post–Vatican II religious women and felt that the radical changes in religious life signaled
the downward spiral of the church. In one of my notebooks I wrote:
"Many religious are trying to blend disparate elements into an odd
mixture: a spiritual charism blended with pop psychology, Vatican
II, and Thomistic theology. It simply won't work." I felt that religious
women had abandoned the true call to follow Christ by buying into

materialism and secularism; the spirit of poverty was lost and so too was the spirit of obedience and humility.

These virtues seem to be still at work, however, in the Franciscan Servants, and it was one of the reasons I was attracted to the community. When I went to formation programs and saw religious women in polyester pants with a black veil, I would chuckle out loud. In my view, this asynchronous dress was part of the new religious cacophony.

I was a religious snob who vowed to remain a "true religious" by wearing the habit (albeit, a modified habit), following a structured prayer life, and practicing the virtues in community. My sense of religious superiority actually blinded me to the goodness of contemporary women religious, including the efforts of some of my own sisters in community. I had no concept of the Leadership Conference of Women Religious (LCWR), an association that encompassed most of the congregations of women religious in the United States, and was ignorant of their struggles to move religious life forward in the late twentieth century. My views on religious life were based on retrieving the traditional monastic foundation focused on austerity, asceticism, and flight from the world of secularism. The idea that modern science or evolution could shape religious life or the church would have struck me as outrageous.

I bought into the patriarchal church lock, stock, and barrel because it reflected the way God ordered creation. Besides, it was the church of my Italian grandparents and the church of my beloved Saint Anthony devotion. God made the church with men as priests and women as mothers, sisters, and servants. To even question if the church should be or could be otherwise was a question for heretics, not for the orthodox. In fact, to raise such questions could incur eternal damnation. Science had absolutely no part in religious life, and I had to make a choice: either find a way to live between two disparate worlds (science and religion) or relinquish science in order to live more fully in God's salvific plan. I had no idea how this dilemma would play out.

On to a New Career

The novitiate brought out the prankster in me, and Michelle and I had a lot of fun dressing up in the old nuns' habits left behind by those who had died. The two of us decided that we would "return" to authentic religious life by wearing the long black habit, a Franciscan cord and rosary, and sleeping on the floor of our rooms. Our novice director was not happy with this behavior and did not know how to handle us. We were part of the Franciscan internovitiate program at the Graymoor Atonement House in Garrison, New York, where novices from all different Franciscan communities came together to learn about Franciscan history and spirituality and to form friendships across community lines. One week the instructor told us to wear comfortable clothing for the program, since the following week we would be doing yoga-type exercises. Michelle and I thought we would liven things up so we put on our dead sisters' habits, including the coif (the headpiece that surrounded the face) and rosary, and wore them to the event.

Our novice director was not amused. She had brought a sweat suit for the occasion, while we were in long habits. We drove in silence to Graymoor that week, and I could sense her controlled rage. Little did we realize that our pranks were making her increasingly angry, and she could lash out unexpectedly. We began to live with heightened anxiety, never sure what might trigger the next outburst.

The community was controlled by a triumvirate consisting of three women: the superior, the administrator of the nursing home, and the novice director. Together they exercised their power in a top–down patriarchal model of mandate and response. The superior caught wind of my strong character and felt that I was controlling Michelle or at least having an undue significance on her, and so I went from being the lovely Carmelite transfer to being the nagging thorn in the side of the novitiate. The triumvirate decided that one possibility to alleviate stress was to send me off to school. They made this decision after consulting with Father Benedict Groeschel, who was my spiritual director at the time, and who helped in my transition from Carmel to the community in New Jersey. Father Benedict knew of my struggles in community life, especially living with simple women who argued over bottle caps and vacuum cleaners, and who were like children under the watchful eye of authoritative parents. So he met with the power team to work out my future.

The community at Villa Maria was a hybrid of two worlds: the world of the old church and the new; the culture of Germany and of

America. The sisters found it difficult to navigate in the murky waters of the emerging post–Vatican II church. They were not sure if they should keep old wineskins or seek new wineskins, and tried to navigate a fledgling ship on the high seas of historical change. They maintained community order by relying on a chain of command that functioned like a stream of water, beginning with the German mother general and flowing into the United States through the power team of three women who presided over our community. In the twenty years I stayed with the community, the triumvirate never yielded their power. But as my mother liked to quote, "Absolute power corrupts absolutely," and in due time the consolidation of power in the hands of several sisters would lead to the demise of the community.

Discovering the Women of Vatican II

In a strange way I felt that God had led me to the Franciscan Servants and that God was in the chaos of the community, so when the community suggested that I study theology, I was intrigued. I had absolutely no intention of becoming a theologian or a theology teacher, nor did the community have such aspirations. I was in a community dedicated to helping women in need by operating a nursing home and a home for mentally disabled women (in Yardville, New Jersey). It was not a community dedicated to education, and I had no desire to seek such a religious community, since I thought they tended to be the "liberal ones."

Villa Maria was my home, and I accepted the dysfunction that came with the life. I knew that going to graduate school was outside the norms of the community, but the opportunity to be more independent and study again was attractive. The community asked me to study spirituality, but I requested to study theology, since that sounded more like an academic discipline. I applied to four schools (Princeton Theological Seminary, Drew University, Seton Hall University, Fordham University) and was accepted at all four schools (with scholarship offers at Princeton and Drew); however, the sisters insisted that I attend a Catholic school for a master's degree in theology. Since I graduated from Seton Hall and did not want to return there, I wound up matriculating in the Department of Theology at Fordham University in the Bronx.

Whereas most students began their graduate studies with no obligations other than schoolwork, I began graduate school as a second-year novice, which meant I had to return to New Jersey each week to participate in community formation activities and in the Franciscan internovitiate program, as well as help serve in the nursing home dining room on the weekends. I did not think twice about this unusual arrangement. It seemed like a breath of fresh air in what was sporadically a toxic community environment. In fact, the distance created between me and the community (simply by going to school in the Bronx) enabled me to see more clearly the dysfunction of my community.

As a second-year novice, I was required to live in community during my studies at Fordham. The Ursuline nuns ran a large girls' school several blocks from the university, and someone suggested that I inquire about a room in their convent. In early August I took a drive to the Bronx to inquire about temporary residence with the Ursulines. The Villa Maria sisters kindly gave me a dented blue Buick that had been in four accidents, and it seemed like an appropriate vehicle for driving in the Bronx, an area of New York City known for gangs, drugs, and violence. The drive itself was about an hour drive, crossing the George Washington Bridge onto the Bronx River Parkway. At first it was a harrowing drive, but after a while, I learned the city patterns of lawless driving, navigating my way down Fordham Road, dodging buses, taxis, double-parked cars, and avoiding speeding police cars or ambulances.

I arrived in the parlor of the Ursulines in my Franciscan habit and the woman who welcomed me inside the parlor look quizzical. What did I want and how fast would I be leaving? The Holy Spirit was probably working overtime that day since the sisters agreed that I could live with them; however, there was no room in the main convent. I could have a room, however, in the house down the road where the community administrators, known as the "leadership team," lived. I was overjoyed.

The Ursuline nuns were founded in 1535 by Saint Angela Merici (1474–1540) in Brescia, Italy, for the education of girls and the care of the sick and needy. I would be living with Ursulines of the Roman Union, whose foundation was a monastic life hybridized with secular education. Prior to Vatican II, the nuns followed the strict routine of the cloister while attending classes at night or over the summer to prepare themselves in their respective fields for teaching young women. They were known as excellent educators and ran girls' academies in various parts of the country. The more I heard their stories, the more inspired I became. My first encounter with them, however, was, "Oh my God, they wear secular clothes!" And their first reaction was, "What is wrong with this young woman dressed in a habit? Has she not heard of Vatican II?" So our initial encounter was friendly but also marked by curiosity, if not downright suspicion. I found myself face to face, sharing the same table, with precisely the type of religious women I had criticized, if not outright rejected, for the last eight years. God certainly has a sense of humor and probably rolled over with laughter while I navigated my new journey.

I began my classes at Fordham in the fall of 1990 without a single thought that my habit distinguished me from everyone else. Studying theology was like being a fish who had found an ocean of water. I was ecstatic with my classes in patristics, foundational theology, history of Christian spirituality, and American Catholicism among others, and I would return to the Ursulines each day with stories and insights to share. They were genuinely interested in what I was studying, and our conversations could last for hours. It was from these women, whom I had initially rejected on the basis of appearances, that I began to learn the value of friendship, conversation, and true dialogue, crossing the thresholds of personal limits and entering into the world of the other. They would share their stories of cloistered Ursuline life mixed with the stress of graduate school at night or during the summer, getting degrees in law, history, theology, and Chinese studies, and I would share my stories of Villa Maria and theology classes at Fordham. As I grew in friendship with these women, the scales on my eyes began to lift, and my heart expanded with an incarnational breadth. I was inspired not only by their achievements but by their commitment to the gospel life.

When I ate at the main house, I often sat with Sister Lucy, who still wore a short veil and had a large set of teeth that protruded every time she smiled. She told me her story of wanting to be a missionary to China when she joined the Ursulines at the age of eighteen; however, when her time came to go on mission she was sent instead to the hinterland of Alaska. She agreed to go to Alaska for only one year but wound up staying for forty years, teaching children from surrounding Eskimo villages. She was asked to become a science teacher at the age of sixty-three, but knew nothing of science, so she enrolled as an undergraduate at the University of Montana and matriculated for six summers. She was truly a remarkable woman, as were many of the sisters I met. Sister Catherine slept in a tiny room outside the main dining room with only a curtain for her door. Her ministry was to the poor in the Bronx, and she lived like one of the poor in her own community. Though I did not want to admit it too readily, these women were incredible in work and witness.

However, I could only reside in the Bronx for the duration of my coursework. At the end of my last course each week, I had to return to New Jersey to participate in the novitiate formation program and help in the nursing home on the weekends, either doing dishes in the kitchen or serving in the dining room. I would arrive back at the convent to hear the sisters' complaining about one another or to find my friend Michelle—now Sister Francesca—increasingly lonely in the novitiate, while potential vocations came and went. The superior was kind enough to give me an office to do my schoolwork; however, the office sat on the main hallway, and many sisters would stop by to say hello, complain about something or other, or just to see how I was doing (or what I was doing!). Needless to say, I was happy to get in the car on Monday and sit in traffic on the George Washington Bridge or dodge speeding cars on the Bronx Parkway until I could arrive back at the door of the Ursulines once more.

The Royal Doors of Theology

Though my religious dress marked me as a curiosity in the Fordham Theology Department, I excelled in my coursework. My fellow students were friendly in the hallways, but only one student by the name of Arlene Gensler actually reached out to me as a friend and invited me to her small studio apartment at the edge of campus. Arlene was a brilliant woman, a graduate of Brown University and a recipient of a Presidential Scholarship at Fordham. Her area of interest was the patristic fathers, and we shared in common our love of the early church. Arlene's husband worked for IBM computers, and one day she asked if I would like to borrow a computer to do my schoolwork. I had heard of computers but never saw one, and writing papers longhand on a yellow legal pad could be tedious. So I agreed to the new device. Arlene brought the computer to school, and I brought the computer back to the community where the sisters gathered in awe around this strange machine. It took us some time to figure how to turn it on and then how to navigate Word 1.0; however, once we did so, writing papers became a breeze.

Studying theology opened up doors that I never knew existed. I loved the patristic fathers of the church and settled on historical theology as my area of concentration. This was not the fluff stuff that I imagined; this was a serious form of study that followed a certain rigor and logic. My puerile notion of God was dispelled and replaced by deep philosophical and theological insights hewn from the thoughtful minds of the early church. Theology was not a matter of feeling or devotion, as I originally thought, but a science in its own right with its own methods of inquiry, logic, arguments, and insightful conclusions. The medieval thinkers viewed theology as the "queen of all sciences." In their view, every discipline, from the mechanical arts to astronomy and rhetoric, could be traced back to theology. It was from the medieval masters that I learned about the harmonious relationship between the microcosm (the human person) and the macrocosm (the cosmos). This made tremendous sense in view of the unity of God and converted me from a dualist to a monist or, better yet, to a Christian. Instead of separating God and world into separate mental compartments, I could begin to envision an integrative wholeness through the centrality of Christ.

I wrote my master's thesis in one long weekend, from Thursday to Sunday, on the role of happiness in the Rule of Saint Augustine. I knew it would not be a stellar paper because I was working under the gun. My second-year novitiate was coming to an end, and I had to prepare to make first vows as a Franciscan Servant of the Holy Child Jesus. In the meantime, I had fallen in love with the discipline of theology and could not bear the thought of terminating my studies at the level of a master's degree. When I asked the superior if I could apply to the doctoral program, she was delighted and said she had the same idea. I concluded my novitiate formation, finished up my master's degree work, and applied to the doctoral program while helping the community on the weekends in the nursing home.

Conversion at Midnight

My last course ended in early December, and I had a take-home exam for a course in the New Testament that had to be submitted two days after the exam. I was not sure how I could drive back to New Jersey, complete the exam, and drive back to the Bronx to submit the exam within forty-eight hours. I was recounting my dilemma to my Ursuline friend, Sister Jean Hamilton, who worked in campus ministry. Jean was a character in her own right, very smart and witty, but kind of loose around the edges, as exemplified by the baggy jeans and sweatshirt that comprised her daily dress. She had an idea, she said, to help me in my dilemma. "Why don't you use the computer in my campus ministry office to write your exam? This way you can complete it, submit it, and then return to New Jersey." It was brilliant, and I jumped on her offer.

That evening I took all my books and notes to Jean's office to complete the exam. She had cleared her desk to make room for my theological task. I was not expecting Jean to hang around since I knew I would be there for hours, so I said, "Jean, please go home, and I will lock up the office." She insisted on staying to make sure I was ok and had what I needed. I started the exam around 5:00 p.m., and around 7:00 p.m. Jean interrupted me to say she had brought supper. She had gone home, made a casserole, and returned with a delicious dinner. I ate quickly as I was intensely focused and did not want to lose time. She was completely obliging, cleaned up the dinner plates, and then stayed around to read in the room adjacent to her office. It was about midnight by the time I completed the exam, and I found Jean sleeping on the sofa in the adjacent room. "Jean," I said, "I finished my exam. It's time to go home." "Ok," she said, "let's pack up and go." Something happened to me in that moment, as if Christ was there for me in the person of Jean Hamilton. All my judgments and biases disappeared. Now God was in the flesh of a woman who cared for me in an extremely selfless way, making me the object of her deep love and concern. What more could the Incarnation mean? My narrow view of religious life was jolted, and doors opened up to a new vista of the gospel life. I returned to New Jersey, drove myself to a retreat at the Vincentian Center in Princeton, New Jersey, then back to the community to celebrate Christmas and profess my first vows as a Franciscan Servant on January 22, 1991. Martin Philbert played the organ at my ceremony, and friends and family gathered, as I offered my life to God, following the path of Saint Francis of Assisi and Antonia Werr. On my profession prayer card, I had printed *Christus ist mein leben*; Christ is my life. However, it was no longer the Platonic Christ who had captured my heart and imagination; it was the Christ of Sister Jean.

8

A Brilliant Mentor

I WAS ACCEPTED into the doctoral program at Fordham without a hitch and wound up studying with one of the leading Bonaventure scholars of the late twentieth century. Ewert H. Cousins was a remarkable man in many ways, a brilliant mind and humble spirit wrapped together in a childlike wonder of new ideas and insights. His class lectures often spanned from the fourth to the twentieth century in the course of two hours. He would begin with Augustine then move to the Victorines and Franciscans and then wind his way into the thought of Alfred North Whitehead and Pierre Teilhard de Chardin and then back to Francis of Assisi and Bonaventure. He was not a linear thinker but an integrative one, and for the linear thinkers in the class, Ewert's lectures could be painful. But I loved his lectures. His "Etch-A-Sketch" discussions formed the pattern of a spiral rather than a straight line, and that was the way I conceived theological connections as well.

Studying with a Prophet and Mystic

E wert was by training a philosopher and received his doctorate in philosophy at Fordham University. He entered the New Orleans province of Jesuits at the age of eighteen and later left to pursue his graduate studies. His first wife, Catherine, died of cancer at the age of fifty. He eventually married a classmate of mine in the doctoral program, Janet Kvamme, and the two of them made a delightful couple. Ewert struggled in his final years with advanced neuropathy due to an autoimmune disease, but Janet journeyed with him to the very end and continues to oversee his intellectual legacy.

Ewert was from New Orleans, and his temperate spirit often betrayed his penetrating mind. He discovered the structure of the "coincidence of opposites" in Bonaventure's writings while translating Bonaventure's classic *Itinerarium Mentis in Deum* ("The Soul's Journey into God"). According to this principle, opposites (for example, heaven and earth or divine and human) exist simultaneously in relation to each other and, in a sense, complement each other. Ewert coined the phrase "mutual affirming complementarity" to describe the coincidence of opposites and used this interpretive key, or hermeneutic, to interpret Bonaventure's system of thought. With Richard Payne he helped create the Classics of Western Spirituality series for Paulist Press, and he was also the general editor of the acclaimed World Spirituality Series for the Crossroad Publishing Company.

Ewert built on the insight of the philosopher Karl Jaspers, who wrote in 1949 about what he called the "axial period"—the centuries between 800 BC and 200 BC, when a new kind of thinking arose in the major areas of the world: in China with Confucius and Lao-Tzu, in India with Gautama Buddha, in Persia with Zoroaster, in Greece with Thales, Pythagoras, Socrates, and Plato, and in Israel with the great prophets. Jaspers described this period as an "axial period" since "it gave birth to everything which since then, the human person has been able to be."[1]

Preaxial consciousness was located in the cosmos and in fertility cycles of nature. Primitive or tribal persons "mimed" and venerated nature, which appeared to them as a sacred reality determining one's destiny. This created a harmony between peoples and the world of nature, a harmony expressed in myth and ritual. While primitive people were closely linked to the cosmos, they were also closely linked to one another. One gained one's identity in relation to the tribe.[2]

Axial consciousness generated a new self-awareness that included awareness of self and a new sense of individuality. The human person as subject emerged. Jaspers states that, with axial consciousness, personality was revealed for the first time in history. With the emer-

---

1. Karl Jaspers, *The Origin and Goal of History,* trans. Michael Bullock (New Haven, CT: Yale University Press, 1953), 1, 2, 23, 27.

2. Ewert H. Cousins, *Christ of the 21st Century* (Rockport, MA: Element Books, 1992), 5.

gence of the rational individual came a new sense of freedom by which the human person could make conscious and deliberate decisions.[3] The world religions that emerged in the first axial period, including Buddhism, Hinduism, Judaism, Christianity, and Islam, all share a common existential thread: self-reflection and self-transcendence of the human person.

Ewert recognized that we are now living on the cusp of a new axial age of consciousness, which, following Karl Jaspers, he called the second axial period. In fact, the second axial period occupied much of his thought. While first axial consciousness gave rise to the free, autonomous individual, Ewert recognized a new axial period brought about by science and technology, including television, mass communication, mass travel, and the internet. This "second axial period" is characterized by the rise of global consciousness.

Cousins claimed that our consciousness was jolted onto a new level when, in 1968, the first photograph of the planet Earth, reprinted in all major magazines, triggered immense awe; a tiny blue marble-like globe suspended in space. From space, the Earth seemed like a single tribe of humanity. "For the first time since the appearance of human life on our planet," he wrote, "all of the tribes, all of the nations, all of the religions began to share a common history."[4] He used the term "complexified collective consciousness" to describe the consciousness of this second axial period, indicating that people are becoming more aware of belonging to humanity as a whole rather than a specific group.[5] Second axial period consciousness is communal, global, ecological, and cosmic; an advancement in the whole evolutionary process.

I was honored to be among Ewert's cherished doctoral students; he once wrote on a letter of recommendation that I had been his best student in forty years. I couldn't quite believe it because he had a steady stream of doctoral students, and the dissertations he had overseen lined his office like wallpaper. And truthfully, being first or tenth was not

---

3. William M. Thompson, *Christ and Consciousness: Exploring Christ's Contributions to Human Consciousness* (New York: Paulist Press, 1977), 21, 23.

4. Cousins, *Christ of the 21st Century,* ix.

5. See Pierre Teilhard de Chardin, *The Activation of Energy,* trans. René Hague (New York: Harcourt, Brace, Jovanovich, 1970), 30–31, 101–3; Ewert H. Cousins, "Teilhard's Concept of Religion and the Religious Phenomenon of Our Time," *Teilhard Studies* 49 (Fall 2004): 12.

important to me. I was simply in awe of the way he would elaborate on Bonaventure's Christology or Augustine's understanding of wisdom. There was something about Ewert that made him stand out among his peers. Many of his colleagues in the department thought he was an "airhead" or theologically "light"; one Jesuit colleague quipped, "Oh Ewert! Me and God at 30,000 feet!" Ewert was well aware of where he stood in the department, and let things roll right past his door. He never spoke against his colleagues, although he knew they complained about him. He would simply say, "Oh well." Like Herb Lowndes, my first mentor, Ewert knew the inside of the human heart and played his cards carefully. Why get involved in department politics and waste precious time when one could be exploring new levels of consciousness or Teilhard's notion of Christogenesis?

Only once did I see Ewert's anger visibly expressed, and that was at a doctoral defense. One of his students had written a very fine dissertation on Richard of St. Victor and had one of the leading Victorine scholars from Oberlin College on his dissertation committee. Ewert asked me to attend the defense since I was anticipating my own defense in two years. In a doctoral defense, the candidate gives a summary of his or work followed by a series of extensive questions from each of the five or six members of the committee. The questions circulate in a round-table style, each examiner taking about fifteen minutes each, until the committee has exhausted its inquiry (and the student as well!).

A Jesuit priest served as an outside reader on this particular exam committee (an outside reader is not involved in the formation of the dissertation but examines it upon completion), and when it was his turn to ask a question, he loaded up his cannons and fired away. He first questioned the student as to who translated the Latin texts. When the student responded that he did the translations himself, the Jesuit then proceeded to assert that the translations were incorrect, and thus the conclusions were incorrect as well. The student was stunned and simply froze. He could not speak for what seemed to be an eternal moment. I could tell that Ewert was enraged, but he kept his cool at the table.

I was absolutely shocked by this turn of the events, as was the rest of the committee. What would be the outcome of what initially seemed to be a flawless dissertation? The student essentially lost his voice and could not adequately answer the remaining questions from the examining committee. Once the exam concluded the committee deliberated almost an hour before delivering the decision of "conditional pass."

I went to Ewert afterward and asked, "What was *that* about?" He knew that the Jesuit was really attacking him as an incompetent mentor, as evidenced by the seemingly poor Latin translations (a judgment the Oberlin Victorine expert vehemently disputed). In any case, I had learned a lesson. I knew that I had to load my ammo early because I would have the same Jesuit examiner on my committee two years later.

Learning the Trade of Academic Theology

What is a true scholar? This was the question that most occupied me. There are many scholars who are weighed down by low self-esteem and constantly seek affirmation or who live with delusions of brilliance or who simply insist that the world revolves around them. The competitive streak in theology is different from that of academic science and part of the difference is due to the clerical history of theology, a discipline born out of the monastic culture and developed at the university by clerics. There is an implicit ontological ranking in theology where disciplines such as systematic theology or biblical studies rank higher than spirituality or ethics because they are more philosophically demanding (systematics) or require multiple languages (biblical studies). Scientists compete for grant money, and thus novel ideas are preciously safeguarded. Yet science is ultimately a collaborative discipline, and camaraderie among scientists is much more evident than the individualism and elitism of theologians.

Steeped in the world of Bonaventure, I had absolutely no interest in feminist theology, even though Elizabeth Johnson had joined the faculty at Fordham. Beth was a rising star and known as an outstanding teacher, so I enrolled in her course on "Mary and the Saints." She was indeed an excellent teacher, and many of the women students gravitated around her. However, I found feminist theology unconvincing, especially in light of Bonaventure's metaphysics of love.

True scholars, I came to realize, are explorers, genuine discoverers who have the brilliance of intellect but the wonder of a child, the power of creativity but the adventure of youth. They are often quietly engaged in their work without ever thinking twice about their reputation or status among their peers or students. The true scholar is one who is not afraid to say, "I don't know but I am interested to find out," and sets upon on a new path of inquiry—rendering the intellectual journey one of ceaseless wonder and exploration. I have met some outstanding scholars over the years, humble, ordinary folk with lightening-rod intellects, and I have met a number of scholars with such large egos that sometimes there was not enough oxygen in the room for two people to breathe.

Ewert Cousins was a genuine scholar of utmost humility. He could peer into centuries far behind us and speculate about centuries stretching into the future. We would sit for hours in his cramped office lined with piles of books and dissertations, lost in a flow of ideas that focused on love, the spiritual life, evolution, the world soul, the mystery of God, and life in an expanding universe. In the presence of Ewert, ideas blossomed into new worlds, and I would often find myself occupying multiple universes, as I listened to his seminal ideas flowering in the midst of the Bronx. His depth of spirit was mystical and illuminative, and he expounded Teilhard's God of evolution and Whitehead's dipolar nature of God within the broad cosmic vision of Francis of Assisi's nature mysticism. It was from Ewert that I learned to be an integrative thinker and to soar above the politics of academia with a smile. While his colleagues labored in first axial theology, Ewert was already thinking for a new age.

Discovering Bonaventure

When the community gave me permission to pursue a doctorate, Sister Gregoria asked if I could do something in Franciscan spirituality. "Ugh, I thought to myself. Why study something so boring!" However, once I began to study with Ewert, who introduced me to the world of Bonaventure (d. 1274), everything changed. Bonaventure was the seventh minister general of the Franciscan Order and led the order through tumultuous times after the death of Francis of Assisi. Even though he was a theologian at the University of Paris (like Thomas Aquinas) he had to resign his academic position and take up the role of minister general due to the fact that the prevailing minister general was forced to resign. Much of his theology relates to his pastoral concerns and quest for unity in the order. The great medieval scholar Etienne Gilson once remarked that Bonaventure's theology is so integral that you either see the whole in its entirety or you do not see it at all.[6] Bonaventure studied at the University of Paris, where he learned about the exemplary world of Augustine, the sacramental vision of the Victorines, and the self-diffusive goodness of Pseudo-Dionysius. These thinkers helped shape his understanding of creation and the God–world relationship. Bonaventure's theology was shaped by two main influences: Francis of Assisi and Alexander of Hales, his teacher at the University of Paris. His theology was like a cascading waterfall, originating from a fecund source, flowing throughout the tributaries of creation, and circling back to the great source. His trinitarian theology flowed into his Christ mysticism in a way that creation was imbued with the dynamism of divine love. From Francis he gained insight into the goodness of God and the sacramentality of creation and transposed these insights into his scholastic summa of theology without losing the distinct character of Francis's spirit. Like Francis, Bonaventure did not view the material world as "brute matter" or lifeless and inert stuff. Rather, creation bears the imprint of Trinity itself, dynamic and relational. All of creation—rocks, trees, stars, plants, animals, and humans—is, in some way, related to the Trinity. The beauty of creation is evident in the order and harmony of the things.[7] Creation is not simply a stage for human activity or a backdrop to human longings, but the whole of creation has meaning and purpose. It comes from God, reflects the glory of God, and is intended to return to God, a flowing cosmic symphony.[8] It was through Bonaventure that I would eventually come to appreciate the deep wisdom and insights of Francis of Assisi.

Alexander of Hales, also a Franciscan, inspired Bonaventure to look to the Greek fathers to understand the Incarnation. Rather than focusing simply on the second person of the Trinity, the Word, they asked,

---

6. Etienne Gilson, *The Philosophy of St. Bonaventure* (Paterson, NJ: Saint Anthony Guild Press, 1965), 13.

7. See Ilia Delio, *A Franciscan View of Creation: Learning to Live in a Sacramental World* (St. Bonaventure, NY: Franciscan Institute, 2003), 29.

8. Bonaventure, *Commentarius in librum Ecclesiastes* 1.7 (V, 13b); Bonaventure, *Breviloquium* (*Brev.*) 2.11.2. Engl. trans. José de Vinck, *Breviloquium*, vol. 2, *Works of Bonaventure* (Paterson, NJ: St. Anthony Guild Press, 1963), 101.

what kind of God could become incarnate? Alexander of Hales said that one must consider the doctrine of God prior to the doctrine of the Incarnation because only a particular understanding of God could support the Incarnation. His theological foundation of Christology began not with the person of Jesus Christ but with the question of God and the possibility of a divine nature united to a human nature. He concluded that there is no necessity in God for either creation or Incarnation. Rather, the power to create and the power to be incarnate rests on the divine nature as such rather than on a person of the Trinity.[9] That is, the Incarnation is not due to the existence of the divine Word but because God is personal, relational, and communicative. Since nature refers to action, creation and Incarnation find their sources in the divine nature understood as a principle of action rather than in the divine essence.[10] Kenan Osborne states:

> The Incarnation, or otherwise stated the "insecularization of God"—God entering intimately into the created world with all its history and its materiality . . . is not separate from creation. Creation and incarnation must be seen in their coterminality and interdependence . . . both creation and incarnation are reflections of a credible God.[11]

Bonaventure indicated that God could not communicate himself in a finite way if he was not infinitely communicative in himself.[12] The Franciscan theologians (including Duns Scotus) built a theology based on the intrinsic relationship between creation and Incarnation and "perceived the widest possible relations between the story of Jesus and the larger picture of the world."[13] They saw that the Incarnation is integral

---

9. Alexander of Hales, *Quaestiones disputatae: 'Antequam esset frater'* (Quarachi: Collegium S. Bonaventurae, 1960), 197.

10. Kenan Osborne, "Alexander of Hales: Precursor and Promoter of Franciscan Theology," in *The History of Franciscan Theology*, ed. Kenan B. Osborne (New York: Franciscan Institute, 1994), 31.

11. Osborne, "Alexander of Hales," 31.

12. Zachary Hayes, "Incarnation and Creation in the Theology of St. Bonaventure," in *Studies Honoring Ignatius Brady, Friar Minor*, ed. Romano Stephen Almagno and Conrad Harkins (New York: Franciscan Institute, 1976), 315.

13. Zachary Hayes, OFM, "Christ, Word of God and Exemplar of Humanity," *The Cord* (1994): 6.

to the possibility of creation itself. This was a radically different view from the position of Saint Anselm, who spoke of the Incarnation as a necessary event to repay the debt of sin incurred by the fall of Adam and Eve. The Franciscans thought otherwise and placed their emphasis on divine love: the Incarnation is due to the excess love and mercy of God, not human sin. Because of the relationship between creation and Incarnation, they held that "a world without Christ is an incomplete world," that is, the whole world is structured christologically.[14] Christ is not accidental to creation or an intrusion but the inner ground of creation and its goal.

When I discovered Bonaventure's rich theological vision of God, world, and the centrality of Christ, I knew I had found the theology that reflected my love of the material world and my love of God. For the first time theology made complete sense of the world of matter and the world of spirit, no longer two worlds but one world now seen in the interplay of depth, breadth, and beauty. Christ was the summation of all levels of reality, what the world is and what the world could become in its relation to God. "Christ shares existence with all things," Bonaventure wrote. "With the stones he shares existence; with plants he shares life; with animals he shares sensation; and with angels he shares intelligence." "In his human nature," he said, "Christ embraces something of every creature in himself."[15] When I read Bonaventure my head found my heart and my heart enkindled my soul, and I knew his vision to be more than a theology degree; it was a vision of life.

Teilhard de Chardin: A Kindred Soul

As I was writing my dissertation on Bonaventure's Christ mysticism, Ewert suggested that I look at the writings of the Jesuit scientist Pierre Teilhard de Chardin, a trained paleontologist whose profound Ignatian heart intuited, in a fashion that resonated with the vision of Bonaventure, a deep connection between Christ and evolution. Teilhard's theology was, in a sense, Franciscan Christology now seen through the lens of modern science and evolution. When Teilhard

---

14. Hayes, "Christ, Word of God," 6.

15. Bonaventure, Sermo I Dom. II in Quad. (IX, 215-219), trans. Zachary Hayes, "Christ, Word of God," 6.

discovered Duns Scotus's notion of the primacy of Christ through the Sicilian Franciscan Father Allegra, he exclaimed: "There is the theology of the future!"[16] With Teilhard I began to appreciate the critical role evolution plays in shifting the understanding of God from static to dynamic, from eternal presence to God of the future. Understanding Jesus as the Christ could only make sense in light of evolution, if indeed Incarnation and creation are one and the same act of God's self-giving love.

I remember the first time I read Teilhard's essays on Christianity and evolution. I felt this resounding "yes" rising up within me; my heart was on fire. Spirit and matter embraced in Teilhard's writings in such a way that the Incarnation made perfect sense in light of evolution. When I began giving public talks on his theology, I often got similar reactions; there was a fire in the room! Many people lit up when they heard his ideas on Christ in evolution and cosmic personalization.

One time a woman came up to me after a talk and said, "I left the church a while ago but if the church adopted Teilhard's vision, I would return tomorrow. Do you think this will happen," she asked? "Well," I said, "it is an unfinished universe and thus we must live in hope that God is doing new things—even with the church!"

With Teilhard one either sees the big picture of God and evolution or one does not understand his writings at all. Linear thinkers often struggle with his ideas, and it is a constant effort to help people think in terms of complexity and consciousness. He understood the science of evolution as the explanation for the physical world and viewed Christian life within the context of evolution. Evolution, he claimed, is ultimately a progression toward consciousness; the material world contains within it a dynamism toward spirit. He was convinced that the total material universe is in movement toward a greater unified convergence in consciousness, a hyperpersonalized organism or an irreversible trend toward cosmic personalization.

In my encounter with Teilhard I found my first clue that modern science and religion can share common ground. For the first time, I realized that science and religion were not opposite or separate areas of inquiry; rather, they informed one another because they were two

---

16. Gabriel M. Allegra, OFM, *My Conversations with Teilhard de Chardin on the Primacy of Christ* (Chicago: Franciscan Herald Press, 1971).

sides of the same conjugate, as Teilhard wrote, two lenses seeing the world, two ways of knowing the one world.[17] I was captured by his insights; his religious-scientific worldview would eventually prove to be formative.

I finished my doctoral coursework and had to prepare for the comprehensive exams while also preparing for final profession of vows. The sisters at Villa Maria somehow did not realize that each of these tasks was a full-time commitment. I finished my last course in early December and had to find a retreat house for my final profession retreat and prepare for the ceremony at the end of January. I wound up going to St. Mary's Villa, my former high school, which had become a retreat house—by myself, with no director. It was a very difficult time because my beloved father died the day after Christmas, and I was on retreat for final profession two weeks after mourning his death, with the anxiety of doctoral comprehensive exams looming on the horizon. Since graduate education was outside the scope of the convent, no one seemed to care too much for my welfare. Life went on in the convent like clockwork, following the schedule of work and prayer.

There is truthfully nothing worse than feeling neglected or abandoned or simply unwanted, and I felt all of these. The so-called community appeared as a group of self-absorbed women who could not see beyond their needs or fragile limits. The title of the community, "Holy Child Jesus," which meant attention to the hidden presence of God in the human person, the humility of God in the small fragile forms of life, floated above the daily life of the community, like oil over water.

While dialogue, mutuality, and shared life were idealistic words, the community grinded vocations into psychological models of depression. It was an unhealthy environment with no real accountability and no supervision, yet because of the outer visible signs of religious life, including the habit, the community was considered to be an exemplary religious order by the diocese and surrounding religious groups.

There was a widening gap between myself and the community I was part of, and yet I chose to make final vows because I had the freedom to live Franciscan life outside the community—not a good reason, but nevertheless expedient. I made my final profession of vows on January

17. Teilhard de Chardin, *The Phenomenon of Man*, 285.

24, 1994, in the midst of one of the worst ice and snowstorms in New Jersey history. Major highways were shut down, and there was a state of emergency in the area; however, Ewert Cousins braved the bad weather and came to the ceremony, as did my old childhood friend, Ellen Farkash; my mother and my faithful brother Richard and his family also came, along with a number of friends. Most significantly, however, the mother general from Germany, Sister Reginarda Holzer, made the trip, despite the weather conditions and the travel advisory. Reginarda was elected to her position at the young age of forty-two, and she was now in her second term as mother general. She was a powerhouse of energy and ideas, and she was equipped with a capacious mind. I liked her immensely, and she too was fond of me. While I hoped that she could influence the community for the good, I think she was placing the same hopes in me.

The final profession ceremony was beautiful and wound up on a good note; however, the week after profession, the community asked if I would take over as vocations director, which meant communicating with women interested in religious life and hosting their visits to the convent. I was aghast, as I still had to take the comprehensive exam and submit my dissertation proposal.

The department had agreed that students could bring notes to the comprehensive exam, and so I prepared detailed notes by asking myself different questions and answering them. I managed to ask myself the same questions that the examiners asked of me, and one faculty member thought I might have cheated! If he had known my strict graduate school conditions, it would be clear that there was not a remote chance of such a feat, other than a revelatory vision on the George Washington Bridge. I was thankful to the Holy Spirit, however, for the inspiration I received during that time. I managed to complete the comprehensive exam and obtain approval for my dissertation proposal all within a few months. Now on to writing the dissertation.

9

Solitude and Liberation

For my new role as vocation director, the sisters at Villa Maria provided me with a large corner office in the main convent. It quickly appeared, however, that my primary role was as convent counselor, advisor, and general problem solver. Every day I was constantly interrupted by sisters who would drop in to say hello, complain about Sister So-and-So, tell me about the cats, or ask if we should wear a black habit on a feast day (you would be amazed how black and grey could make a difference!).

I knew things would have to change when one day I heard Sister Elizabeth paging me over the convent loudspeaker: "Sister Ilia, I need your help quickly. Muffy is injured. Please come to the basement now." Muffy was one of three stray cats Elizabeth adopted and cared for with utmost attention. So I quickly dropped my pen into my book and ran to find Elizabeth hovering over this ragamuffin fur ball of a cat whose left ear was missing a tip due to his recent fight. I tried to tell her that I was not a veterinarian, but she would not hear my lament; my job was to fix the ear.

My actual duties as vocation director were often equally diverse. I was constantly receiving phone calls and had to answer letters: Did we provide education, have health insurance plans, retirement plans? Several asked, Could we provide for children of a potential candidate? I was not sure if women were interested in religious life or in seeking asylum.

I knew that unless I made a radical decision for myself, however, I would not complete my degree. So once again, I asked to leave the community to write my doctoral dissertation; and since it was on the

Franciscan theologian Bonaventure, I asked to go to the Franciscan Institute at St. Bonaventure University to complete the work. The institute had one of the best Franciscan libraries in the United States and some of the best Franciscan scholars in the country. Besides, the Franciscan Sisters of Allegany had a huge motherhouse right down the road. Sister Gregoria agreed to this request and, together with Francesca, drove me to the motherhouse in late summer of 1994.

The Allegany Franciscans were kind enough to give me a large room; unfortunately, it was located on the main hallway that led to the dining room. There was constant traffic in the hallway, and within a few days I knew the room would not work. When I inquired about another room in the motherhouse, I was told that all rooms were occupied.

Franciscan Solitude

I was sitting in tears on the edge of my bed one day when Sister Beth stopped by to say hello and see how I was doing. "Not well," I confessed. I told her of my dilemma, and she said, "Well, I am from the Ritiro, which is located in the back of the motherhouse. We are the contemplative branch of our community. We might have room for you in the Ritiro. I will check and get back to you."

Since God had brought me this far, I lived in hope that something would open up. Beth returned the next day with positive news: "We have room for you in the Ritiro!" I was overjoyed and fell on my knees to give thanks to God and then quickly packed up my things for the move.

The Ritiro (a house in which one lives in retirement or withdrawal from the world) has its origin in Francis of Assisi's *Rule for Hermitages*. Although Francis was known as a poor itinerant preacher of the gospel, his first love was contemplative prayer, and he spent most of his life living in solitary places. In fact, his initial conversion was to the life of a hermit, as biographer Donald Spoto notes:

> Hermits lived alone, following the customs of the Byzantine tradition, which included solitude, silence, fasting on bread and water, prayer vigils and, to avoid idleness, craft work. . . . But their desire for solitude did not mean they turned their backs on the world completely, for they were much involved

in trying to alleviate society's problems, serving as wandering preachers, aiding visitors, helping weary travelers and generally assisting the needy.[1]

This eremetical life was deeply imprinted on Francis's spirit, and he eventually forged it with his gospel way of life, creating a unity of contemplation and action that he encapsulated in his *Rule for Hermitages*, composed around 1217. He wrote this *Rule* as a way to preserve the contemplative dimension of evangelical life, so that the inner life of prayer could inspire the outer life of action. The text of the *Rule* is brief, befitting a guideline or scheme. Noteworthy is the purpose of the hermitage in terms of relationships between the brothers and the adherence to monastic liturgical hours. The body of the text is noted here because it was modernized and modified in the life of the Ritiro sisters:

> Those who want to remain in hermitages to lead a religious life should be three brothers, or four at most; of these, let two be "mothers" and have two "sons," or one at least.
>
> The two that are "mothers" should maintain the life of Martha and the two "sons" the life of Mary, and have a single enclosure, in which each may have his cell to pray and sleep in.
>
> And they are always to say Compline of the day immediately after sunset. And they should make sure to keep the silence. And they are to recite their Hours. And they are to get up for Matins. And let the first thing they seek be the kingdom of God and his justice.
>
> And let them say Prime at the appropriate hour and, after Terce, conclude the silence so that they can speak and go to their "mothers," from whom, when they want to, they can beg an alms, like little paupers, for love of the Lord God.
>
> And afterwards, they are to recite Sext and None and, at the appropriate hour, Vespers.
>
> And as to the enclosure where they stay, they may not allow any person either to enter or to eat there.

---

1. Donald Spoto, *Reluctant Saint: The Life of Francis of Assisi* (New York: Penguin, 2003), 62.

Those brothers who are the "mothers" are to make sure they keep their distance from people and, on account of the obedience due their minister, shield their "sons" from people, so that nobody can get to speak with them.

And those "sons" are not to speak with any person other than their "mothers" and their minister and custodian, when he wishes to visit them with the blessing of the Lord God.

The "sons," nonetheless, should now and then take over the duty of the "mothers," according to what arrangement they have come to about taking turns at intervals.

As for everything above-mentioned, let them earnestly and carefully endeavor to observe it.[2]

It was hard for me to grasp at first that the Ritiro sisters lived a contemplative life, especially since my Carmelite experience was less than ten years behind me. Was there really another way to live a contemplative life? Yes, there was, and the Ritiro sisters were completely dedicated to a life removed from the world but not separated from the world. More so, this contemplative life was at the heart of Franciscan life, and this fact, together with the rich Franciscan intellectual tradition, confirmed for me that I had found the right charism for my spirit.

There were only three sisters residing in the Ritiro at the time I moved into it; several other sisters were living outside the community for various reasons. The small number of sisters and the ample space of the dwelling was perfect for my needs. The sisters gave me two bedrooms for my use: one for sleeping and the other for studying and writing my dissertation. They called my study room "the cave," because I buried myself in that room from morning until evening every day, plowing through hundreds of books lining the walls which I retrieved and returned from the Franciscan Institute library. I would come out of the cave for meals and sometimes for a brief recreation in

---

2. Benedikt Mertens, OFM, "Eremitism: An Authentic Element of Franciscanism," in *Franciscan Solitude,* ed. Andre Cirino, OFM, and Josef Raischl (New York: Franciscan Institute, 1995), 139–40; Francis of Assisi, "Rule for Hermitages," https://www.hermitary.com/articles/francis.html. The Rule for Hermitages is an authentic writing of Saint Francis, composed between 1217 and 1221, but the latter date is preferred for historical reasons (Mertens, "Eremitism," 146).

the evening and was fortunate to have the Franciscan Institute within walking distance. Several times a week I would go over and meet with Father Romauld Green, a Scotus scholar, who was willing to review my research with me.

Learning to Breathe

I was still garbed in a modified habit in 1994, and the Ritiro sisters wondered why I continued to wear it; but I, however, still could not quite understand why they would abandon it. Like the Ursulines, they wore secular clothes that looked like what my mother and sisters might wear. How did they express their Franciscan identity, I asked them? What did religious identity mean to them?

We had numerous conversations about the habit during my time with them (when I was out of the cave), and they were good hearted in addressing my questions. There was a transparency about them; they were Franciscan inside and out, and it began to dawn on me that their life of prayer formed their life of service to others. Their "habit" was a "habit of the heart"—a vigilance of God's tender love and care. They gave witness to that love by the way they related to one another and to those they encountered.

Six months after living with the Ritiro sisters, my strong convictions about religious life and what comprised a religious sister once again began to melt around the edges. The Ritiro sisters were all heart and soul; they shared everything they had materially, and they shared unlimited kindness and love spiritually. Because of them, I was able to write my doctoral dissertation on Bonaventure's Christ mysticism virtually uninterrupted, except for the vocation phone calls from the sisters in New Jersey.

By Christmas 1994, I was four months into writing my dissertation but felt obliged to return to the community in New Jersey and fulfill my duty as vocation director. I arranged for seven women to visit the community during the two weeks I would be in New Jersey. It was absolutely ludicrous of me to do so, but the Villa Maria sisters were glad to see me fulfill my community obligation. One young woman eventually joined the community based on that December visit. As the vocation director, I had to ensure that all papers and requirements were completed and to welcome her on the first day of her new life. I was caught between a rock and a hard place, trying to fulfill my job as vocation director while completing a doctorate. I continued to pray for guidance and heard the words of the Holy Spirit: "Return to the Ritiro and write!"

I loved my time with the Ritiro sisters. Like the Ursulines, they were thoughtfully engaged on all levels: spiritual, intellectual, and the world of current events. When I mentioned my admiration for the Ritiro sisters to a sister at Villa Maria she said to me, "People are always nicer on the outside than in your own community"; but there was something wrong with this statement. What was the point of belonging to a community? What actually forms a community if not some type of shared values and shared vision? Underneath the outer layers of habit and horarium, some of the Franciscan Servants were submerged in murky waters of anger and resentment, especially those who had minimal education and viewed the younger sisters as spoiled and self-indulgent.

Living with a religious community can feel like being stuck on a bus or in an airplane with a group of people you are unrelated to biologically but related to existentially. Either there is something that binds the group together or there is perpetual conflict. Vatican II communities worked toward finding a new understanding of religious life that allowed their charisms to develop in a world of change and complexity. Those who did not accept Vatican II followed a monastic structure of religious life coupled with a type of theology that warranted separation between self and world. In between was a third type of community that acknowledged Vatican II but clung to the visible signs of religious life. Villa Maria fell into the third category. While the German sisters *tried* to be on board with Vatican II by allowing younger sisters to work outside the community or, in my case, to obtain a graduate degree, they did not consider the deeper implications for the community or the impact such changes would have on the community life. When broached on the topic of change or growth, those in power would reply: "Look what we have done for you. You should be grateful." (Which I was.) It was like a bad marriage where one partner grows in deep resentment of the other (for a whole host of reasons) expressed in passive aggressive rage ("Look what *I have done for you*, and look what I get in return—*nothing* but more work!").

I could not help but reflect on the changes in myself and in my understanding of God. As I changed, God changed; as I become free and independent as a person, God became free from my expectations and demands. The more I came to need God, the more God came to need me. I was growing out of a divine–human parental relationship into an incarnational mutual relationship grounded in love. As I studied Bonaventure's theological insights, I began to appreciate God as a fountain fullness of love, an unstoppable, irresistible wellspring of love who is the source of all life, a divine ocean of love from which my life flowed like a river onto the unfolding fabric of space-time. I came to "know" God as the infinite mystery of my life—entwined, entangled—and I began to realize that the choices I make affect the life of God.

When, back in 1984, I first crossed the threshold that separated the world and the cloister, I had renounced a profession I loved in order to live for God alone. I did not realize it at the time but my response to the call of God was a response to the call of my deepest self; God was not outside or above me, but God was (and is) the breadth and depth of my life. The search for God is the search for one's true identity, as Merton so eloquently wrote.[3] Our names are written in the stars ever before we take our first breath. There is a mysterious dimension to every person that belongs only to *that* person and is discovered in the vast silence of one's own heart: "Be still and know that I am God!" (Ps 46:10).

I began to realize, however, that stillness in God does not mean stillness of daily life. I found myself moving from house to house and from community to community (one year I moved ten times!), packing and unpacking suitcases. I stopped asking God when things would settle down because I came to realize that religious life is like a Sunday Italian dinner with the relatives, constantly moving their arms and talking and eating in a chaotic movement of dynamic activity. Rather, stillness in God means "leaning in" and "resting" on God, as if emptying out one's closets of everything one owns and giving it all away and then standing with nothing to lean on but the flow of life itself. This life is God. God is the present bubbling with life, overflowing into the future.

---

3. See Merton's chapters "Things in Their Identity" and "Pray for Your Own Discovery" in his *New Seeds of Contemplation*, 29–46.

Crossing a New Threshold

Iwrote my doctoral dissertation in one academic year, never sending chapters to Ewert Cousins or to the committee; rather I sent the entire manuscript, 464 pages, in late June and awaited their decision. It was a rather bold move on my part since the whole thing could have been rejected; however, the doctoral committee accepted my manuscript with only minor changes. I got an adjunct position at Seton Hall University in the fall of 1995, teaching a course on Catholic theology while I prepared to defend my dissertation, which was scheduled for late fall.

Being back at Seton Hall in a modified habit teaching theology was not lost on my long-term memory, but God is a deeply forgiving and compassionate God who doesn't remember the sins of our lives, only the love we try to live. In the words of the prophet Hosea, "Come back to me with all your heart, don't let fear keep us apart. . . . Long have I waited for your coming home to me and living deeply a new life" (cf. Hos 11:1-9). My goal was to live deeply a new life.

The theology class at Seton Hall was a large undergraduate group, mostly freshmen and sophomore students. I was a nervous wreck about teaching this class because I had absolutely no preparation as a teacher. I knew how to do spinal cord laminectomies and research medieval texts, but I had no idea how to convey theological material to undergraduates. It was a terrifying experience, but I worked hard to ensure that my students learned something three days a week.

The decision to accept this teaching position was made easier by the superior at Villa Maria, who laid out my alternatives one day in her office. "Well," she said, "you will be graduating soon with your doctorate, and now you will have to work. You can either work in the nursing home or get a teaching job."

Work in the nursing home? Seriously? I did that for two summers while taking summer classes at Fordham. I was the charge attendant on a floor of about twenty women, giving out medications and changing diapers while making sure no one fell. One time I had to give a hot water bottle to an elderly woman and promptly forgot about the bottle. When I returned, she had a nice red mark on her bottom. No, I could not work in the nursing home without incurring a lawsuit at some point. So I opted to teach with no pedagogical tools under my belt except my Fordham education and Sicilian common sense.

I defended my dissertation on December 8, 1995. Among the committee members was the same Jesuit who had unexpectedly upended the examination of a hapless student two years before because of the quality of his Latin translations. With that memory in mind I had carefully prepared all arguments and reviewed my Latin translations with a fine-tooth comb.

Despite the snow, the Ritiro sisters drove to Fordham from Allegany, New York, and their presence was deeply appreciated. From the New Jersey community, Sisters Gregoria and Francesca came and brought different types of foods for a reception afterward. The dissertation exam went so smoothly I thought something was wrong. I kept waiting for the poison darts to be thrown and was ready to counterattack. But after two rounds of questions, Ewert asked the committee if there were any further questions to be raised and the committee said "no." I had answered everything sufficiently. I could not believe that the exam had gone so smoothly and quickly and turned to Ewert: "Is this it?" I asked. Are we done?" "Yes," he said. "We are done." I exited the room, the committee convened, and in about five minutes the verdict was rendered: I was now a doctor of theology.

The community in New Jersey had no idea that I had completed my doctorate. It was never mentioned in community, and there was no celebration of the event. The graduation ceremony took place in May, and by then both Gregoria and Francesca had transferred to South Africa. Francesca had struggled in the community after I left for graduate school. While she excelled at Seton Hall (valedictorian of her class), she could not find her place in the community. The community in South Africa looked like a better option for her, and she accepted the challenge.

When May graduation rolled around, I was not sure what to expect. I wanted to participate in the ceremony because of Ewert Cousins, and I could not think of a more appropriate symbol than Elisha accepting the mantle from Elijah—the disciple from the master. The sisters at home in New Jersey, however, knew nothing of my completion of a doctorate. The May graduation ceremony was announced in the community the day before the event as another task among community activities: "Laundry can be picked up in the basement this afternoon, rosary at 4:00 p.m., and Sister Ilia will graduate tomorrow. End of announcements." The older sisters came up afterward and said, "I didn't know you were graduating!" Or some said, "Congratulations, Sister Ilia. I don't know what for but congratulations."

On the day of graduation, the superior, the postulant, and my cousin Jane drove to the main campus at Fordham University for the ceremony. We celebrated with dinner at a local restaurant, and I was happy with all that had been accomplished. While there was no celebration in the community or card or gift, I had the greatest gift of all: the presence of God and good common sense to keep my eyes open for new opportunities.

Moving to Washington, DC

My job choices were narrowed down to the nursing home or teaching, so I opted to continue teaching. In the spring semester of 1996, I applied for an adjunct position at Trinity College in Hartford, Connecticut. Within no time, I was called for an interview and landed the temporary position on the spot. I was recounting my good fortune to one of my classmates, another Franciscan sister, as we were standing in line for our May Fordham graduation. She too had been a student of Ewert Cousins and told me how she hoped to go to Washington Theological Union in Washington, DC, to teach. I had never heard of the school and learned it was a graduate school for theology and ministry. Apparently two professors had just left their positions, and there was an opening for a Franciscan scholar. "Well, good luck," I said, "sounds great. I hope it works for you."

We both graduated and went our separate ways. But then in the beginning of June, I received a phone call from a Franciscan friar telling me about the position at Washington Theological Union (or WTU). "You should apply for the position," he said. "You are well qualified for it." I had not thought of applying when I first heard about it, but this friar's encouragement was enticing, and I thought to myself that perhaps I would be a good fit for the position. I sent in my application and did not think twice about it. In early August I received a phone call from the dean at WTU requesting that I come down for an interview.

I drove to Takoma Park, DC (across the street from Takoma Park, Maryland), passing the exit for Johns Hopkins on Route 895 South and thought to myself, "God certainly has a sense of humor." I pulled into the parking lot of WTU and walked to my interview in my black veil and modified habit.

Washington Theological Union was founded in 1968 by several male religious communities who wanted their men trained in a post–Vatican II theological education. They originally established the school in one of the institutions owned by a religious order in Silver Spring, Maryland, before purchasing a warehouse in Takoma Park and renovating it according to the growing needs of the school. When I walked through the door of WTU in the summer of 1996 there were over three hundred men and women studying theology in various graduate degree programs, although the lodestar was the master of divinity degree. There was also a thriving sabbatical program, and many religious women and men from around the world came to WTU to do a sabbatical. The president of the school was a Franciscan named Vincent Cushing, and when he greeted me at the door in his pin-striped shirt and blue tie, with a big Irish face and broad smile, my first thought was "Hah! A liberal school of theology!"

The interviewing committee was composed of three priests, all dressed in shirts, ties, and sport jackets, and there I was in my modified religious habit. Apart from some of the Jesuits at Fordham, I was not used to seeing priests in sport jackets and ties, and the novelty of the moment made me wonder whether or not I would fit into the school. But the committee was very congenial, and I immediately liked the men gathered around the table.

The interview went smoothly, and when it was finished the committee asked me to step outside. I was not sure what to expect nor did I have any high hopes; I simply accompanied God's joy ride. Vince opened the door and called me in and said, "We would like to offer you the position. We need a good Franciscan scholar, and you come highly recommended." I was elated. Never for a moment did I think I would land a job on the spot. When the sister who originally told me about the position found out I was offered "her job," she thought it was rigged. I assured her it was not, but alas it was not in my hands.

With the WTU offer in hand, the plan was to go to Trinity College in the fall semester as adjunct assistant professor and to begin the position at WTU in the spring semester, beginning January 1997. I looked at the way my life was unfolding up to that moment and realized that all my plans for religious life—die to the world and live for Christ alone—had been "undone." "Why make plans," I thought, "when God thrives on chaos?"

The temporary position at Trinity College in Hartford meant again finding a community to live with, and this time it was the Sisters of Saint Joseph of West Hartford who opened their doors and offered me a room. This was my third post–Vatican II community, and I was primed for the questions about my habit and my community in New Jersey. The sisters were friendly but less engaged than the Ursulines or Ritiro sisters. Now I was a professor at the local college, and the demands on me were greater, so my only contact with the sisters was at mealtime. However, my few social contacts with the sisters reaffirmed what I had learned from the Ursulines: Vatican II called women and men to engage the presence of God in history, not in a wooden life removed from the world. History means change, and thus the challenge for communities was to find a way of integrating service, community, and charism without resorting to parental lines of authority or childlike dependency. It was and still is a difficult balance, and in due time I would realize that an entirely new theology is needed for religious life if it is to grow into a way of life in evolution.

Among the Sisters of Saint Joseph of West Hartford, I was very inspired by one sister who had just returned from her mission on the Ivory Coast. This sister had ventured to Liberia four years before to join three other sisters as a nurse, working in a makeshift hospital in a poor village. She recalled the many electrical outages in the infirmary and caring for cholera victims while submerged in a flood of water.

One evening a paramilitary group stormed into the village, and the sisters received a forceful knock on their door. They opened it to find two men pointing guns at them. "Step outside," one of them yelled. So the sisters, dressed in tee shirts and shorts, stepped outside and were told to line up. It appeared that they were all about to be shot, when this sister from West Hartford had the courage to step forward from the line and ask rather flippantly: "You're not going to shoot us now, are you?" Her disarming presence (and courage) caused the lieutenant to have a second thought, and he changed his mind. Instead, the sisters were blindfolded and placed on a truck and driven to an unknown location. They opened their eyes to find themselves barricaded in the village church, along with many other men, women, and children.

This sister recounted how the nuns found themselves hiding under the pews, grasping the arms of those around them, including their Muslim brothers and sisters. They were locked in the church for about a week with barely enough food and water, unaware that the military had burned to the ground all the houses in the village. They lived moment to moment, unsure if the next breath would bring life or death.

After about five days, the church doors swung open and the military leader told the people to leave the village by foot. Arm in arm, men, women, and children started to walk, and they kept walking for days and weeks on end until they reached the Ivory Coast, about four hundred and fifty miles from home. The sisters were among the exiles who made this trek with nothing but the shirts on their backs. When they reached the Ivory Coast, they started a community farm—Muslims and Christians—planting seeds for a new life together.

When the community in the United States was notified of the sisters' whereabouts, they ordered the sisters to return home. It was clear, however, that the sister recounting this story had left her heart with her exiled community on the Ivory Coast. Once again, I was inspired by courageous women who took up the call of Vatican II and risked their lives on behalf of the gospel. I had to step back from my narrow (but ever-expanding) world to confront my biases and theological walls. The problem with Vatican II was not the women and men who responded to the mandates of the council: it was me.

Grappling with Science and Religion

I was asked by the chair of the Religion Department to teach an undergraduate course on science and religion since I had graduate degrees in these areas. I naïvely accepted the assignment, not knowing that science and religion was a growing field since mid-twentieth century that had amassed a wealth of literature. I found myself pouring over books night after night wondering how I would get through the course. Science and religion are two pillars that support the entire edifice of life. To adequately get a grasp on their relationship I could not begin with modern science but with the question of what comprised science itself; thus, I had to go back to the ancient Greeks and review their cosmology and metaphysics. The best snapshot I had of a unified relationship was obtained in the Middle Ages, when the microcosm-macrocosm relationship governed the thought of the various schools: Chartres, the Victorines, Franciscans, and Dominicans.

I understood that after the sixteenth century and the church's rejection of Galileo's *Dialogue on the Two World Systems,* the harmonious relationship between science and religion fell apart. A brilliant mathematician and scientist, Galileo shifted the question from "why" something happens to the question "how," introducing a radical change in science and philosophy. Aristotle was influential on natural philosophy and provided four ways of explaining causality, indicating that every existent is oriented toward a final cause (*telos*). Hence, for Aristotle, final causality was the primary cause of movement. Galileo shifted the emphasis from final causality to efficient causality, not *why* does something move but *how* does it move. By shifting the emphasis from final cause to efficient cause, Galileo initiated a new understanding of nature according to mechanistic explanations of events rather than teleological ones, a shift that posed a challenge to the church. From the church's perspective, God was first cause, not nature. The real concern, however, was that Galileo defended the Copernican system at the same time that Luther and Calvin were rebelling against the church. Hence, Galileo appeared to be as flagrant as the Reformers.[4]

Cardinal Bellarmine insisted that "the doctrine attributed to Copernicus (that the earth moves around the sun and the sun stands at the center of the world without moving from east to west) is contrary to Holy Scripture and therefore cannot be defended or held."[5] The Catholic Church rejected Galileo's treatise, and, following the 1633 inquisition, he was placed under house arrest for life. (Of course house arrest in Florence, Italy, was not the worst possible fate!) The church found itself in a vulnerable position with regard to science, especially since the

---

4. Joshua Moritz, *Science and Religion: Beyond Warfare and Toward Understanding* (Winona, MN: Anselm Academic, 2016), 19–38.

5. The 1633 injunction by Cardinal Bellarmine is noted in N. Max Wildiers, *The Theologian and His Universe: Theology and Cosmology from the Middle Ages to the Present* (New York: Seabury Press, 1982), 98n30.

Galileo affair overlapped with the Protestant Reformation; the authority of the church seemed threatened on all sides. Science was detaching itself from its Christian roots, and the implications were enormous.

The resistance of the church to modern science and the loss of human centrality in creation spawned a radical empiricism and a milieu for scientific materialism to emerge. The Jesuit-trained philosopher René Descartes tried to preserve God from the clutches of a changing world by locating true knowledge not in creation but in the self-thinking subject. While up to and through the Middle Ages, creation was a source of revelation and knowledge of God, Descartes separated matter and spirit by a thought experiment. If knowledge depends on the material world and the world is full of change then one cannot attain true and certain knowledge from nature. However, if knowledge depends on the individual thinking self (in Descartes's famous line, "I think, therefore I am"), then self-thinking must be the basis of true and certain knowledge. The German philosopher Immanuel Kant used Descartes's philosophy to build a new ethics based on the "turn to the subject." The only thing one can know, Kant said, is the starry heavens without and the moral order within. Descartes's brilliant insight spawned the rise of rationalism and empiricism; scientific knowledge began to wrest from nature its inner secrets and to shape nature into a vast machine.

As the new science story emerged between the seventeenth and twentieth centuries, the human person was not part of the cosmic story. Whereas the ancient universe gave the human person a special role in creation as image of God, the world of modern science subsumed the human person into the dazzling world of scientific data. Essentially, nature was stripped of its sacred character. As the cosmos assumed a new world picture through modern science, religion remained tied to the medieval cosmos. The marriage of Greek metaphysics and Christian faith gave rise to an understanding of God, humanity, and creation that was too neat and orderly to be disrupted. Christian doctrine was inscribed within the framework of a perfect, immutable, hierarchical, and anthropocentric order—the Ptolemaic cosmos. The widening gap between the church and modern science undergirded the concern of Pope John XXIII, who saw the church as a ship at sea, unmoored to the changes of history; hence the need for a new Vatican council that could realign the church, theologically and pastorally, with the modern world.

Despite the massive shift in theological worldview ushered in by the Second Vatican Council, the timing was too late. Science had already undergone a significant paradigm shift that began in the early part of the twentieth century and was exploding by the advent of Vatican II. Einstein's theory of relativity, the rise of quantum physics, Darwin's evolution, the discovery of the gene, and many other findings gave rise to a new view of the human person within the context of development and change. Evolution was now the bread and butter of modern science. Teilhard de Chardin clearly understood the implications of evolution for all aspects of life:

> They truly are blind who do not see the scope of a movement whose orbit, infinitely transcending that of the natural sciences, has successively overtaken and invaded the surrounding fields of chemistry, physics, sociology, and even mathematics and history of religions. Drawn along together by a single fundamental current, one after the other all the domains of human knowledge have set off toward the study of some kind of *development. . . . Evolution is a general condition, which all theories, all hypotheses, all systems must submit to and satisfy from now on in order to be conceivable and true.* (italics added)[6]

The Catholic Church was built on stability and immutability and was not prepared for a cosmic order based on change. To this day, it struggles to retain universality in a world of increasing complexity due to the forces of evolution.

How to Reconcile Science and Religion

As I was studying and teaching on the relationship between science and religion, I found myself smack dab in the midst of these forces: church, science, religion. I was born and raised in a church formed by Greek metaphysics and the Ptolemaic cosmos (evidenced by the Roman architecture of churches with starry domes and an elderly God looking down from on high), but I was educated in the world of science, which included evolution and quantum physics. Was the God I prayed to the

---

6. Pierre Teilhard de Chardin, *The Human Phenomenon*, trans. Sarah Appleton-Weber (Brighton: Sussex Academic Press, 1999), 152.

same God who inspired Darwin's theory of natural selection or Einstein's theory of special relativity? Was God stable and fixed as portrayed in the church I prayed in or as our liturgical hymns proclaimed—"Holy God! Holy and Mighty!" Or was God as whimsical as my life? Did God *play* dice or did God merely create the dice players? These were difficult questions, and I could not find satisfactory answers.

I was happy to come across some critical thinkers like Ian Barbour and John Haught who used a set of categories to try to make sense of the relationship between science and religion. Barbour's fourfold typology is probably the best known. Science and religion, he said, can be understood according to one of the following relationships: Conflict, Independence, Dialogue, and Integration. The popular view is that science and religion are in conflict, an idea rooted in the hostility of church authorities and religious thinkers to Galileo and Darwin, but reinforced in the twentieth century by biblical literalism and fundamentalism.[7] Barbour pointed out that science and religion can also be seen as independent of each other, each having nonoverlapping domains of teaching. However, dialogue between the two disciplines could lead to mutual enrichment, and a cross-fertilization of insights could lead to integration, as Pope John Paul II wrote: "Science can purify religion from error and superstition; religion can purify science from idolatry and false absolutes. Each can draw the other into a wider world, a world in which both can flourish."[8]

In fact, it was John Paul II who saw the need to bring the church into a closer relationship with modern science. In his 1988 letter to George Coyne, SJ, the director of the Vatican Observatory at the time, he asked: "Is the community of world religions, including the Church, ready to enter into a more thorough-going dialogue with the scientific community, a dialogue in which the integrity of both religion and science is supported and the advance of each is fostered?" He continued:

For a simple neutrality is no longer acceptable. If they are to grow and mature, peoples cannot continue to live in sepa-

7. Moritz, *Science and Religion,* 19–38.
8. John Paul II, "Letter of His Holiness John Paul II to Reverend George V. Coyne, SJ Director of the Vatican Observatory," http://w2.vatican.va.

rate compartments, pursuing totally divergent interests from which they evaluate and judge their world. A divided community fosters a fragmented vision of the world; a community of interchange encourages its members to expand their partial perspectives and form a new unified vision. . . . The Church does not propose that science should become religion or religion science. On the contrary, unity always presupposes the diversity and the integrity of its elements. Each of these members should become not less itself but more itself in a dynamic interchange, for a unity in which one of the elements is reduced to the other is destructive, false in its promises of harmony, and ruinous of the integrity of its components. We are asked to become one. We are not asked to become each other.[9]

The pope's letter was like opening a window to the morning light, inviting a new exchange between science and religion that could enliven both bodies of knowledge. This was the type of exchange I was looking for, as John Paul II's insights were oriented toward a unified world:

Understanding is achieved when many data are unified by a common structure. The one illuminates the many: it makes sense of the whole. Simple multiplicity is chaos; an insight, a single model, can give that chaos structure and draw it into intelligibility. We move towards unity as we move towards meaning in our lives. Unity is also the consequence of love. If love is genuine, it moves not towards the assimilation of the other but towards union with the other. Human community begins in desire when that union has not been achieved, and it is completed in joy when those who have been apart are now united. . . . Theology is not to incorporate indifferently each new philosophical or scientific theory. As these findings become part of the intellectual culture of the time, however, theologians must understand them and test their value in bringing out from Christian belief some of the possibilities which have not yet been realized. . . . The matter is urgent. Contemporary developments in science challenge theology far

9. Ibid.

more deeply than did the introduction of Aristotle into Western Europe in the thirteenth century. Yet these developments
also offer to theology a potentially important resource. Just as
Aristotelian philosophy, through the ministry of such great
scholars as St Thomas Aquinas, ultimately came to shape some
of the most profound expressions of theological doctrine, so
can we not hope that the sciences of today, along with all forms
of human knowing, may invigorate and inform those parts of
the theological enterprise that bear on the relation of nature,
humanity and God?[10]

The church was calling for more dialogue between religion and
modern science, but how would this be realized? Where were the signs
of this dialogue, and where was such dialogue taking place? On the
one hand, John Paul II's letter was inspiring, and, on the other hand,
it raised a lot of questions. Who were the theologians doing this kind
of integrative work? Why did the Vatican's Theological Commission
not include the pope's mandate on theology and science in its key
documents?[11] There were conflicting messages in the church, and it was
not clear that a dialogical relationship between theology and science
was accepted as part of the church's development in the world. Even
in the academy, theology spanned a wide range of interests with no
real effort to connect these interests with modern science. If theology
should be in constant dialogue with modern science, as John Paul II
indicated, then should we not be talking about God and evolution, or
matter as a form of energy, or the entanglement of God, human, and
cosmos? Yet, few signs of ongoing dialogue were (or are) readily visible.
Something was right and something was wrong.

Religious life was a good indicator of what was right and wrong in
the church vis-à-vis the modern scientific worldview, and exploring the
impasse created by a patriarchal ecclesial culture would be part of my
own journey.

---

10. Ibid.
11. For information on the Vatican's Theological Commission see http://www.
vatican.va/roman_curia/congregations/cfaith/cti_documents/rc_cti_index-doc-pub
bl_en.html.

10

Nuns Towers

I SPENT THE CHRISTMAS OF 1996 with the community in New Jersey. Every time I returned *to* the community, however, I realized I was turning *from* the community, kindled by a new vision of religious life. The sisters were aging, and by 1996 most of the American women who had joined the community had left it for various reasons. Francesca was in South Africa, and the one postulant in formation was preparing to enter the novitiate. The sisters would ask me to give spiritual talks to the community, and I was happy to do so, but the talks could do no more than mollify what was a deeply dysfunctional group of aging women.

By the time I completed my doctorate at Fordham, I had an ambivalent relationship to the community. On the one hand, I was given every opportunity to teach and travel, and, on the other hand, I was resented for the opportunities I was given. I was grateful for the experiences they had made possible for me, despite the tension of living outside the community. The inscrutable ways of God, however, are never to be underestimated. The divine mystery is embedded in our lives and will always draw us on to new life, if we do not block the movement of the Spirit. "Every culmination is merely a beginning," theologian Jean Daniélou wrote, "and every arrival a point of departure. Everything appears forever new, everything begins again."[1] Deep within I knew

---

1. Jean Daniélou, *La colombe et la ténèbre. Textes extraits des "Homélies sur le Cantique des Cantiques" de Grégoire de Nysse* (Paris: Editions de l'Orante, 1967), 416; Marc C. Nicholas, *Jean Daniélou's Doxological Humanism: Trinitarian Contemplation and Humanity's True Vocation* (Eugene, OR: Wipf & Stock, 2012), 122.

something was coming to an end and something new was beginning, but I had no idea what path the road ahead would take.

Life at Nuns Towers

I had to find a place to live in Silver Spring, Maryland, since I would begin my new position at WTU in January. The community requested that I live with other sisters, but when I got to Takoma Park, I could not find a community to live with. There were about five women religious on the faculty at WTU, and they all lived in single apartments. The women faculty dressed in secular clothes (and well dressed I might add), while I was in my modified habit. They could not understand why I would wear the habit, but I still held on to my conviction and the need for religious identity. Four of the women lived in an apartment building called Montgomery Towers, which was a little over two miles from school. A sister who had been in pastoral ministry was leaving the area, and I was told her apartment would become available. I called the community in New Jersey to tell them of the situation. The superior was reluctant to give permission to live alone in an apartment, but since there were few other options, she acquiesced.

I went to see the apartment on the sixth floor of Montgomery Towers, where I soon discovered that the building housed not only the women theological faculty of WTU (all but one) but almost twenty-five other sisters as well. I soon dubbed the building "Nuns Towers," and the name caught on. The sixth-floor apartment that was being vacated was perfect. It had a large living room, bedroom, dining room, and a small kitchen, which was just right for "heating and eating." The back of the apartment was a wall of glass windows, and my view was a panoramic scene of wooded trees. There was a small balcony off the living room, and in the summer I could sit out on the patio and drink a beer.

The sister who was leaving the apartment looked at my veiled head and asked, "Are you going to be ok living here by yourself?" I assured her that I would be fine, and she was kind enough to leave behind some furniture and rugs. She also told me that the apartment that I was about to call home was the same apartment where Sister Laura Ann Quinonez wrote the book *The Transformation of the American Catholic Sisterhood*, the book that angered (then-)Archbishop McCarrick so much that he took it to Rome to lobby for a new body of religious women who would exemplify fidelity to the Catholic Church. In opposition to the transformation of the American Catholic sisterhood (the basic tenets of which are now consolidated in the Leadership Conference of Women Religious, or LCWR) emerged the formation of the Council of Major Superiors of Women Religious.

I was moving into the midst of women who were part of the most significant changes in religious life since the Middle Ages. However, I did not know what these changes would mean for me. I was committed to a traditional form of clockwork religious life, but I could not quite trade the clock for a mandala or a game of Scrabble. "Traditional religious life is mechanized," one sister confessed, and I had to agree. The structure that made religious life appealing was the same structure that now seemed to be stifling religious life, and the women of Vatican II were rethinking new forms of religious life in a world of change.

I have to admit, however, that the monastic schedule was written on my soul, and I followed the same routine day in and day out: up early, morning prayer, put on habit, go to work, return home, evening prayer, eat, study, get up, and do it all over again. There is no doubt that a routinized life is very appealing: predictable, repetitive, controlled, and with little thinking involved. I met a young woman who decided to join a traditional religious community, and I asked why that community. Her response was startling: "I am attracted to this community because I am tired of thinking and making choices. I am happy to have someone else think for me." I was surprised to learn that in this community even morning meditations were assigned by the mother superior!

It seemed to me that a life on automatic pilot is not a *life* but an illusion of security. Ironically, it was the routinization of religious life that the church was trying to correct at Vatican II, calling for a renewal of charisms in the church and new forms of apostolic and missionary activity to meet the needs of the world. This meant opening our windows to the world and renewing our religious lives in accord with the current needs of the world. (Truthfully, religious women in the United States had been doing this since the nineteenth century.)

But as with theology itself, the church was ambivalent in its directives. On the one hand, the habit was considered important to religious identity, and, on the other hand, the church was asking religious women and men to inculturate, to identify with the people they were serving. The mixed signals from the church reflected the church's ambiguous relationship to the world. How does the church understand universal salvation in Christ? How does God's reign unfold in history? These questions continue to be conflicted in the church. Those who favor Greek philosophy tend toward a church of spiritual ideals, and those who are open to history favor change and flexibility. To this day the church insists on holding together two conflicting paradigms for religious life: on the one hand is the monastic structure based on Greek metaphysics and, on the other hand, the dynamics of evolution. Over time I would realize that it is impossible to reconcile these two paradigms; a choice for one or the other paradigm would have to be made.

The Women of Nuns Towers

My position as assistant professor of spirituality at WTU was invigorating. I loved the students, and my colleagues were warm and engaging. I taught courses in Franciscan theology and spirituality, as well as general spirituality. We hired a young professor by the name of Bill Durbin to teach church history, and Bill's primary interest was religion and science. We quickly became good friends and decided to start a certificate program in religion and science. My initial course in religion and science at Trinity College in Hartford was still on the back burner of my mind, and Bill's arrival allowed that interest to be rekindled. I applied for a Templeton Course Award for a course called "Following Christ in a Scientific Age" and received the award while serving on various science and religion committees, including the Metanexus Forum on Science and Religion in Philadelphia and the Association for the American Academy of Sciences, Dialogue on Science, Ethics, and Religion in Washington, DC.

I was introduced to some of the leading thinkers in the field and started reading more widely in the area. As much as I read, however, I found no satisfactory answer to the relationship between science and religion. What I discovered was a lot of intellectual arguments on science and religion, insightful ideas but not transformational ones.

To my own surprise, I was becoming a good teacher as well as a public speaker and was invited to give talks to many Franciscan communities and schools in the United States and abroad. This opportunity allowed me to visit different communities and to see how religious life was faring on the threshold of the twenty-first century. The prognosis was not good. More women were leaving communities than entering them. Communities were thinning out and reorganizing their structures and properties to accommodate the losses. The world was opening new doors for women in culture and society, and gender itself was undergoing an evolution of epic proportions, the extent of which we are just beginning to realize.

I had the luxurious freedom of returning from school each day and simply reflecting on the wealth of changes around me. The sisters of Nuns Towers were an education unto themselves, and they became my mentors simply by sharing wine and cheese together at social gatherings. Many of them had been leaders in the transformation of the American Catholic sisterhood. Women like Maria Reily, OP, of the Center for Concern, Catherine Pinkerton, CSJ, of Network, Amy Hoey, RSM, of the USCCB-Lay Ministry program, Janet Mock, CSJ, who was with the Religious Formation Conference and would soon become the executive director of LCWR during the Vatican investigation of women's religious communities. Being with these women made the history of Vatican II come alive with their stories and explanations of how and why radical decisions were made following the mandates of the council. The realization of the church "in the world" called women to don secular clothes and put away the habit; to fight for the poor; to accompany prisoners on death row; to lobby for the homeless; to fight for the justice of immigrants—the list of engagements on behalf of the gospel was incredible.

If my walls of traditional religious life were made of ice, the warmth of the women of Nuns Towers was quickly melting my frozen boundaries. I could not help marvel at the risks they took to create new forms of life, to fight for justice and peace, some even willing to go to jail in their struggle against nuclear disarmament or global warming. I thoroughly enjoyed their candid stories, their openness amidst struggles to be themselves, and, truthfully, their capacity to enjoy a social hour together with wine and cheese and shared meals. Surprisingly, many of them came from large communities with motherhouses (although motherhouses were starting to close), and I was surprised to learn that when they returned to their communities, they returned to a scheduled way of life. However, these women of Vatican II were light years ahead of me in their understanding of the gospel life in the twenty-first century. I was obstinate on wearing the habit because removing the habit meant exposing my vulnerable nature to the whims of the world. I feared that I would lose the essence of my religious identity.

One day Catherine Pinkerton and I were sitting across from each other at one of our social parties. Looking at me straight in the eye she said, "Ilia, we need to educate you in the changes that have taken place over the last fifty years." Pointing at my black veil, she said, "Once you hear the stories you won't want to wear that 'thing' anymore." I listened but was inwardly resistant. What was the resistance, I wondered? Could I adequately express my religious commitment without a black veil? The women of Nuns Towers seemed to do so effortlessly. What was my problem?

One day I arrived home after class and had the opportunity to sit quietly in my apartment, as the sun was setting outside, like an orange watercolor line running across the strip of brown trees. I was basking in the solitude and the beauty of the burnt-orange scene glowing outside the large windows. In a moment, I had a profound inner experience of God's deep inner presence and a sense of real freedom. The words of the *Benedictus* were in mind but now directed to me: "I have come to *you* and set *you* free." Life in God, I realized in that moment, is not about clothes or schedules or power lines of authority; it is about freedom, the freedom to live in the unquenchable intimacy of God's love.

The moment caught me off guard, and one of the inner walls of self-protection fell to the ground. I realized in that moment that the habit did not define who I was as a Franciscan; love alone did. "God is the reason for loving God," Bernard wrote, "and the way to love God is to love without measure."[2] Or as Saint Francis sang, "The love of him who loved us is greatly to be loved."[3]

---

2. Bernard of Clairvaux, *On Loving God* I.1, in *Bernard of Clairvaux: Selected Works,* trans. G. R. Evans (New York: Paulist Press, 1987), 174.

3. Thomas of Celano, "The Remembrance of the Desire of a Soul," in *Francis of Assisi: Early Documents*, vol. 2, ed. Regis J. Armstrong, J. A. Wayne Hellmann, and William J. Short (New York: New City Press, 2000), 373.

To commit one's life to Christ is to commit oneself to radical love. Love alone bears witness to itself. I had encountered enough religious women to know that the habit could be deceiving because the outward appearance of holiness could be mistaken for the inner content of wholeness. Francis of Assisi understood this reality and did not choose to wear a monastic habit but the dress of a beggar. "Do not look at the outside," he wrote to Clare of Assisi, "for the inside is better . . . because it is of the Spirit."[4]

Religious life can never be a life of appearances; the life of holiness must be connected to the life of wholeness. "If the heart is sound, the whole body will be sound," Jesus proclaimed (see Matt 6:22). Religious life is a perpetual fitness center for the soul or a "training center of love." The pursuit of holiness is learning to integrate the threads of our many loves into the single-hearted love of God. "You truly exist where you love," Bonaventure wrote, "not merely where you live."[5] Where we grow in love is where we find our true being because it is where we find our freedom; and where we find our freedom is where we grow into our true identity in God.

"Religious" life is a life tethered to God and should be a life of growth in freedom and thus growth in courageous love, a life bountiful in love and thus the most daring life possible. "If you make my word your home," Jesus said, "you will learn the truth and the truth will set you free" (John 8:31). Freedom in love is what gives courage to love in new and radical ways, ways that reflect the life and passion of Jesus, so that the world may move from ungodly darkness to God-centered light. This freedom in love radiated brightly in many of the women of Nuns Towers.

---

4. Francis of Assisi, "The Canticle of Exhortation to Saint Clare and Her Sisters," in *Francis of Assisi: The Complete Works,* trans. Regis J. Armstrong, OFMCap (New York: Paulist Press, 1982), 40.

5. Bonaventure, *Soliloquium* 2.12 (VIII, 49). Engl. trans. Zachary Hayes, *Bonaventure: Mystical Writings* (New York: Crossroad, 1999), 140. Bonaventure writes: "O my soul, I think that you exist more truly where you love than where you merely live, since you are transformed into the likeness of whatever you love, through the power of this love itself."

The Habit of the Heart

Let me not be too glib here, for I was deeply attached to the habit. God knows, the world needs signs, and I must admit, I do not find the habit a problem in itself. It was the way the habit could hide the truth of the person that became problematic for me, in the same way that an alcoholic could be affable in public and have a violent temper at home. Was the habit a protection of dysfunction or a liberation of identity? In the postmodern sense, it was whatever I wanted it to be. I was the one who gave meaning to the habit; the rest of the world did not really care what I wore. I began to see that the habit expressed a core set of values for me in the same way that tattoos or pierced eyebrows or sculpted hair express a set of values for younger generations. In a world stripped of signs, clothing and body piercing are marks of identity. Our postmodern milieu evokes a branding of oneself or wearing brand clothes as marks of identity, to single out the distinctiveness of the human person in an otherwise algorithmic mass of humanity. But we are no longer in Christendom, and we would delude ourselves to think that the religious habit signifies the presence of Christ or the mark of holiness in the general public at large.

I remember getting stuck in an airport in Taiwan one time with a group of Buddhist nuns. They all wore their silk, rust-colored monastic robes with thong sandals on their feet and prayer beads around their hands; they looked completely other worldly and quaint. I was not thinking "these women signify the Buddha to me" or "they must be holy women with prayer beads wrapped around their fingers." I simply thought, "How quaint are these women." The postmodern milieu thrives on difference; the plurality of human expressions is signified by the phrase "whatever," or "cool," especially when it comes to clothes. As to what makes a difference to a postmodern world? Signs of interruption or resistance: like Sister Dorothy Stang, dressed in T-shirt and jeans, who stood before the hired guns of the loggers to protect the poor and their Amazon home and answered their threat by pulling out her Bible; or the young student who threw herself in front of a tractor-trailer to prevent bulldozing low-income apartments in Palestine; or Archbishop Oscar Romero saying Mass in the face of death threats.

Francis of Assisi thought it was shameful just to talk about the martyrs without wanting to imitate them. The martyr is still the most significant sign of holiness, and the church would do well to reclaim this sign of "second baptism" instead of worrying about habits. Postmodern martyrdom may not mean necessarily physical death, but it could mean resistance that leads to jail or speech that leads to rebuke or protest that leads to being ostracized from an established community. To give witness (the meaning of "martyr") means to stand in the transparency of truth, unafraid of the consequences, because truth ultimately sets free; hence, the martyr lives for freedom in God. The postmodern world longs for holiness and recognizes the martyr in the expression of self-engagement. The world otherwise is ambivalent, if not apathetic, about religious garb.

One time I attended a funeral with a Franciscan friar who was wearing his brown robe, the Franciscan cord (a fisherman's rope with three knots), and Birkenstock sandals. At the end of the funeral a woman ran up to him and said, "Brother, I am so happy to see you!" They talked briefly, but we had made plans to go out to dinner afterward, so he excused himself, walked to his car, took off his Franciscan robe and cord, and threw them in the car. Underneath his religious garb he wore a beautiful black turtleneck sweater and looked quite dashing as we headed out to our evening dinner in DC.

There is an irony to wearing a religious habit in a consumer culture because consumerism is based on labels and fashions. In his provocative book *Consuming Religion*, Vincent Miller describes the religious habit within the consumer mentality of "brands." For example, the monk in his brown Franciscan habit vowed to a life of poverty is wearing Birkenstock sandals that cost $150.00. The habit itself is made of gabardine material and would cost about $300.00 to purchase in a store. Our New Jersey community wore a Sunday habit that was imported from Germany; the cost of the habit in 1992 was about $150.00. In a consumer culture where appearances are everything clothes are signs of status and class.

This raises an interesting question: what is the status or class of the religious woman or man vowed to consecrated life wearing a $300 habit? Does the eradication of the body lost in the yards and folds of material signify a higher class (due to a "higher" calling) or an elite spiritual class? Does the habit neutralize the body and reduce it to a secondary functional role of housing the soul? Does the habit bond the members of a community together in such a way that it excludes all those not in habit and thus not in the community? Does the habit signify inclusivity or exclusivity? These were (and continue to be) the questions about the sign of religious identity represented by the habit.

It was also clear to me that the habit did not have an identical function for men and women. For men, it was like a uniform one puts on "for the job" and removes once the job is over and one is "off duty." Women simply did not have this luxury because of the simple fact that the veil had a deeper significance of second-class humanity. In his letter to the Corinthians Paul writes:

> But I want you to understand that the head of every man is Christ, the head of a wife is her husband, and the head of Christ is God. Every man who prays or prophesies with his head covered dishonors his head, but every wife who prays or prophesies with her head uncovered dishonors her head, since it is the same as if her head were shaven. For if a wife will not cover her head, then she should cut her hair short. But since it is disgraceful for a wife to cut off her hair or shave her head, let her cover her head. For a man ought not to cover his head, since he is the image and glory of God, but woman is the glory of man. For man was not made from woman, but woman from man. Neither was man created for woman, but woman for man. That is why a wife ought to have a symbol of authority on her head, because of the angels. (1 Cor 11:2-10)

Similarly, the habit had a different function for women than men. It was not a uniform but a protective garb against the sinful elements of lust and vice. In his book *The Religion of Technology*, the late Canadian historian David Noble indicated that religion and science trace their primordial myths back to the fall of Adam and the restoration of Adam to divine perfection. Adam was created before Eve and thus received the breath of life directly from God; Adam was the true image of God, and Eve was a weak imitation. Since Eve was the reason Adam lost his divine likeness as well as his share in divine knowledge and divinely ordained dominion over nature (the "Fall"), Eve was the problem and not the solution. Hence, restoration of perfection relies on the male; through man, God completes his work.[6]

Patriarchy is based on the primacy of the male seed. Similarly, a theology based on patriarchy means that power flows from God the Father to Adam down to the lowest level of beings who are furthest from God—women and the creatures of the earth. As weak and incomplete, women have traditionally occupied the lower rungs of the ladder, which is why the habit has functioned differently among women than among men. Whereas a male religious priest can remove his habit and still maintain his integrity, a woman who removes her habit exposes herself for what she truly is (in the eyes of the church), fleshy and the source of sin. Adam and Eve still loom large in the church, as if God created Adam and said, "It is good," then created Eve and said, "Wow, what do we have here?"

Liberating Identity

Interestingly, a lot of the seminarians at WTU who belonged to male religious orders wore a habit, but one of my greatest discoveries was that a significant number of them were gay; several left their religious communities to join their partners, while others just felt the need to verbally express their sexual orientation without necessarily acting on it. Homosexuality was simply part of the fabric of the WTU milieu because it was becoming increasingly woven into the fabric of postmodern life. I had never really encountered homosexuality prior to my tenure at WTU and was at once shocked and liberated by it.

Bishop Thomas Gumbleton, the prophetic and generally marginalized auxiliary bishop of Detroit, once gave a lecture at WTU on the challenges of the church today, and shortly afterward I received a call from a local bishop who had sent priests as "spies" to the lecture to report on topics contradicting church teaching, such as women's ordination and homosexuality. The bishop wanted to know what exactly I had heard and did it corroborate the information he had received.

This was my first inkling of a church with heavily guarded doors. The truth is, many of the men who identified themselves as gay were

---

6. David Noble, *The Religion of Technology: The Divinity of Man and the Spirit of Invention* (New York: Knopf, 1997), 1–25.

wonderful friends, and I came to love them in the freedom of their personhood.[7] When the school received a formal visitation by a leading archbishop and his entourage who were trying to purify the seminarians of all potential sources of sin—including homosexuality, women, and laity—I was absolutely floored by one of the examiners, a Jesuit priest acting on behalf of a "whitewashing" church who was, unmistakably, gay. I was not concerned about his sexual orientation; however, I was concerned that he was hypocritical, chastising the seminarians while expressing the very behavior he condemned.

Ironically, while WTU was receiving pressure to reform the education of seminarians, the archbishop of Washington, DC, was the now-defrocked Theodore McCarrick. The push for priestly formation without women or laity fit the secret cultic environment of the church, which only recently has been brought to light. The fall of Theodore McCarrick recapitulates the problems of a cultic and closed male priesthood, a perfect milieu to contain webs of secrecy and lies. In 2002, McCarrick helped draft the Vatican policy on sexual abuse, calling for "zero tolerance." One news reporter wrote:

> Resplendent in their red hats and elegant black robes, the American cardinals stepped into the Roman sunshine and swept down the stairs of the fortress like Pontifical North American College. . . . Cardinal Theodore E. McCarrick was in no hurry, however. On a shady patch of grass off to one side, the 71-year-old Washington archbishop chatted amiably with reporters last Tuesday. After a half-hour, his press secretary gently stepped in to warn him that he had to move on—or he might miss the bus. At a time when many leaders of the U.S. Roman Catholic Church have been criticized as arrogant, secretive and uncaring, McCarrick has given the scandal-battered institution what it so badly needs: an attractive public face. Assuming the role of leading spokesman for the U.S. cardinals during their meetings with Pope John Paul II on the sexual abuse crisis, McCarrick came across to many as candid, compassionate and committed to strong reform. In one interview after another, he spoke of a

---

7. For an enlightening recent discussion see Andrew Sullivan, "The Gay Church," January 29, 2019, http://nymag.com.

uniform national policy of "zero tolerance" toward priests who molest minors.[8]

In the past year, the news broke that Cardinal McCarrick had sexually abused a young boy over four decades ago, and since then, other stories of his abuse have emerged. One news feed reported:

> Cardinal Theodore McCarrick, the former archbishop of Washington and longtime globe-trotting diplomat of the Catholic Church, has resigned his position as a cardinal, the Vatican announced Saturday. McCarrick, 88, was found by the church in June to be credibly accused of sexually abusing a teenager nearly 50 years ago. Since then, additional reports of sexual abuse and harassment by the cardinal, over a span of decades, have been reported. The victims include one then-minor and three adults, who were young priests or seminarians when McCarrick allegedly abused them. Pope Francis ordered McCarrick to remain in seclusion, and in prayer, until a church trial considers further sanctions. McCarrick is the highest ranked U.S. Catholic clergy member to ever be removed from ministry due to sexual abuse allegations, and the first cardinal to fully resign his position since 1927.[9]

How did the church become so disconnected from Jesus, the Christ? I found myself at a complex intersection between church and world. Every breath was becoming a choice and decision. What was I as a Franciscan sister? What did I stand for? What were my core values? The courage and witness of post–Vatican II women convinced me that the habit was a valuable sign but not essential to my identity as a Franciscan.

One day I went to the Salvation Army and bought a basket full of secular clothes; I removed my veil and modified habit, put on a pair of pants and went to school. Some of the students were shocked and did

---

8. Caryle Murphy and Alan Cooperman, "Vatican's Man of the Hour," *Washington Post*, April 28, 2002.

9. Julie Zauzmer and Chico Harlan, "Cardinal Theodore McCarrick, Facing Sexual Abuse Reports, Resigns from the College of Cardinals," *Washington Post*, July 28, 2018.

nor recognize me at first, but most (if not all) of the faculty supported my new look. It was a transitional moment, but a liberating one. For the first time in twenty years I felt part of the whole mass of people I was connected to, whether in the bank or post office or standing on the street waiting for the light to turn green. I lived for God, God lived in them, and I lived in them, and they in me. I had committed myself to Christ, not to a Platonic ideal—Hopkins's Christ, who "plays in ten thousand places," the Christ of broken hearts and shattered dreams, of stars and baby seals, of lovers and mourners. I became liberated without because I became liberated within. I no longer sought God's love but found myself living in God's love, a love entwined with my very breath. My challenge was learning to live in freedom while learning to love in freedom while remaining faithful to the vows I had made.

I leaned on the divine heart of God because I knew an impending split with the community in New Jersey was underway. Every time I returned to community in New Jersey, I found the group to be shrinking and imploding from lack of exposure to the world. While I was discovering new levels of life, the community was barely holding on to life. The one young woman who entered when I was vocation director had difficulties in the community and was sent to Germany to complete her formation; she left after final vows. The fact is, every single American woman who entered the community (after 1980) eventually left the community.

The German sisters knew about the problems but were helpless from afar, so they simply let the field go fallow. I came to a point where I had to take a year's leave of absence to discern my path of religious life. The German superior graciously granted the leave, and I found myself on my own, in my apartment, in my jeans and T-shirt, learning to live in the present moment.

11

Self-Discovery

I CONTINUED TO TEACH and travel around the country giving talks and workshops, returning to the solitude of my apartment each time in a spirit of deep gratitude to the God of generous love who was at the center of my life. I was grateful for where my journey had brought me, even though I could not quite find a community conducive to my spirit. I wondered if there was something wrong with me, or if I had simply made bad choices. It wasn't that I did not appreciate the value of living in community; however, the constant grind of meeting the needs of others was exhausting. I knew one thing, however—that I loved the solitude of my apartment. Resting in solitude, I could sit in the silence of my own being and drink deeply from this wellspring of divine love that sustained me.

While I am sure some sisters in my community saw this as a selfish way of life, I saw it as a liberation of the soul. In fact, without the need to constantly satisfy the demands of the community, I could devote more time to writing and theological reflection. I wrote books on Bonaventure and Franciscan prayer and articles that explored Bonaventure's metaphysics of love and his distinction of being and goodness. I thrived in this milieu, but I was also lonely at times and missed the socialization that living in community affords.

We make choices at every moment of our lives, and I had made a choice. I came to realize that life is an ongoing creative process, not a preset form to be filled in by the colors of our lives. Each moment we choose a possibility and put it into motion, and the act of every choice shapes our lives. Traditional religious life had a prescribed form; one learned to live in the given form. Now I was in the midst of a

151

new set of values, a formless form, discovering the space of freedom and the capacity to choose in ways that would constitute—moment to moment—the most authentic expression of my life as a person.

Falling in Love Anew

There was a young sister who had moved into the area, having taken a local job in Silver Spring, and we became good friends. I enjoyed her company because she was a good listener, and we would spend long hours going for walks in the park or listening to music or just sitting quietly on my patio watching the trees play in harmony. But something else was happening; without warning I was falling in love with her. I did not consider myself gay, in fact, I had a fear of lesbians, as if they might attack me if left alone with one in a room. I had absorbed the cultural biases of the church and society lock, stock, and barrel. I thought there was something wrong with gay people, although I did not accept the notion of "intrinsic disorder," as the church described it. I simply thought being gay is "weird." That is, until I found myself kissing another woman alone in an apartment, and it was the most natural thing to do. And then a second wall started to crumble, the wall of gender identity.

We are born into a set of values, and those values are deeply inscribed in us like genetic dispositions. I was born into an Italian-American culture where matriarchy reigned, but males were first in everything: first to sit down, first to eat, first to get a job. Sexuality in my childhood milieu was no more a question than religion. You are what God made you to be: end of story. I never once questioned my gender or sexuality but strove to live according to the implicit guidelines of my Italian-American culture, which basically came with two options: meet a nice boy, get married and have kids, or become a nun and give your life to God. I tried the first but knew it was not for me; I tried the second and found myself in the midst of depressed, angry women.

Now here I was alone with another woman in a relationship, and it was the most liberating of all options. I followed through on this new option during the time I was on leave from the community and found myself completely at home in it. My authentic self was allowed to surface from the layers of the cultural-mandated self, and for the first time I confronted my own gender identity. Still, it seemed odd to use the label "gay," as if putting myself in a category of marginalized people. It was simply a liberating expression of my sexual identity—not to the exclusion of men, since I still enjoy the friendship of men and take note of handsome men. Rather, it was the truest expression of what I am as a person. From this new experience I began to see the LGBTQ community in a whole new light, not as weird mutations of humanity but as authentic human persons who are at home in their own sexual identity.

Of course, the church has problems with gendered identity because Aristotle defined male and female in terms of matter and intellect and the early church added to these distinctions the biblical notion of being created in the image of God. Without embracing evolution as the way God creates the ensouled human person, the church simply cannot accept that nature undergoes modifications over time. Instead, the church holds an ambivalent relationship between modern science and ancient Greek philosophy in a way that stifles nature's development and God's creativity. The misogynist tendencies of the church and the suspicion of human flesh (because of sin) have created a distortion of sex and sexuality in the church, as if the body might be a machine simply for procreation.

Sexual dualism has marked much of the Christian tradition in which spirit is higher and superior to the body, while the body is inferior and weak. The result of this dualism has been sexism and patriarchy. Aristotle identified the male with the spirit (mind), and women with the body (matter), wherein the higher powers, such as the mind, must control the lower ones. Implicit in sexual dualism has been the notion of divine impassivity—the *apathy* of God. If the body is marked by passion and if spirit is passionless, then bodily hunger (*eros*) has no connection with the divine. God is without hunger, and the human hungers (of which sexuality, with its drive to connection and intimacy, is one of the most basic) seem to have no connection with our experience of God.

Yet, incarnational theology emphasizes that the most decisive experience of God is not in doctrine, creed, or ideas but in the Word made flesh—and in the Word still becoming flesh, which means that sexuality is intrinsic to the experience of God. Such experience has been described by Nikos Kazantzakis: "Within me even the most metaphysical problem takes on a warm physical body which smells of sea, soil, and human sweat. The Word, in order to touch me, must become warm flesh. Only then do I understand—when I can smell, see, and touch."[1]

Sex is not the problem; the problem is the church's refusal to accept a healthy view of sex and sexuality as intrinsic to salvation. The word "sex" has a Latin root, *secare,* which means literally "to cut off." To be "sexed" literally means to be cut off, to be severed from or to be amputated from the whole. Sex is a dimension of our very awareness. We wake up in our cribs lonely, cut off, severed from the great whole. Sexuality is a sacred energy given us by God to overcome our incompleteness, to move toward unity and consummation with that which is beyond us, outward beyond the self, to celebrate, give and receive delight. Sex is a wide energy, and we are healthy sexually when we have love, community, communion, family, friendship, affection, creativity, joy, delight, humor, and self-transcendence.

Sexuality is not simply finding a lover or a friend. It is about overcoming separateness by giving life and blessing it. Teilhard saw love and sexual energy as part of the process of cosmic personalization. Individuals emerge from isolation and enter into union with another in a way that is more spiritualized than individual personalities. Love attains a higher consciousness through a deeper centeredness or union of souls. Teilhard wrote: "Love alone is capable of uniting living beings in such a way as to complete and fulfill them, for it alone takes them and joins them by what is deepest in themselves."[2] In its maturity, sexuality is about giving oneself over to community, friendship, family, service, and creativity; personal union in love contributes the energy of passion to a universe seeking to become more personal through consciousness and convergence. For Teilhard, sexuality and spirituality are intertwined; sexuality, like spirituality, is intrinsic to cosmic life.

I did not see being in a relationship with a woman as a form of disorder but as an expression of personhood, and I began to empathize with those who constantly feel the need to defend themselves against the cultural and religious stigma of homosexuality or the fear of being labeled "disordered" or simply the cruelty of others who define nature dogmatically.

---

1. Nicholas Kazantzakis, *Report to Greco* (New York: Simon & Schuster, 1965), 43.
2. Teilhard de Chardin, *Phenomenon of Man*, 265.

The movie *Boy Erased* portrays the damage wrought by fundamentalism and biblical literalism when God is used to define a narrow bandwidth of nature and we ourselves play God in trying to control nature. But I also remembered that I vowed my life to God. Could I continue to live a single-hearted commitment to God? And what might this single-hearted commitment look like?

In the end I simply could not finalize any human relationship because my heart belonged to God. There was a powerful, invisible divine power woven into my gendered body. I could love a woman and I could love a man, but at the end of the day, I simply loved God and my heart turned toward God like a wilted flower turning toward the sun. This great mystery of love invaded my life over and over again, never letting me rest in human relationships, constantly causing interruptions in my pursuit of human love, always pulling me back toward the infinite center within, where this divine mystery of love radiates a warmth of deep presence. God was truly the jealous lover, and I would find myself saying at times, "Go away, God, I just want to be left alone and live a normal life." But over and over again I perceived this humble figure of the compassionate Christ standing at the door of my heart: "Look! I stand at the door and knock. If you hear my voice and open the door, I will come in and eat with you, and you with me" (Rev 3:20). Or as the prophet Jeremiah wrote so beautifully, "I have loved you with an everlasting love, and I will continue to draw you to myself" (Jer 31:3).

The God of My Heart

No matter how hard I tried to get away from the grip of God's love, I was caught up in this powerful divine embrace—not only because God does not like to share his jealous love but because God's love has a particular aim. From all eternity God loves *this* person for *this* reason in *this* way, the secrets of God alone. Bernard of Clairvaux, on whose feast day I was born, wrote, "The reason for loving God is God Himself; and the measure of love due to God is immeasurable love."[3] This saying spoke to me deeply. As a Franciscan on the edge of religious life, my experience of human love and divine love revealed to

---

3. Bernard of Clairvaux, "On Loving God," trans. G. R. Evans, http://people. bu.edu/dklepper/RN413/bernard_loving.html.

me a deep passion of life at the heart of life, a passion that enkindled my heart; in truth, I wanted to love God without measure.

Love is a fire of transformation that constantly needs wood to keep the fire alive. Real fire is destructive; throw yourself into a fire and you will be destroyed. God's fire is destructive too because it can swiftly eliminate all self-illusions, grandiose ideas, ego-inflation, and self-centeredness. Throw yourself into the spiritual fire of divine love and everything you grasp for yourself will be destroyed until there is nothing left but the pure truth of yourself. I was living in a church that tried to control the definition of nature, but I was learning through a winding path of love that nature is elusive and dynamic and that creative personhood demands attention to the movements of the spirit. "One must have chaos in oneself to be able to give birth to a dancing star," Friedrich Nietzsche wrote.[4] The birth of a star is a violent and chaotic event, with gas flowing in and being ejected outward at speeds up to hundreds of kilometers per second.[5] I was living from an inner chaos out of which a new star was being born.

Life in Silver Spring was a rich soil for fertile growth. I was out of the mold of the religious nun and now on a trajectory toward a future I could not anticipate by thought alone; I would have to live into it. A sister from the Midwest moved into our building and was living on the floor above me with another sister from Minnesota. Lisa was gentle and sweet, and we quickly became friends. I was not really looking for a friend, but Lisa had a knack for persistent friendship. She would make food and put it in my refrigerator when I was traveling, or clean my apartment so that I could return to a dust-free environment. She soon became my best friend and companion for the journey. I had been thinking about starting a new Franciscan community for years, although I had no idea what a new form religious life might take. I shared my hopes and dreams with Lisa, as well as my deep disappointment with institutional religious life. She was from a large Polish Franciscan community in the Midwest where work and prayer were the

---

4. Friedrich Nietzsche, *Thus Spoke Zarathustra: A Book for Everyone and No One,* trans. R. J. Hollingdale (New York: Penguin, 1961), 3–5.

5. "A Star Is Born," https://medium.com/@ResearchFeatures/a-star-is-born-understanding-the-physics-of-star-formation-daee12447763.

staples of the life. She was educated as a nurse, then sent to graduate school at the University of Virginia to become a nurse practitioner; however, upon completion of her graduate degree, the community asked her to relinquish her nursing career to move into administration in one of their nursing homes. Such was the way of canonical religious life in an apostolic community; when the call to obedience was given (that is, a request from on high) one acted without question. I did not have this experience, thanks to the wide net of community I was enmeshed in. The New Jersey sisters were liberal in granting new opportunities, and in this way they were a real blessing.

My desire to start a new community was less about obedience than it was about poverty. The more I engaged with the secular world, the more I saw traditional religious life as a closed system, a type of welfare system where one could get three square meals, health insurance, car insurance, a retirement policy, a car full of gas, and a monthly stipend. To be fair, everyone who works in the community either turns over their income to the community or simply works without pay so that the laborers support the community, including those who are unable to work—a type of Christian communism that takes Acts 4:32 as its inspiration. On the positive side, corporate communal wealth (and by this I mean many religious communities are multimillion dollar corporations) makes possible retreat houses, schools, social agencies, and other institutions that benefit society.

A corporate religious system must be a closed system to function in a monetized culture. Those who work and those who do not work both benefit from the same system of wealth. A religious brother or sister, for example, who does not have a full-time job or is out of work for one reason or another could take a year-long sabbatical while being supported by the community. I have met a number of religious women and men who have taken a six-month or a year-long sabbatical in California, North Carolina, Maine, Rome, Ireland, and various parts of the world, either studying, traveling, or both. Truthfully, it sounds wonderful.

I could not reconcile a vow of poverty, however, with a life of corporate wealth when millions of people around the world struggle each day to make ends meet. It was not the wealth per se that bothered me. I realize that the wealth of religious communities must meet the needs of the community members, as well as support the institutions that care for children, the poor, the sick, and the elderly.

I also know that a number of communities, especially women, are facing the constraints of financial security due to dwindling numbers. As I listened to stories of lay men and women "making ends meet," however, I could not reconcile corporate wealth with a rise in unemployment or the grinding hours millions of people spend trudging to work each morning to support their families. It was simply the fact that the average person must work to eat, as St. Paul wrote: "Those unwilling to work will not get to eat" (2 Thess 3:10). To lose one's job is to lose a roof overhead and possibly a sense of self-worth and dignity. I felt that the vow of poverty must be more authentic in a monetized culture. My feeling was confirmed one day when I was in the supermarket on the checkout line and asked the cashier how her day was going. She looked at me out of a set of baggy eyes and said, "This is my third job and I am exhausted." I knew I had to rethink my commitment.

Awakening to a New Reality

Lisa and I began to make plans to form a new way of Franciscan life, but we had no idea of what "the way" would be. We both belonged to established institutions, and the uncharted path forward was daunting. Our communities were initially supportive of our venture and gave us a three-year period for the experiment. We had no money to buy a house, and neither community would support us financially, so we kept an open eye for reasonable rents. One day out I received a call from the guardian at the Holy Land Monastery in Washington, DC. "I hear you are looking for a house to start a new community," he said. "We have a house for you." I could not believe it! Later, I found out that the sisters living in the house ran into a dispute with the guardian over rent, and he was happy to see them move on. We moved to the Brookland section of Washington, DC, into a renovated farmhouse that had once been the novitiate of the Franciscan friars. We were clueless as to what we were actually trying to accomplish but convinced that we were on the right way.

I continued my teaching at WTU, and Lisa started work at Christ House, a shelter for the homeless in the Columbia Heights area of DC, resuming her skills as a nurse. She later took a job as executive assistant to the archbishop of the military services and remains a devoted employee to this day. We rented the house from the friars and furnished it with furniture and housewares from the Salvation Army and Goodwill.

The friars, who were delighted that we had moved in, made every effort to upgrade the house to our liking. Carpenters, electricians, painters all filtered through our humble abode, transforming it from a disjointed farmhouse into a lovely Cape Cod home. I had some money in the bank from my outside talks, and now I could begin to save money from my teaching position. I knew nothing about money since I never dealt with it in Carmel and only in a limited way as a Franciscan Servant of the Holy Child Jesus. Lisa was in a similar position and did not have enough money to buy a car. I lent her mine and bought a used Honda Civic to drive around town. The rusted Honda functioned, but it was an accident waiting to happen. However, we had no credit to our names and quickly awoke to the reality of a financial system that runs on plastic cards. At midlife, we were basically starting from scratch. A few phone calls and some family connections helped launch us financially, and I decided to invest in a reliable car, a silver Toyota Corolla, the first car I ever bought (not counting the first car my parents actually purchased for me upon graduating from college).

The last time I had been at a car dealership was in New Jersey when the community generously saw the need to purchase a new set of wheels. While preparing to pick up my graduation gown at Fordham one afternoon, my banged-up Buick literally died out in the left lane of I-95 North at the speed of seventy miles per hour (the electrical system shut down). A Spanish-speaking trucker driving a large rig saw me standing helplessly on the side of the highway in black veil and habit and probably thought he was having a vision. He was kind enough to stop, call for help, and took me to a nearby garage where my car was towed. It was quite an experience: the neon-lighted waiting area was manned by two women in pants that seemed to be spray painted on, their long fake eyelashes batting frantically as they stared at me, slumped in the torn leather chair opposite them.

One of them yelled out: "Awe you a nun?" I didn't want to alarm her because her fingernails were long enough to be pointed daggers. "Yes, I am," I said. "My car died." "Oh my gawd," she exclaimed, "I can't believe you're a nun!" I was released unscathed from the Hoboken garage shop and had to return home to get another car; however, there were no cars available because the community had just retired a few old ones. The next day, the superior and I drove to the Volkswagen dealership around the block, and I picked out a beautiful, brand-new white Jetta on the lot and drove it back to the convent. I never thought twice about the sticker price, but it was paid for in cash on the spot.

Now I was counting every dollar that passed through my hands, and at times I longed for the community support. We agreed that our new way of life would be self-supporting so that members would maintain their own financial needs and budget. We did form a community 501c(3) (thanks to the Franciscan friars, who urged us to do so) and contributed to the community fund according to our means, a practice we continue today. Our vow of poverty was not a corporate vow of poverty but a vow of interdependence in relation to one another and to the goods of the earth.

We opted to be a noncanonical community and thus not bound by the canonical evangelical counsels of poverty, chastity, and obedience. Instead we revised the vows according to our way of life: poverty as interdependence, chastity as single-heartedness, and obedience as attentive listening. Our new community adventure was extremely risky and daring because we had so few resources to rely on but a lot of trust in God. Rather than thinking in terms of success or failure, I thought in terms of evolution; we were letting go to engage a new structure of relationship in order to participate in the emergence of Christ. I did not think that the new community would be the ultimate community but a step toward a provisional way of religious life whose form could change over time. Every once in a while Lisa and I would look at each other and exclaim: "What were we thinking!"

Living without Possessing

I had a whole new sense of poverty outside the community, the poverty of vulnerability, the poverty of mortgages, the poverty of taxes, the poverty of insecurity. The decision to break new ground in a spiritual adventure outside the norms of religious life was audacious. Establishing credit at the age of fifty was an eye-opener. We had no retirement funds and had to ensure that our places of employment could ensure us retirement and health benefits.

I managed to get at least one credit card, which opened the doors to the world of finance. I thanked God for my chutzpah, as we skated on thin ice. My brother Richard was helpful in learning the steps of financial independence; luckily he was an investor who knew the stock market inside and out and was financially successful. Richard was the executor of my mother's estate and took the liberty of reinvesting her portfolio several times over. She left this world unaware that he had quadrupled her portfolio, enabling each of her four children to receive a sizable inheritance; in a sense, my mother bought the house we eventually purchased from the friars.

Our new community was like a tiny mustard seed planted in Washington. We held weekly soup and Bible sharing sessions and entertained all sorts of women who came through our doors. We quickly realized that between the two of us we would have to do everything from planning, cooking, cleanup, prayers, vocational talks, all while working full time. In addition to full-time teaching and trying to build community, I found myself taking on more outside talks to meet our financial needs. Within a few years, two other women joined us and for various reasons have stayed on the journey. We are far from the ideal of a new way of religious life because the rapid changes in the world call for a radicalization of the life that is difficult to conceive. Religious life cannot be born anew today without a new theology consonant with evolution and a restructuring of the church as an open system. That is, religious life needs temporary boundaries so that when the right time comes to let go, new structures of relationships can ensue. Stability lies in change, not in remaining the same. I have come to realize that the road to God does not lie in stability but in creativity, and the forms of religious life that can renew creative centers, both personally and collectively—centers at home in a world of flux and shifting boundaries—will be the communities that will grow in the future.

The Death of My Mother

My mother died the year before we moved to the Brookland area of Washington. Mom insisted on living alone in Florida in her last years, but in truth she was lost without my father, who died ten years earlier. Her Sicilian genes gave her a fighting spirit; even at the age of ninety she would dress up to go to church. But I knew her mental state had deteriorated when one weekend I visited her in Florida to help after she fell and injured her back. When I returned home and called to see how she was doing, I received a startling response. "Oh," she said. "I am doing fine. A nice man came to visit me and brought me some heating pads for my back." "Wonderful," I said, not having the heart to tell her that it was I who had just visited and brought her the heating pads.

My sister and I realized that Mom's energy of life was slipping away, so we decided to visit her at Christmas, sensing that it might be our last time together. The mother we knew as a dominant force in the universe was now a tiny, frail woman who was a bit confused and forgetful, a wisp of the mother who once ran the Hickory Dock Nursery School and lobbied for justice and equal rights. It was Christmas time, and that Sunday we decided to take her to the mall after Mass. Mom was dressed in a black leather skirt and jacket, black fishnet stockings, and high heels. She loved to go to this nearby mall and eat a soft pretzel and lemonade.

Anne Marie and I found a comfortable spot at a table in the mall with Mom, her lemonade, and pretzel. She was quite content, and I thought that maybe my sister and I could browse around the stores while Mom was eating her pretzel. So off we went to the surrounding stores, getting lost in racks of shoes and clothes. About an hour later I exclaimed, "Anne Marie, we need to get Mom and go." We returned to the table where we left Mom in her black leather skirt and fishnet stockings, but there was no Mom. We looked everywhere and in every store, and after an hour's search we had to call the police. Because of her age, they sent the Alzheimer's unit, and we stayed for another hour answering all sorts of questions. I called my brother Richard in Medfield, Massachusetts (Italian families always call the responsible male), and he had the good sense to call Mom's house.

She answered the phone with a lilt in her voice, "Hi, Richard, how are you doing?" "Mom," he said, "Denise and Anne Marie are looking for you." "Oh," she said, "I got tired waiting and went outside to look for a ride. This nice man in a big truck took me home." My ninety-one-year-old mother went outside the mall and hitched a ride with a trucker who apparently said, "Lady, you know this is dangerous." I could not believe that a four-foot-nine, ninety-one-year-old would take such a chance, but it also confirmed that the stuff of my genes is something between diamond rock and dynamite.

It was not long after the hitchhiking experience that Mom fell again and needed to go to rehab. My siblings and I thought it might be the right time to move her to an assisted living facility. Richard located one several miles from his home in Franklin, Massachusetts, and since Mom refused to go voluntarily, we essentially had to kidnap her. My siblings and I arrived in Florida upon her return from rehab. Without wasting time, we wrapped her up in warm clothes and walked her onto an airplane bound for Boston without explaining the purpose of the trip. "Where are we going," she asked, snuggled between my two brothers with my sister and me as bookends. We sat her on the plane in such a way that she could not look out the window; all she saw was her children: "Isn't it great that we are all together," she exclaimed.

We settled her into a lovely, warm room in the quaint New England living care facility. She lasted about two days before she looked out the window and could not find a palm tree anywhere. "Where am I?" she screamed on the phone to Richard one day. As hard as he tried to explain the situation, she rebelled and insisted that she return to Florida. But it was not possible, and deep down she knew it.

After three months of being confined in the living care facility (and not finding a palm tree) she gave up her will to live. She was hospitalized with congestive heart failure, and we all gathered around her; but she survived the hospital stay and died peacefully in her sleep in the living care facility with only Richard's family around her. I was not able to be present in the final moments of her life and deeply regretted it. She insisted on being cremated and to have a poem by Elizabeth Frye read at her grave site:

Do not stand at my grave and weep;
I am not there. I do not sleep.

I am a thousand winds that blow.
I am the diamond glint on snow.
I am the sun on ripened grain.
I am the gentle Autumn rain.

When you awake in the morning hush,
I am the swift, uplifting rush
Of quiet birds in circling flight.
I am the soft starlight at night.

Do not stand at my grave and cry;
I am not there. I did not die.[6]

Although she complained routinely about my father throughout their fifty-six years of married life, she missed him deeply after his death. She died on April 10, the day before my father's birthday (April 11), and on the same day that Teilhard de Chardin died in 1955, the year I was born. There are things written in the stars that we can never understand, nor do we ever see them, but they are there guiding us in this wild and chaotic journey of life. The lives of Mom and Teilhard were somehow intertwined in the dancing star out of which I was born.

I continued to teach at Washington Theological Union, but the school was undergoing significant shifts in enrollment, declining vocations, as well as a decline in international sabbatical students, following the tragedy of 9/11. Since tuition was the bread and butter of the school, it was uncertain how long the school could survive. Moreover, the twenty-four-year tenure of Vince Cushing as president during the growth years of WTU made it difficult to find a president who could lead the school with vision and creativity. In a period of five years, we had four different presidents, one of whom walked out of the position during spring break because of a conflict with the board of trustees. The position of dean did not fare much better, and we went through

---

6. This poem by Elizabeth Frye was never copyrighted, and the poem was in dispute until 1988; however, scholars have since verified it as an authentic work of Frye. The version my mother bequeathed to the family was taken from page 62 of a memorial service document for the United Spanish War Veterans service held at Portland, Oregon, on September 11, 1938 (the "40th Encampment") published by the U.S. Congress in early 1939.

at least six deans during my time at the school. Given the shifts in religious life and the role of the laity in the church, I felt that a new vision was needed for the school, but the faculty and board were not in agreement as to what the new vision might be. I saw the word "closure" invisibly written on the walls that housed so many students and seminarians, and I knew something had to change; but I was not sure what change would mean for me.

12

Woodstock Theological Center

O NE DAY I WAS SITTING at my desk and the phone rang. The voice was deep and a bit hesitant. "Uh," he began. "I am looking for Sister Ilia Delio." "Well, that would be me," I said. He continued, "My name is John Haughey, and I am with the Woodstock Theological Center at Georgetown. I am interested in your work in science and religion and would like to invite you to give a paper to our group." I hung up the phone, looked at God and chuckled. "Really, God," I thought. "You truly are amazing."

The following week I made my way to Georgetown University and found the Woodstock Theological Center on the second floor of the main building, Healy Hall. I was met by John Haughey, a tall man with long, dangling legs who looked like a walking Slinky. He was a Jesuit priest who had taught theology at some of the best Jesuit universities around the country. Now approaching eighty, he was in his wisdom years and devoted his time to thinking deeply about theology and culture and topics in science and religion. He was sharp as a knife and delightfully humorous, and we bonded immediately.

Woodstock was founded in 1869 in rural Maryland by the Jesuits as a college for novices and young Jesuits. After Vatican II, the college was moved to New York City, and then dissolved. Its library was moved to Georgetown in 1973, where it reorganized as a research institution and became known as the Woodstock Theological Center. Scholars were devoted to researching issues of social justice, religion, and ethics from a Roman Catholic perspective, while being open to interreligious dialogue and studies. The center produced writing on topics like nuclear weapons, public policy, religious freedom, ecology, Christian–Muslim relations, globalization, lobbying, and just war. The famed twentieth-century theologian Karl Rahner visited Woodstock during his visits to the United States, and what would become my office had been the home of the top-tier journal *Theological Studies* prior to my arrival.

The Jesuit Expansion

The Woodstock group of Jesuits was rich and diverse and included scholars from a variety of fields. The senior scholars wanted to diversify the core areas of research and were interested in a senior fellow who could devote full time to the area of science and religion. I did not realize during my initial visit that they were checking me out. Within a week's time, John called and offered me an affiliation with Woodstock as an associate fellow. He thought this would be a good arrangement so that I could get to know the group and see if full-time research would be an avenue of interest for me down the road.

In 2009 I joined the Woodstock Theological Center, participating in their seminars and Lonergan salon, which met once a month. It was a fascinating mix of people, many of whom were notable experts in their areas of economics, journalism, sociology, philosophy, Islamic studies, lay ministry, and the list went on. Woodstock took me to new levels of thinking and widened my worldview beyond the walls of WTU. The following year I accepted the invitation to become a full-time senior research fellow at the Woodstock Theological Center, and for the first time in many years I could devote my efforts to questions in science and religion.

John Haughey became my principal dialogue partner and best friend. We spent hours discussing philosophical and theological questions, such as the implications of matter and consciousness, the pros and cons of panentheism, and whether or not artificial intelligence would take us to a new level of human existence.

The breadth of intellectual life at Georgetown was exhilarating and the scope of our discussions illuminating. I had the opportunity to engage with (among many others) theologians Denis Edwards and Michael Amaladoss, SJ (who spent their sabbaticals at Woodstock), sociologist José Casanova, the writer Paul Elie, and philosopher Jürgen Habermas, who visited Woodstock as part of a seminar. John and I spearheaded a year-long project on transhumanism that resulted in a small publication called *Humanity on the Threshold*. It was this project that catapulted my interest in technology and human becoming and eventually led to my teaching an undergraduate course at Georgetown called Facebook and Jesus.

The Woodstock Theological Library, located in the basement of Lauinger Library at Georgetown, was one of the best theological libraries in the country; it also housed some of the archives of the Jesuit scientist Pierre Teilhard de Chardin. Part of those archives landed in the office of the program manager of Woodstock Theological Center. One day he walked into my office and said that he had some boxes in his closet pertaining to Teilhard's writings and asked if I would be interested in them. "You bet," I said, and within an hour I had four large boxes of Teilhard's writings sitting at my feet. It was an exhilarating moment, and I felt like a kid in a candy shop. I quickly sorted through the materials and discovered copies of notes where Teilhard had scribbled diagrams, words, and thoughts, reflecting his developing ideas. Eventually I had to return the materials to the archives (where they properly belonged), but for the time being I was thrilled to see how Teilhard formed his thoughts by reading across a broad spectrum of materials.

Deepening Teilhard's Vision

Woodstock Theological Center provided the opportunity to develop an intellectual depth on theological questions in view of science, technology, and culture that was not available in other settings. The center was steeped in the philosophical theology of Bernard Lonergan (d. 1984), the Canadian Jesuit who explored in detail the role of consciousness and understanding in the desire for God. His complex writings flowed from a brilliant mind originally trained in mathematics and classics and later in theology. Lonergan placed a significant emphasis on attention and consciousness as the first step of knowing God.

The Woodstock Jesuits used these insights (and many others) to explore various questions of faith and culture. As I engaged in these seminars, I could not help but be affected by the deep interiority called for by the Jesuit intellectual approach to knowledge. Ignatius of Loyola, who founded the Jesuits in 1541, developed a set of Spiritual Exercises that would enable his men to grow in holiness while on mission, preaching the gospel around the world. Ignatian spirituality is based on spiritual discernment, whereby one uses the imagination to participate in the life of Christ. It is a rather rigorous process, yet one that could easily form the mind to think out of a deep interiority and thus more capacious consciousness.

Many people ask how I have come to an integrated view of religion and evolution, and my first response is that I learned this integration through Teilhard de Chardin. Teilhard, who grew up in France, joined the Society of Jesus at eighteen years old and was formed in the Ignatian tradition during his training in England. I think the process of spiritual discernment played a significant role in his vision of faith and evolution. His "method of theology" was not too different from that of Lonergan: attend to experience, reflect on that experience through the intelligent mind, ponder the reflections inwardly through the structures of consciousness, and express what is contemplated by articulating new horizons of insight.

Understanding Teilhard through Lonergan's "method" allowed me to recognize that without the interior component of contemplation and reflection, the dialogue between science and religion is nothing more than a set of categorical statements and ideas. Without contemplation there is no integration of experience. As Lonergan said, "Knowing is not merely taking a look."[1] Knowledge is a comprehensive process of attention, consciousness, and reflection. The integration of knowledge requires subjectivity as an integral component of objectivity. The knowing subject forms the horizon of the world. Teilhard himself came to realize that science and religion form a "conjugate," a complexified whole, in which the two disciplines are two ways of knowing the one world. The artificial separation of these spheres of knowledge, in his view, undergirds our contemporary moral confusion and divided world.

Teilhard was as much a contemplative as a scientist; he was a mystic and a priest. His mind seemed to operate as a dynamic process in which, as physicist Henry Stapp wrote, "Each creative act brings into

---

1. Michael T. MacLaughlin, *Knowledge, Consciousness and Religious Conversion in Lonergan and Aurobindo* (Rome: Gregorian and Biblical Press, 2003), 64.

existence something fundamentally new."[2] Teilhard held an integral connection between mysticism and evolution and thought that mysticism secures what is needed for the future. Mysticism is the most intense spiritual energy and thus the most intense energy of centration. The awakening of the mystic to the presence of the Sacred is the beginning of a new vision of reality, as Martin Laird writes:

> This experience of the Sacred draws the mystic out of self into a new arena where the spiritual rhythms of Reality are rich and resonant. The mystic enters the center of a network of cosmic influences and is astonished at the depth and intimacy of relationship with the universe. In this arena, the mystic becomes aware that his or her fundamental duty and desire is to be united with God. But in order to be united the mystic must first of all *be,* and so the mystic sets out actively on a course of development.[3]

Consciousness played a fundamental role in Teilhard's vision. He saw it as part of the core energy in the universe that accounts for "radial" energy, or the energy of transcendence, which is "inside," so to speak, of everything that exists. Corresponding to this energy is another energy, which Teilhard called "tangential" energy, or an "outer" energy of attraction, that is, center-to-center attraction. Teilhard put these descriptive terms in a quasi-scientific framework to indicate that physical matter has the capacity to unite and transcend.

Consciousness and attraction led Teilhard to posit love as the fundamental energy of the universe. "Love is the most universal, the most tremendous and the most mysterious of the cosmic forces,"[4] he wrote, "the *physical* structure of the universe is love."[5] By this insight he indicated there is an irresistible and unyielding force of attraction in the universe with a specific character of personal, center-to-center

---

2. Henry Stapp, *Mind, Matter and Quantum Mechanics* (3rd ed., Berlin: Springer-Verlag, 2013), 94.

3. Martin Laird, OSF, "The Diaphanous Universe: Mysticism in the Thought of Pierre Teilhard de Chardin," *Studies in Spirituality* 4 (1994): 219.

4. Pierre Teilhard de Chardin, *Human Energy*, trans. J. M. Cohen (New York: Harcourt Brace Jovanovich, 1969), 32.

5. Ibid., 72.

attraction, which he called "love-energy." Love-energy is anti-entropic, present from the Big Bang onward though indistinguishable from molecular forces. "Even among the molecules," he wrote, "love was the building power that worked against entropy, and under its attraction the elements groped their way towards union."[6] Love energy is intrinsically relational, the affinity of being with being in a personal, centered way. If there was no internal propensity to unite, even at the level of the molecule itself, it would be physically impossible for love to appear higher up in human form.

If love is the "heart" of life and consciousness is the "mind" of love, so to speak, then where the mind is, so too our treasure lies; consciousness is the source of our freedom in love. Teilhard was influenced by the French philosopher Henri Bergson and his principle of *élan vital*, a principle that undergirds the capacity of nature to change. Teilhard identified this principle as "Omega," the presence of something in nature that is wholly other than nature; distinct yet intrinsic, autonomous and independent, yet deeply influential on nature's openness toward more being and consciousness.[7] Omega is God deeply entwined with the vagaries of nature. God is not divine substance controlling creation but the radical subject of everything that exists. God loves the world with the very same love with which God *is*. God's love fills up each being as "this" particular expression of love. Since no one finite being can adequately express the fullness of divine love, the excess of God's love spills over everything that exists as its future. Transcendence is the fecundity of love, the "yearning" of everything that exists for the fullness of love. Saint Paul alludes to this idea when he writes, "We know that the whole creation has been groaning as in the pains of childbirth right up to the present time" (Rom 8:22). God is struggling through the limits of nature to emerge in the freedom of consciousness as the glorious presence in creation. Teilhard said that God and creation form a complementary pair; creation contributes to God what God lacks in God's own life, namely, materiality. Hence, the fullness of God is realized in evolution, and evolution is fulfilled in God.

---

6. Thomas Mulvihill King, Teilhard's *Mysticism of Knowing* (New York: Seabury, 1981), 104–5.

7. Teilhard de Chardin, *Phenomenon of Man*, 257–60.

In light of the dynamic relationship between God and evolution, Teilhard spoke of religious experience as having evolutionary significance through centration of the universe. The openness of matter to divinity means that at higher levels of consciousness, the human person can "receive" the divine. The fulfillment of this capacity to receive divinity "centrates" the universe because the unitive experience with God unites all spaces of separation in the universe by filling them with the presence of divine love. What does this mean for us? It means faith has a cosmic function. The act of faith centrates the cosmos through higher levels of consciousness that integrate and unify. Laird writes: "Far from escaping the evolutionary structures of the world, the mystic refines those structures. Through divinization the mystic becomes a doorway through which Christ-Omega enters and transforms the world in the Divine Milieu."[8] In other words, *only* inner transformation can escape outer cosmic entropy and thus centrate energy on higher levels of complexity. Through inner transformation, the mystic nurtures a zest for life by becoming more inwardly whole, thus contributing to the unfolding cosmic wholeness and drawing others into new levels of community. Beatrice Bruteau wrote, "The more conscious the individual becomes, the more individual becomes *person*, and each person is person only to the extent that the individual freely lives by the life of the Whole."[9] The integral relationship between consciousness, personhood, and evolution resonates in Karl Rahner's famous dictum: "The devout Christian of the future will either be a 'mystic,' one who has experienced 'something,' or he will cease to be anything at all."[10]

Engaging a New Vision of Catholicity

Teilhard approached the scientific world of experience from his inner world of religious experience. His critics (of which there are

---

8. Laird, "The Diaphanous Universe," 222.

9. Beatrice Bruteau, "Trinitarian Personhood," in *The Grand Option: Personal Transformation and a New Creation* (Notre Dame, IN: University of Notre Dame Press, 2001), 77.

10. Karl Rahner, "Christian Living Formerly and Today," in *Theological Investigations* VII, trans. David Bourke (New York: Herder and Herder, 1971), 15, as quoted in Harvey D. Egan, *Soundings in the Christian Mystical Tradition* (Collegeville, MN: Liturgical Press, 2010), 338.

many) completely misunderstood his ideas by judging them from analytical philosophical or scientific perspectives. After spending a lot of time with Teilhard, I think no one should make a judgment on his ideas unless she or he is a person of contemplative prayer and attuned to the mystical dimensions of reality. Teilhard himself tells us that he saw matter with the eyes of faith; he listened to the sounds of old bones dug up from layers of sand and silt and perceived the sound of the Spirit in these "incarnational" bones. God, he said, is being born in and through the stuff of matter.

His method of experience was phenomenological, not analytical. Yet, his lack of philosophical tools to support his theological insights has caused his cosmic vision to be marginalized in both the academy and in the church. Theologians continue to shrug him aside as a delusional lunatic or simply a quack. For those who are not wedded to Greek philosophy or logical arguments, Teilhard's insights are breathtakingly novel and creative. No other thinker of the twentieth century has achieved his comprehensive view of religion and evolution. While science and religion continue to limp along (both in the church and the academy), the Teilhardian vision is proving attractive to various people who are seeking God in a world of change and complexity. As I travel around the globe, I find many small groups forming around his vision; in fact, the emergence of spiritual seekers prompted me to form the Omega Center in 2016 as a way to deepen Teilhard's vision. Given the evolutionary forces of our current age and the rise of new spiritual trends, I anticipate that his vision will eventually generate a paradigm shift in church and world.[11]

John Haughey understood Teilhard as a fellow traveler, a Jesuit brother, as if they might have shared a mental room sometime in the past. It was from the way he spoke about Teilhard that I knew he had tapped into something that other scholars missed, the deep contemplative soul of Teilhard.

I once asked John during a long lunch break how he came to his insights. "I just think," he said. "I just sit and think." But then he said to me, "Trust your own thoughts. Don't rely on others all the time. Trust your own experience because the Spirit of God is working through that

---

11. I began the Omega Center in 2016 as a way of deepening Teilhard's vision of love at the heart of the universe.

experience." His advice was novel for an academic because the world of scholarship is based primarily on footnotes. But John's advice was simple: "Think from yourself and trust what you think."

I took his advice to heart, because he was a brilliant thinker. His book *Where Is Knowing Going* is a landmark for Catholic higher education, building on Lonergan's notions of interiority and consciousness and providing a new and robust understanding of catholicity as wholemaking, the consciousness of making things whole. Because of John, I could see Teilhard's vision as a vision of catholicity, wholemaking in an evolutionary universe. I remember the day the "catholicity" light turned on for me. I ran into John's office and had to search for him buried behind piles of books and papers. "Now, I get it," I exclaimed. "Teilhard is not marginally catholic but deeply catholic," I said, "maybe the first real catholic after Jesus (who of course was not catholic!)." In fact, "the whole Big Bang universe is catholic," I quipped during one of our afternoon discussions. But I meant it—a truly "catholic" cosmos is not the conversion of all people to Catholicism but the liberation of all people as wholes within wholes, a consciousness of wholeness that includes all earthly forms of life. Not the institutionalization of the gospel but the deconstruction of the Temple and the new awareness of the holiness of life as the personal and communal wholeness of life.

Jesus ushered in a new consciousness of divine presence, a new heart and mind, a new creativity that was both present and future oriented. Catholicity can never be institutionalized because the openness of life to more life demands an ongoing conversion of creative consciousness. Jesus was clear that his mission was not to supplant Temple worship but to fulfill the covenant of God's faithful love: "I have come not to abolish the law but to fulfill the law" (Matt 5:17). He drew a link between a new Temple made not by human hands but by the Holy Spirit (John 2:19), a point that Saint Paul emphasizes as well: "Do you not know that you are God's temple and that God's Spirit dwells in you?" (1 Cor 3:16).

Catholicity is not a term that has entered into the consciousness of the church that seeks to be "missionary" and "universal," abstract terms that are not fully integrated into the reality of a Big Bang cosmos and biological evolution. The lack of catholicity that flows from an integrating view of theology and science is giving rise to an aging church. Whenever I speak about faith and evolution, inevitably I get questions from younger people as to where they can find these ideas in the church. "Umm," I answer, "hope is a verb with its sleeves rolled up; hang in there, church is what is being born."

The Catholic Church is entrenched in a hierarchy that seeks to maintain universality in a world of evolution and shifting consciousness. The church propounds a type of hierarchy that is acosmic, independent of evolution, despite Vatican II and its call to open the windows to history. A static and fixed structure demands fixed laws and dogmas independent of developmental time and shifts in consciousness. Such a structure, however, cannot hold indefinitely.

Evolution is speeding up around the world due to advances in computer technology. The globe is now an electronic brain, giving rise to complexified consciousness (that is, higher degrees of relationality or information) in areas such as socialization and religious consciousness. In an evolutionary milieu, all structures are local and depend on environmental factors. In a universal structure, such as the church, local entities subsist in higher-order entities that operate on static, fixed principles, the same principles that support patriarchy and clericalism. For the church to thrive in the future, it must restructure itself according to the provisional matrices of evolution; such change would mean a deconstruction of hierarchical power and a reconstruction of leadership across horizontal lines.

What we are witnessing today is the resistance of an entrenched hierarchical church against the forces of evolution. Teilhard de Chardin was clearly aware of the problem of a static church and struggled with the ambivalence of Christianity: "If we Christians wish to *retain* the very qualities on which God's power and our worship are based, we have no better way—no other way, even—of doing so than fully to accept the most modern concepts of evolution."[12] Evolution is not a theory for discussion; it is (and has been for over a century) the best scientific description of unfolding life and must be the starting point for understanding all aspects of life, whether biological life (including human life), divine life, or spiritual life.

---

12. Teilhard de Chardin, *Christianity and Evolution*, 128.

Max Wildiers, a Dutch Franciscan, had a keen grasp of Teilhard's vision. In his introduction to Teilhard's essays on Christianity and evolution he stated: "The conflict we are suffering today does indeed consist in the conflict between a religion of transcendence and a secularized world, between the 'God of the Above' and the 'God of the Ahead,' between a 'religion of heaven' and a 'religion of the earth.'"[13] Teilhard himself wrote: "Christians should have no need to be afraid or shocked by the results of scientific research, whether in physics, biology or history . . . science should not disturb our faith by its analyses. Rather it should help us to know God better."[14]

Until we come to know God in evolution we shall find the world a problem. Teilhard envisioned the evolutionary process as one moving toward higher levels of consciousness and ultimately toward evolution of spirit, from the birth of mind to the birth of the whole Christ.[15] He urged Christians to participate in the process of Christogenesis, to risk, get involved, aim toward union with others, for the entire creation is waiting to give birth to God. He opposed a static Christianity that isolates its followers instead of merging them with the masses, imposing on them a burden of observances and obligations, and causing them to lose interest in the common task. "Do we realize that if we are to influence the world it is essential that we share in its drive, in its anxieties and its hopes?"[16] "We are not only to recognize evolution," he wrote, "but make it continue in ourselves."[17]

In the midst of these activities, the Jesuits decided to close Woodstock due to lack of financial resources. I was subsequently hired by Georgetown College as director of Catholic Studies and visiting assistant professor. Thanks to the generosity of a beautiful family who donated a million dollars to Catholic Studies, I envisioned building the program into a vibrant theological-cultural enterprise. My hours in

13. Wildiers, foreword to Teilhard de Chardin, *Christianity and Evolution*, 10.

14. Pierre Teilhard de Chardin, *Science and Christ*, trans. René Hague (New York: Harper & Row, 1968), 36.

15. Pierre Teilhard de Chardin, *The Future of Man*, trans. Norman Denny (New York: Harper & Row, 1964), 309.

16. Henri de Lubac, *Pierre Teilhard de Chardin: The Man and His Meaning*, trans. René Hague (New York: Hawthorn Books, 1965), 124.

17. Ursula King, *Christ in All Things: Exploring Spirituality with Pierre Teilhard de Chardin* (Maryknoll, NY: Orbis Books, 1997), 80.

conversation with John Haughey left a deep impression on me. John kept asking, "Where is knowing going?" and I too wondered about the purpose of higher education in relation to the rapid pace of evolution. A Catholic university should ask one question, John indicated, "What is the good you are trying to do?" "Yes, John," I would respond, but I would add, "is knowledge leading to love?" John's insights helped me see the potential value of the Catholic university today in nurturing a new wholeness through the dynamic process of collaborative dialogue. As Gerald O'Collins notes, to be human is to have "a ceaseless drive toward meaning and truth . . . there is a dynamic thrust to the human intellect that constantly presses toward the fullness of meaning and truth in the Absolute."[18]

Teilhard stressed the importance of knowledge in the evolution of wholeness. "To think is to unify," he said, "to make wholes where there are scattered fragments; not merely to register it but to confer upon it a form of unity it would otherwise be without."[19] He warned against abstract knowledge divorced from physical reality; abstract knowledge, he said, forms ideas but leaves the physical world adrift. Such knowledge can only lead to fragmentation. How we know and what we know are essential to the way evolution proceeds; ultimately, knowledge makes a difference in how we love. In Teilhard's words, "To discover and know is to actually extend the universe ahead and to complete it."[20] My goal of building Catholic Studies into an interdisciplinary program oriented toward a consciousness of the whole did not materialize at Georgetown; however, the insights I gained were invaluable.

In expanding Teilhard's vision through hours of conversation and reflection my inner world became my outer world. My childhood Catholicism was now converted to a worldly Christianity. As much as I still loved Plato, Aristotle, and the church fathers, I loved them for the way they probed into the mysteries of God and nature. I too was doing the same. Teilhard helped me realize that the only way to heaven

18. Gerald O'Collins, SJ, *Rethinking Fundamental Theology: Toward a New Fundamental Theology* (New York: Oxford University, 2011), 38; Gregory Kalscheur, SJ, "A Response to Kenneth Garcia: Healthy Secularity and the Task of a Catholic University," *Theological Studies* 73, no. 4 (December 2012): 924–34, at 932.

19. King, *Mysticism of Knowing*, 36.

20. King, *Mysticism of Knowing*, 35.

is *through* earth; not a flight *from* the world but a deepening entrance *into* the world, where the storm of bleeding hearts yearns to rest in the heart of God. Through Teilhard and John Haughey, two Jesuits, I saw the profound import of the Incarnation for our complex world of evolution, globalization, capitalism, and technology. I tried to lay out the foundation of this vision in several books, including *The Unbearable Wholeness of Being* and *Making All Things New*; but I have yet fully to articulate what I see.

One of the final highlights at Georgetown was commemorating the sixtieth anniversary of Teilhard's death. I took part in this commemoration and joined a panel discussion on the relevance of Teilhard for today. Afterward, we performed Teilhard's "Mass on the World," a beautiful priestly oblation and celebration of cosmic life.

In the meantime, I applied for an endowed chair in Christian theology at Villanova University. It was a gambit with no further expectations than the breath of God's will. I entered the open space of chance and spontaneity because that is where God delights. I was offered the Connelly Chair in Theology and moved to Villanova in the fall of 2015. Shortly after accepting the position, I was running to catch the train to attend a meeting at Villanova and tripped over my suitcase while flying down the concrete steps. After a short leap in the air, I crashed head-first on to the stone pavement. A beautiful young dark-skinned man with black-rimmed glasses picked me up and looked at my torn chin. "Are you ok?" he asked. I looked into his deep brown eyes through my bent glasses and saw pure compassion. "No, I am not," I said. He took me by the arm and gently walked me to the metro police station nearby. He waited with me until the ambulance arrived. This person was no mere "image of God"—such a trite, arid, overused idea. This young man was the radiance of divinity—stunning love in the midst of DC and "Black Lives Matter" posters. Quite honestly, I think I saw Jesus that day, and I knew that the breath of God would continue to move me along this journey of life.

13

Christian Cyborg?

O NE OF THE FINAL COURSES I taught the undergraduates at Georgetown was the course Facebook and Jesus. I wanted an attractive
title that could pull students into a meaningful discussion on social
media and artificial intelligence and the significance of these for human
personhood in the twenty-first century. We covered key areas of transformation in religion and culture that are undergoing change, signified
by terms such as cyborgs, transhumanism, and posthumanism. Since
teaching impels one to "digest" the material, I had to begin to understand the foundations of these concepts in a meaningful way. Students
who take this course (or the variation of it at Villanova) almost always
begin by saying that technology is a tool for our use. I question them
on this statement and then ask them to hold on to it and revisit it at the
end of the semester. What I try to show from various perspectives is
that technology is not simply a "tool" for human use but an extension
of what we are; once I make this point, I have their attention.

The Lure of Artificial Intelligence

T he root of dualism can be found in Descartes's mechanical philosophy. Descartes thought of the human person as one composed
of a physical body and immaterial mind, giving rise to two distinct
entities: body and mind. This notorious dualism of body and mind
extends into our everyday thinking with statements such as these:
"These athletes are prepared mentally and physically," and "There's
nothing wrong with you; it's all in your mind."[1] If the mind is distinct

---

1. Daniel Dennett, "Review of Damasio, Descartes' Error," http://ase.tufts.edu/
cogstud/papers/damasio.htm.

from the body, could the mind be housed in another medium? Alan
Turing pondered this question. A British intelligence officer and crypt-
analyst, Turing originally developed the computer to decipher German
codes during World War II, but he also wondered if a machine could
be made to mimic human intelligence. In 1950 he developed a test in
which a computer was set up to fool judges into believing that it could
be human. The test was performed by conducting a text-based conversation on a subject. If the computer's responses were indistinguishable
from those of a human, it had passed the Turing test and could be
said to be "thinking." John McCarthy coined the term "artificial intelligence" in 1956, defining it as "the science and engineering of making
intelligent machines."[2]

The philosopher Carl Mitcham said that up to the twentieth century
the philosophical challenge was to think about nature and ourselves
in the presence of nature. Today the great and the first philosophical
challenge is to think about technology and ourselves in the presence of
technology.[3] Artificial intelligence begs the question, "What is nature?"
Is "nature" the same as "information"? Is "nature" distinct from "information"? The word "nature" comes from the Latin *natura,* which is the
translation of the Greek *physis,* literally meaning "birth" or "growth";
existence is not static but has dynamic principles of development. Discussions of artificial intelligence (AI) as being "outside nature," posing
either as an existential threat or an inert tool, miss the deeper meaning of AI as integral to nature, insofar as information is integral to the
pluripotentiality of nature itself.

Nature is paradoxical if not outright elusive. All scientists can
attest that just when they think they have understood an aspect of
nature, their theories slip into new questions. Quantum physics, one
of the main pillars of modern science today, is strange and mysterious. The physicist Niels Bohr, one of the key proponents of quantum
physics, once exclaimed, "If quantum mechanics hasn't profoundly
shocked you, you haven't understood it yet."[4] Physics is like poetry,

---

2. Leora Morgenstern and Sheila A. McIlraith, "John McCarthy's Legacy,"
Journal of Artificial Intelligence 175 (January 2011): 1–24.

3. Carl Mitcham, "The Philosophical Challenge of Technology," *American
Catholic Philosophical Association Proceedings* 40 (1996): 45.

4. Quoted in John Gribbin, *In Search of Schrödinger's Cat* (Toronto: Bantam

he claimed; it is descriptive of deep realities but cannot exactly define the realities.

Teilhard de Chardin used the word "nature" more than a thousand times in his writings, often replacing the word "nature" with other words such as "earth," "world," "planet," "cosmos," and "universe."[5] A more formal definition of "nature" would include the existing system of things; the universe of matter, energy, time, and space—the physical world, all of creation. Or perhaps it is the summary of everything that has to do with biological, chemical, and physical states and events in the physical universe. But these definitions do not adequately account for the fact that nature is as much defined by computations and algorithms as it is by physics, chemistry, and biology.

Technology is part of evolutionary life, and by this I mean that nature has within it the capacity to create tools and find new means to optimize life. The ontological distinction between "nature" and "technology" no longer holds, as scientists now recognize a connection between *bios* and *techne*, yielding to what we can aptly describe as the "plasticity of nature." Nature is pluripotent; it has infinite potential to be some*thing;* and every time nature becomes some *thing,* the thing itself transcends the givenness of nature. Hence, nature is *techne* in that "toolmaking" is part of nature's inherent capacity to optimize life and creatively transcend itself.

Lynn Margulis, a renowned microbiologist who died in 2011, argued that the blurring of technology and biology isn't really all that new. She observed that the shells of clams and snails are a kind of technology dressed in biological clothing. Is there really that much difference between the vast skyscrapers we build or the malls in which we shop, even the cars we drive around, and the hull of a seed? Seeds and clam shells, which are not alive, hold in them a little bit of water and carbon and DNA, ready to replicate when the time is right, yet we don't distinguish them from the life they hold. Why should it be any different with office buildings, hospitals, and space shuttles? Put another way,

---

Books, 1984), 5; Simon Singh, *Big Bang: The Origin of the Universe* (New York: Harper Perennial, reprint, 2005), 492.

5. Libby Osgood, "The Nature of Nature: An Examination of Teilhard de Chardin's Use of the Term Nature" (2018), 1. Unpublished paper shared in a personal communication.

we may make a distinction between living things and the tools those things happen to create, but nature does not.[6] Nature does not distinguish between the clamshell and the clam, or the first flint knife and the human that made it. Rather nature is a social construct of multiple meanings so that neither the artifice (the knife) nor the organism (the human) alone is adequate by itself as a cultural root symbol.

Nature is deceiving, playful, and mysterious; it has a sacred depth that evades the scientific grasp. The language of "tool making" misleads the capacity of nature to be harnessed as information in the form of AI and sets up a binary system of opposites, for example, the human person versus the computer. If indeed "nature" includes algorithms and computation, then nature and artificial intelligence are not opposing terms but descriptive of the same reality. We can consider computer technology as part of the wider biological process of emergent complex relationships. Nature constantly creates new connections, and computer technology is part of the broader framework of interconnections.

The Plasticity of Nature

Studying the culture of technology and artificial intelligence has opened up for me a new window of understanding that undergirds shifts in gender and human personhood. I found a new level of meaning through the friendship of Martine Rothblatt, who was introduced to me through our mutual friend, Frank Sasinowski, a Washington lawyer and student of Richard Rohr. Martine was born Martin Rothblatt to a Jewish family in a suburb of San Diego, California, and obtained her degree in communication studies and later a law degree as well from the University of California Los Angeles. She pioneered the development of Geostar and founded several communications satellite companies before establishing Sirius XM satellite radio. She then went on to build a multimillion-dollar pharmaceutical company, United Therapeutics, of which she is currently CEO and full-time chairwoman. More to the point, Martine was transgendered at the age of forty while married and raising a family of four children.

I had never met a transgendered person prior to Martine, and I was

6. Chip Walter, "Cyber Sapiens" (October 26, 2006). http://www.kurzweilai.net.

not sure what to expect at the luncheon that Frank arranged for us at the Four Seasons Hotel in Washington, DC. Frank and I arrived early and waited for Martine. She emerged from the rear, a large, tall woman, with long brown hair in a pony tail, and a black turtleneck sweater. I was rather nervous at our first meeting, but she was completely disarming. Here was the highest-paid CEO in corporate America sitting at the table drinking water and eating bread with a Franciscan sister and her lawyer friend. Her unassuming presence expressed a deep spirit of peace. We talked at length about Teilhard de Chardin, especially since Martine has a spiritual foundation called "Terasem," which has a technocultural vision inspired by Teilhard's notion of the noosphere, the linking of minds through technological means.

One time I invited Martine and her wife, Bina, to dinner at our home in Washington. Bina had made quite a stir in the news as Bina48, the robot Martine built to experiment with mindclones, that is, electronic cloning of the mind. The program *60 Minutes* did a segment on Bina48 with the real Bina talking to the robot Bina. When I showed this program to my students, they cringed at the idea of a humanoid robot, but I explained that Martine is aiming to show that what we are biologically can be reconstituted electronically and uploaded into a new medium, thus creating an extension of presence beyond the boundaries of space/time. I assumed the person who came to dinner was the biological Bina, as she had a beautiful smile and a spontaneous effusion of gratitude for our hospitality. Knowing the real Bina helped me realize that Martine is not trying to replace the human person but extend the human person into future forms, not so much negating death but enhancing life.

Martine's writings on brain uploading and digital immortality have invited many criticisms, but as I read the criticisms, I found a deep misunderstanding of her brilliant insights. She understands the plasticity of nature and the way nature can be harnessed toward a more environmentally sustainable world, not only electronically but ecologically as well. She recently inaugurated the world's largest net-zero office building, called the Unisphere, containing 210,000 square feet of space in Silver Spring, Maryland, powered, heated, and cooled completely from on-site sustainable energy technologies. This office building uses 1 MW solar panels (1,000 kilowatts of power), fifty-two geothermal wells, a quarter-mile-long earth labyrinth, and electrochromic glass to operate with a zero-carbon footprint while graphically communicating its net-energy status in real time to the building occupants.

I recently visited the Unisphere, and it is an incredible structure of ingenuity, creativity, and sustainable engineering. It is one of the many visions Martine continues to realize for the transformation of the world, and I am often inspired by her luminous ideas, which she shares in a spirit of humility and peace. She lives out of a deep personal freedom without need to justify herself. She is a visionary and futurist who seeks to realize the potential of human nature to expand into a more unified presence in the world, a sustainable presence that can live more consciously in love.

My friendship with Martine has caused me to rethink a few things. For one, Aristotle cannot be entirely correct, and by this I mean there are no fixed essences of things, or, to put this another way, prime matter is not shaped by form. Rather, prime matter is prime energy or consciousness. Recent studies on consciousness support the notion of panpsychism, which states that consciousness comes first and then matter, rather than the other way around. The physicist Max Plank noted in the early twentieth century: "I regard consciousness as fundamental. I regard matter as derivative from consciousness. We cannot get behind consciousness. Everything that we talk about, everything that we regard as existing, postulates consciousness."[7] Even Teilhard thought that evolution is the rise of consciousness—not the rise of material forms.[8] Matter depends on consciousness, and consciousness gives shape to matter. There is no consciousness apart from matter, and hence everything, including religion, begins with consciousness.

The primacy of consciousness fits nicely with Saint Anselm's ontological argument for the existence of God: God is that than which no greater can be thought.[9] There is no God without consciousness; it is impossible to conceive of God apart from consciousness. God is ultimate consciousness. If Planck is correct and matter begins with

---

7. Max Planck, "Quantum Physics," *The Observer* (January 25, 1931): 17.

8. Teilhard de Chardin, *Phenomenon of Man,* 221.

9. Saint Anselm, *Proslogian, Monologium, An Appendix on Behalf of the Fool Gaunilo; Cur Deus Homo,* trans. Sidney Norton Deane (La Salle, IL: Open Court, 1948).

consciousness, then matter "matters" to God; indeed everything matters to God. Traveling in the circles of evolutionary thinkers such as Teilhard de Chardin and Martine Rothblatt, I have come to realize that new levels of consciousness give way to new forms of life and new understandings of God.

As I stand on the threshold between the church and the wider sphere of science, I see two problems facing the church. The first is the speed of evolution, which is accelerating because of more efficient computing power and which will continue to accelerate with quantum computing (as my mother used to say, "Stop the world! I want to get off!"). This factor alone makes it unlikely that the church can survive indefinitely into the future in its present form; the church must either reorganize along the lines of evolution or resign itself to becoming a minor sect.

The second problem is more challenging because it confronts the philosophical bedrock of theological doctrine, and that is the question of nature itself. The Incarnation is based on the union of divine nature and human nature; human personhood is based on Aristotelian concepts of nature marked by matter and form. Nature bears within it a natural law of the good written on the human heart. Thomas Aquinas once said, "A mistake about creation is a mistake about God." However, "an insight about creation is an insight about God."[10] If nature is a dynamic birthing process of evolving life, what is our understanding of God? The medievalists said that revelation is the one divine Word expressing itself in the Book of Nature and the Book of Scripture. If science tells us that nature is informational, dynamic, relational, evolving creative forms, then what is God? If creation is one whole unity in God then should not our understanding of nature (the work of science) influence our understanding of the things of faith? Apart from science, any explanation of God can be logically explained, but it is not necessarily true. Truth means that the transparency of what is seen and what is believed is the same reality without contradiction or confusion. Without modern science, modern faith floats on a sea of abstractions.

The church today, for example, continues to define the human person in the same way it defined personhood in the thirteenth century, following the definition of Boethius (d. AD 524), who wrote: *Persona est rationalis naturae individua substantia*; that is, "A person is an indi-

---

10. I am grateful to Matthew Fox for this insight.

vidual substance of a rational nature."[11] We know we each have a rational nature, but are we "individual substances"? Is there another way to conceive the particularity of personhood in light of modern science?

Evolutionary biology confirms that the modern human person is a member of the species *Homo sapiens*, which emerged out of Africa. Recent studies show that we did not emerge as one lineage from one spot in Africa, however (*pace* the Adam and Eve myth). Instead, the lineage of *Homo sapiens* probably originated in Africa at least 500,000 years ago—evolving from interlinked groups across the entire swath of Africa toward contemporary human morphology over tens of thousands of years. This slow and expansive change was influenced by ecological and genetic shifts.[12] Studies in evolution show that factors such as climate change caused changes in the environment so that adaptation to the environment resulted in variations over time, giving rise to new types of hominid species. The project on human origins at the Smithsonian museum states the following:

> Paleoanthropologists—scientists who study human evolution—have proposed a variety of ideas about how environmental conditions may have stimulated important developments in human origins. Diverse species have emerged over the course of human evolution, and a suite of adaptations have accumulated over time, including upright walking, the capacity to make tools, enlargement of the brain, prolonged maturation, the emergence of complex mental and social behavior, and dependence on technology to alter the surroundings. The period of human evolution has coincided with environmental change, including cooling, drying, and wider climate fluctuations over time.[13]

---

11. The definition is given in Boethius's *Liber de persona et duabus naturis* 3.2 (Patrologia latina 64; ed. J.-P. Migne; Paris, 1844–64), 1343. This definition was given in an attempt to defend the Council of Chalcedon's definition of the one person and two natures of Jesus Christ contra Eutyches and Nestorius.

12. Ephrat Livni, "How to come up with better ideas, according to scientists who developed a new theory of human evolution," https://qz.com.

13. Smithsonian, "What Does It Mean to Be Human?" http://humanorigins.si.edu.

One thing is clear: the human person did not just appear, out of nothing, in a garden. Rather, personhood is a biological and evolutionary phenomenon that continues to change, based on environmental factors and biological relationships. In evolution essences are provisional, not fixed; boundaries are made and unmade, and hence fragile. Whereas the church defines what constitutes a person, evolution (and AI as an expression of evolution) makes no such demands. Life is not an established structure but a work of art in which the work itself includes the imagination of God and the serendipity of nature in an ongoing creative process.

The Symbol of the Cyborg

The idea that technology is not a tool but an extension of our nature has been developing since the mid-twentieth century. The cyborg arose in the 1960s as humans were sent into space. In order to survive in space, human astronauts had to be strapped to machines to maintain normal physiological functions. Manfred Clynes and Nathan Kline who coined the term "cyborg" in a 1960 article and envisioned that a cyborgian man-machine hybrid would be needed in the next great techno-human challenge of space flight.[14]

The term "cyborg" is an abbreviation of "cybernetic organism" and expresses the capacity of biological nature to be joined to or hybridized with non-biological nature such as an oxygen tank, contact lenses, or any of the devices we use to enhance physiological or biological function. Donna Haraway's 1985 "Cyborg Manifesto" brought prominent attention to the concept of cyborg as a symbol of hybridity, indicating that nature is not fixed but permeable and dynamic. Cyborgs appear where boundaries are transgressed. Estonian theologian Anne Kull writes, "The conceptual boundaries of what it means to be human or what we human beings mean by *nature* have never been less secure."[15] Emerging from and integrated into a chaotic world rather than a position of mastery and control removed from it, "the cyborg has the poten-

---

14. Manfred E. Clynes and Nathan S. Kline, "Cyborgs and Space," *Astronautics* 9 (1960): 27–28.

15. Anne Kull, "The Cyborg as an Interpretation of Culture-Nature," *Zygon* 36, no. 1 (2001): 50.

tial not only to disrupt persistent dualisms (body and soul; matter and spirit) but also to refashion our thinking about the theoretical understanding of the body as a material entity and a discursive process."[16]

The significance of the human cyborg means that subjectivity is emergent rather than given, distributed rather than located solely in the mind; "boundaries have meaning only for particular, locatable, and embodied subjects."[17] The most powerful thing that happens in the cyborg boundary-crossing is that the categories we use to distinguish human being, nature, culture, and technology are rendered obscure. What the cyborg signifies is that there are no fixed or lasting ontological distinctions. The cyborg symbolizes the extension of nature into new forms. They destabilize our fixed understandings of nature because the cyborg has as much affinity with technology as it does with wilderness. Cyborg bodies cut across a dominant cultural order, not so much because of their "constructed" nature but because of their kinship with both culture and nature. In a sense we have never been *purely human*. We are (and have always been) a mix of technologies that help us to survive and thrive in the world.

Cyborgs indicate that the old mechanistic framework is giving way to something new. This new entity *will not* be a major rehabilitation of the organismic model of nature; rather, a new hybrid is emerging which is both machine and organism and is less substantive than an information-processing entity. These emerging hybrid entities are neither wholly technological nor completely biological and have the potential not only to disrupt persistent dualisms but also to refashion our thinking about the theoretical understanding of the body as a material entity and a discursive process. The cyborg has radicalized the modern subject, dismantling the centered and masterful subject as an affirmative project, ending not in the absence of the subject but in new and positive conceptions of social subjectivity. Integral to this new conception is the idea that a cyborg body is not bounded by the skin but includes all external pathways along which information can travel. Boundaries have meaning only for particular, locatable, and embodied subjects.

In short, a new type of person is emerging in the twenty-first cen-

---

16. Anne Kull, "Cyborg Embodiment and Incarnation," *Currents in Theology and Mission* 28, nos. 3–4 (2001): 282.

17. Kull, "Cyborg Embodiment," 281.

tury and we are challenged by the idea that technology is evolving nature in new ways. This idea scares people and the first reaction is, "I am not a cyborg!" A religious person might add to this exclamation: "This has nothing to do with God. We should be concerned about the spiritual life and salvation, not cyborgs!" But the truth is, there is no God apart from evolution and there is no God apart from cyborgs. If God makes things to make themselves (as Thomas Aquinas suggested) then self-making is written into the heart of nature. Reality is a process constituted by the drive for transcendence. The nature of reality is to explore possibilities that are not yet actual. Nature, in a sense, is never satisfied; it always presses on for novelty and to be something more.

If we consider how quickly we are evolving with computer technology we can begin to realize that God has set up a system in which the entities who will transcend humans in the chain of evolution are entities we humans are designing and creating, so that their act of transcending us is at the same time our own act of transcending ourselves. Far from being opposed to God, AI is the way human nature is realizing new possibilities; when we participate in the drive for new possibilities, we are also participating in God. If nature is being revised, repackaged, and rediscovered, so too our understanding of self and God must evolve.

Horizontal Personhood

Generation Z (born between 1990 and 2019) has an intuitive grasp of cyborgs and transhumanism, although they are often unaware of their own technospheric minds. Once they see themselves in the mirror of technology, they are startled at what they see and what they are becoming—but they are not scared or thwarted by it. They are born into a world that has been rewiring and rerouting its planetary circuits since the beginning of the twentieth century (thanks to mass communication and air travel). Today, the amount of information available is accelerating relationships of shared information through the vast webs of networks. My intuitive self speculates that younger generations probably have larger brain centers of integration and are "wired" horizontally, that is, across complexified fields of relatedness. Their sense of personal relationship is based on shared information, so that even personal identity is relational rather than self-reflective. There are gains and losses in the emergent personhood of younger generations.

One gain, in my view, is that differences of gender, race, or religion are being transcended by shared interests; that is, a young person is not too concerned if his or her video playmate or social media friend is black, white, Asian, gay, transgendered, or bi-gendered. Such ontologies are essentially irrelevant and favored by what I call an ontology of "betweenness"; that is, shared information that links two or more persons together is the basis of existence. Betweenness has a different logic of relationality from the classical "you and me" relationship insofar as "betweenness" or the informational relationship is not constituted by "*me* and *you*" as two distinct entities, but by "me *and* you" as one shared entity formed by our "betweenness," or informational flow.

I think something along these lines accounts for the emphasis younger generations place on authenticity, transparency, and community (although I am also aware that the internet can be used deceptively to hide identity and information). It is not unusual to have undergraduate students come up after class to identify themselves as gay or indicate that one of their siblings is transgendered, as if they have a need to confess their identity or simply to be transparent in who they are. Authenticity and transparency seem to be a trademark of this generation, even as they struggle to define themselves.

While shared information establishes personhood, one of the losses of the internet generation is self-knowledge and self-reflection, the ability to know oneself within oneself rather than outside oneself. It is not a coincidence today that exoskeletal (online) life coincides with an increased interest in yoga and meditation and may also underlie the increased rate in teen suicide as well. The information overload of online life demands a balance of peace and quiet, but there are few guides or religious frameworks for harnessing the mystical dimension of life within the AI technosphere. Teilhard had insights in this regard and spoke of the noosphere (the realm of interconnected minds) as the place where love can deepen, but his ideas have yet to be integrated into a way of life, for they require a dynamic relationship between God and evolution.

A New Human on the Horizon

What I am learning from studies on artificial intelligence is that connections form relationships and relationships form persons. Younger generations are focused more on relationships and less on ontological distinctions that can lead to rejection based on race, gender, or religion. From childhood on, younger generations learn to communicate via some form of artificial intelligence, and I suspect that children who are more deeply involved in complex levels of communication (internet, TV, phone, travel, etc.), beginning in early stages of development, are more likely to form relationships across informational lines rather than lines of difference (for example, male vs. female, black vs. white). The primacy of information undergirds a type of emerging nondual consciousness. Those who are oppositional (such as white supremacists) tend to be influenced by strong religious backgrounds and are likely to have less exposure to complex levels of information. By this I mean they are probably from small towns or rural areas where church and community are more important than iPhones and video games.

On the whole, I find that younger generations want to help make the world a better place. Many Gen Z-ers express a desire for a just and sustainable world and are concerned about world poverty and hunger. They have an inclination toward catholicity without realizing it, expressed for them as a desire for inclusive, ecological, and planetary life. These concerns are not necessarily driven by institutional religion but by an inner sense of belonging to a whole.

One time a student at Georgetown University got up before the class in a black miniskirt, black tights, and leopard shoes to announce a fundraiser for a clean-water well in South Sudan. "We *have* to help them," she told her classmates, "they are our brothers and sisters!" This young woman was not religious or speaking from a religious perspective. She simply had a strong sense of solidarity with the poor in Africa (probably aided by the Jesuit motto, "men and women for others," hanging on flags all around campus!).

Many community-minded students reflect a "network consciousness" that corresponds to second axial-period consciousness. This new consciousness emerging at the beginning of the twentieth century has been accelerating in the twenty-first century with increasing computerization of the global world. The complex levels of information circulating around the globe are shifting levels of consciousness toward more complex integrative levels; "multi-tasking" has become more of a norm than an exception.

I suspect that Gen X and Gen Z (the "iGen" or internet generations) have different neural maps than the baby-boomer generation, and thus these younger generations are "wired" for a different planet, a more unified planet. If the human brain evolves based on environmental factors, and the primary environment today is information, then we can assume the human brain is evolving according to new patterns of informational flow giving rise to an "ibrain" rewired for nondual, horizontal relationships.

Younger generations are undergoing significant shifts in response to vast interplanetary networks of information, and new levels of consciousness are emerging, giving rise to a new type of person, a "*techno sapiens*," a technologically hybridized and interactive person who thinks across interactive lines, which I would describe as interconscious, interspiritual, and glocal (simultaneously local and global).

It is time to face our new reality. Personhood has never been static or given but has always been a creative process. A person is not the accumulation of the past, the spatialized substance that has some volume or weight to it, but the creative activity of life as it projects itself to the next instant. To be a person does not mean to "do this" or "follow that"; rather, it is a matter of living in the flow of life and creating the future. The emerging person today is not the same person as yesterday but a new type of person constituted by a new consciousness of gender, race, and religion, a person not defined by genotype but by a new cybernetic phenotype, as Rothblatt writes: "Personality, values, and other attributes are increasingly being captured in cybernetic form, they are becoming virtual entities of their own; personhood is being gradually complexified with technology."[18] We are alarmed by this reality because we have no real sense of evolution nor do we think of ourselves in evolution. The church continues to treat evolution as a theory and not as a fundamental reality; hence, we do not have a theology to accommodate technological nature or the rise of the new technological person.

I anticipate that the second axial person will continue to technolo-

---

18. Martine Rothblatt, "On Bemes, Memes and Conscious Things." Rothblatt continues by saying, "these "bemes"—units of beingness—are analogous to memes (culturally transmissible ideas) and genes but go far beyond them. Common sets of bemes will lead to a new "Beme Neural Architecture" (BNA), analogous to DNA. But while DNA expresses matter in a limited way, substrate-independent BNA expresses mind, and can replicate with a speed and flexibility far beyond DNA, extend our consciousness, and survive beyond our fragile DNA," http://www.kurzweilai.net.

gize. The widening gap between the institutional church and younger generations will stretch into a yawning gap that will yield either a new type of church or a new religion of the earth, as Teilhard suggested. The new emerging person, the *techno sapiens*, will be oriented toward interspiritual, interracial, and intergendered life. This new type of person will not necessarily forfeit humanity to a triumph of technology; rather, as Rothblatt has already shown, technology can be used to enhance a new ecological unisphere, an ultrahumanism and planetization, so to speak, if we develop technology toward these goals. Nor will *techno sapiens* life mean a renunciation of religion and faith, although a new understanding of these core cosmic dimensions of life is needed. Bruteau claims that personhood, transcendence, and creative freedom may become "the real interior meaning of the act of faith."[19] Would it not be hopeful to suggest that new identities of personhood might reflect a new presence of spiritual values (since technology can be developed toward spiritual aims, as Rothblatt exemplifies), so that persons may be identified as ecological, compassionate, planetary, or interspiritual, whether or not they are black, gay, Hispanic, binary, or transgendered? What makes the coming age so truly new is that it will be ushered in by a genuinely radical rearrangement in our life experience. Nature presses on to be more creative and novel. The ultimate reality of life *is* self-transcendence itself.[20] Bruteau put it this way: "A genuine revolution must be a gestalt shift in the whole way of seeing our relations to one another so that our behavior patterns are reformed from the inside out. Any revolution worthy of the name must be primarily a revolution in consciousness."[21] I could not agree more. "We ourselves are the future and we are the revolution. If and when the next revolution comes, it will come as we turn, and the world turns with us."[22]

---

19. Beatrice Bruteau, "Freedom If Anyone Is in Christ, That Person Is a New Creation," in *The Grand Option*, 172.

20. Philip Hefner, *Technology and Human Becoming* (Minneapolis, MN: Fortress Press, 2003), 85.

21. Beatrice Bruteau, "Neo-Feminism and the Next Revolution in Consciousness, " *Cross Currents* 27, no. 2 (1977): 170–82.

22. Beatrice Bruteau, *The Grand Option*, 32.

14

Thoughts on Love

"WHAT IS A HUMAN PERSON?" I asked my adorable cat, Rosie, as she sat on my desk staring at me with her bright green eyes, her grey furry body yearning to sit on my lap. Rosie was not interested in my question; she simply wanted to be loved. She jumped into my lap and coiled up like a snail in the comfort and protection of my slouched body in the chair, basking in the warmth of my human flesh. My animals have taught me much over the years about what it means to love and to live in the moment. We humans are weighed down by the dead bones of our memories, the dust balls of past hurts and angers, the twisted knots of fear and rejection; the sins of our youth; the inability to free ourselves from things held captive by our minds, not realizing that everything we were yesterday is everything we are in this moment increased by one. Yesterday is an illusion of the mind; there is only today, this moment in which I exist—this moment to love, for it is love alone that gives me life. Not merely the sentiment of love (not to be denied or suppressed, of course) but the depth of love that is awareness of this breath, this desire, this idea, this movement toward everything that draws my being into greater fullness of life, a bubbling of being in which this moment opens out to the next. God is love, the fountain fullness of our lives even in the midst of great suffering and sorrow, for if there was no fullness of love there would be no hope or tomorrow.

The Core Reality of Love

I exist because I stand outside myself in this power of God's love that sustains me, or better yet is the entangled fire of my life. Yet, my heart is not nearly full, not even after having taken in and tended to all those calamitous moments of darkness and sorrow and pain; my heart still has a vast open space to receive and forgive even more, for this love that fills my heart is infinite. God is constantly loving me and receiving me into the expanse of the divine heart with all my wounds and dead bones; hell is what I do to myself in my own terrified mind. For if one fragile and limited being, such as myself, could experience even one such moment of absolute forgiveness and acceptance, I cannot imagine the breadth and depth of God's eternal compassion. I am aware of where I stand and cannot know those whose childhoods have been trampled upon by abuse or neglect, where love is difficult to grasp and hold on to. The desire is there, but it slips through the cracks of pain and scars imprisoned by the mind, which never heals; thus love is never free. I belong to these persons, however, and they to me so that love is never self-serving or manipulated or cheapened but forged into the beauty of what we can be together.

When I speak about love as core reality to colleagues in theology (or science) I often get a look of annoyance or the raised eyebrows that signify dismissal. The academy can be like the church, intellectually self-preoccupied with the precision of logical arguments. I want to shout out, "Hey, I am seeing from a different perspective; I am looking out from a different window." But, instead, I often remain silent because love cannot be defended by analytical arguments; love has its own internal logic.

That I should come to see love as the "axis" of second axial consciousness is no mistake. One can see with a new pair of eyes only if one is standing outside the center. From my first breath of earthly life, I have been standing at a different place and seeing the world with a different set of eyes. It is what prophets do. My place in the world has been consistently outside looking in and inside looking out, whether in religious life or in academic life; my existence has thrived on the fragile threshold of ever-changing life. And it is because of where I stand that I see the church and science as a marriage made in heaven but divorced on earth—the need to belong together yet unable to find a fruitful relationship together.

It is not because religion and science are so radically different that they have nothing in common. Quite the contrary, they are closely aligned in their pursuit to control the purpose and future of human life. David Noble said that both science and religion seek to restore the fallen Adam to divine likeness. Whether or not Noble's idea is true, religion and science are in competition, not conflict. Each area has a grip on the human person in the form of doctrines, theories, and creeds, and each area contributes to the human narrative in ways that can appear to conflict with each other. It is not really a conflict; each side simply wants to tell the story of the whole by itself. Religion and science vie for human attention and allegiance. By stoking the fires of ignorance (cloaked in theological jargon or scientific formulas) the human person needs both areas to navigate the waters of life and to avoid drowning; hence both sides gain power without conceding to the other. It is no accident that science and religion are both predominantly male fields, driven by lines of patriarchal power.

Through winding roads of relationships, failed paths, and unexpected detours, and most of all, by allowing God to breathe in me the Spirit of new life, my views on science and religion and church and world have been turned inside out. Something broke within me, as if exiting the dark birth canal of isolated existence into a new light of personhood and freedom. This breakthrough, I have come to realize, relates to the way consciousness can change and shift to higher levels of integration. It is a breakthrough in consciousness that continues to emerge on new levels, inviting me to new understandings of self, identity, gender, and personhood.

The Buddha said something to the effect that the mind creates the world and not the other around. And to this I can attest. The mind is that field of awareness that includes the brain, the body, the emotions, and the connections between the particular being of "self" and the wider environment in which the self is connected. All of nature is endowed with the energy of love (which is grace), and yet only by being open to love (and by this I mean living in receptivity to love) can one know love as the precious gift of nature itself. In this receptivity of love I began to let go of my fixed ideas and narrow definitions of God, church, and world, and I invited into my heart and mind a new universe of life and a new way of seeing the world. I did not seek a new worldview; rather I went in search of truth and found love at the heart of all things. I have come to realize that all knowledge is true knowledge—whether in the sciences or in the humanities—if it moves one to fall more deeply in love.

The power to transform the world cannot come from either science or [institutional] religion; that is, it cannot come from without, it must come from within. I think this was the main point of Jesus's message, which may be more relevant today than ever before. The head must find a new way to stand in the heart, and the heart must find a new way to stand in God. In this respect, a renewal of monastic life as inter-spiritual and secular life may be essential for the future of the planet. We may consider this new life along the lines of Saint Francis, who spoke of living in the cloister of the world, in which the body is the cell and the soul is the hermit. But neither a renewal of monastic life, alone, nor a new church is enough to change the world. Nothing can change the world except the one who makes the world, and that is the human person. If I ask, what makes the human person "person," I must answer, love alone. It is love that makes us what we are. We are created out of love, in love, and for love, as the Spanish mystic Raimon Lull so beautifully wrote:

> The lover was asked to whom he belonged.
> He answered, "To love."
> "What are you made of?" "Of love."
> "Who gave birth to you?" "Love."
> "Where were you born?" "In love."
> "Who brought you up?" "Love."
> "How do you live?" "By love."
> "What is your name?" "Love."
> "Where do you come from?" "From love."
> "Where are you going?" "To love."
> "Where are you now?" "In love."
> "Have you anything other than love?"
> "Yes, I have faults and wrongs against my beloved."
> "Is there pardon in your beloved?"
> The lover said that in his beloved were mercy and justice,
> and that he therefore lived between fear and hope.[1]

It is our capacity to love and the purity of that love that shapes the world into a vessel worthy of God, and it is our capacity to destroy love and crush it that makes the world a living hell of endless terror. We frail humans constantly live between these two realities.

---

1. Raimon Lull, *The Book of the Lover and the Beloved,* trans. Mark D. Johnston (Warminster: Aris & Phillips, 1995), 39.

The Mystery of Love

I went in search of love because love was in search of me, and it found me when I was not looking. I was seized by the power of love in a way that defies logic or words. I tried to run away from this grip of love, but each time I thought I had escaped, my heart became entangled and at times confused by all that was not love. Eventually I had to yield to this power of love. Thus, while trained as a scientist, I let go of all my worldly ambitions so that I could respond to this call of love. Teilhard thought that love is the most mysterious energy in the universe because it cannot be reduced to simple laws of attraction. I came to the conclusion (still a working hypothesis, of course) that love has its own inner logic and that the greatest paradox of love's logic is laid bare in the mystery of the cross. I have come to realize that this furnace of the crucified Christ, in which love and suffering are deeply intertwined, is the root reality of all life, because it is the root reality of God.

I had no idea that when I entered a Carmelite monastery in 1984 that I would find myself in the heart of the crucified Christ, not by sitting quietly in the chapel wrapped in meditation but in the difficult discovery of my own frail humanity. Day in and day out I struggled with my ego and all that was (and still is) enfolded in my ego: self-worth, judgments, anger, and strong opinions. I tried to let go of all the human spider webs that kept me bound within myself and isolated from others, especially those I called my sisters. I was instructed to let go and cling to God, but my letting go was an intellectual act of the will; deep down, I clung to everything with an iron grip. When I eventually studied the work of the Franciscan theologian Bonaventure I was attracted to his insight: "There is no other way into God than the way of Christ crucified."[2] Really, I thought, no other way?

The mystics tell us that love, pain, suffering, and death are the stuff out of which life is formed. How is this possible, I wondered? How could the pain of the human heart contribute to the formation of life? One does not have to look far to find hearts that are torn, crushed, sliced open, bleeding, and wounded to the core; sometimes they become so

---

2. Bonaventure, *Itinerarium Mentis in Deum* 7.6. Engl. trans. Ewert H. Cousins, *The Soul's Journey into God, The Tree of Life, The Major Life of St. Francis* (New York: Paulist Press, 1978).

damaged that it seems impossible for such hearts to really love again. And yet, that possibility is always present. Love lives on the wings of hope, even if they are clipped by sorrow. It is as if beneath the surface of our lives there dwells a dimension of inexhaustibility, a depth dimension that overflows with meaning, the *experienced ultimacy* of being and meaning, the realm of ultimate concern. The name of this infinite and inexhaustible depth is God. One cannot find this divine depth in books or conference meetings. One must search within to find this depth of love, whose name betrays an insuperable wisdom.

When I was in Carmel we recited the prayer of Saint Thérèse each morning: "May my life be an act of perfect love." Was my life an act of perfect love? For the longest time, I thought it meant never getting angry or talking ill of others, or never having a bad day. For years, I struggled with the weight of my humanity, seeking to become something other than human. It has taken me decades of learning, searching, and pondering the deep mystery of love to realize that love itself is the essence of matter. Matter on its own is static, dead weight. One has only to lift a dead person to know this fact. Matter cannot resolve its own internal mysterious connections; it cannot explain itself. The reason for my own existence cannot be explained by my own existence; hence, I must make a choice, I either belong to another or I do not truly exist. And since I know that I exist, I must belong to another.

When I explained this idea to my cat, Rosie, nestled in the hammock of my thighs, she understood perfectly, because her little furry body was sleeping soundly between the legs that held her and love her. Teilhard de Chardin also had this insight in the early twentieth century when science was just beginning to blossom into a new paradigm with the recognition that matter and energy are interconvertible. Given the primacy of energy and the force of attraction in the universe, Teilhard speculated that the principal energy in the universe is love. I imagine Teilhard in the dead silence of the desert, sitting alone by a kerosene lamp in the evening, pondering the deep mystery of love, a core energy, he thought, that accounts for attraction and consciousness. "The physical structure of the universe is love."[3]

But what *is* love? A few years ago Cynthia Bourgeault and I spent an evening in Arizona before a gathering of people sharing our insights

---

3. Teilhard de Chardin, *Human Energy*, 22.

on love. (I thought of the scene in Saint Augustine's *Confessions* where he and his mother, Monica, were in Ostia speaking on the things of God, two hearts joined in a single spirit of ecstatic love, drawn beyond ourselves by the power of God.) We spoke of love as the core energy of life, the ineffable center of the heart drawing each person to search for relationship, for belonging to another, for unity and wholeness. Love is unitive, and union is the basis of personality because union differentiates. The more we are in union with another the more we become ourselves because the core constitutive relationality of "self" is the basis of union, as Teilhard claimed. In love we become a personal icon of God.

For the longest time, however, I had a fear of love in the same way that I had a fear of fire. I was attracted to the idea of love but unsure about the reality of love. I was in the cave that Plato described, weighed down by the chains of my everyday flesh and hoping that I could catch a glimpse of the sun/Son so that I could be released from my bodily imprisonment and, like Saint Thérèse, become a perfect oblation of love. The more I tried to rise above my so-called fallen nature, the more I was weighed down by that nature. Then one day I woke up and fell in love with myself, and on that day, I fell in love with a living God and not a Platonic ideal.

Teilhard thought that love is the most mysterious and unknown energy in the universe. It is *this* center drawn to *that* center; *this* person drawn to *that* person. There is no logical explanation for this core energy of life; it is deeply personal and yet whimsical; mysteriously felt but cloaked in words; an energy field that is somehow entangled with an infinite energy of divine love—for God alone, who is absolute love, is completely personal and ineffable intimacy. Love is rooted in the fundamental nature of reality itself whereby the *eros* of divine love stretches forth from the heart of God onto the unfolding canvass of life. Love forms every star, atom, leaf, daffodil, bird, earthworm, cat, giraffe, tiger, and human; everything that exists is born from love. Even consciousness is born of love so that mind is not intellect alone but includes the body and senses and emotional life. Love makes the world go around because love makes the world; matter is formed by love.

Christian mystics understood love as the core of reality and spoke of a deep relationship between love and knowledge. "Love is the highest form of knowing," Saint Augustine wrote.[4] Gregory the Great said, "Love itself is a form of knowing" (*amor ipse notitia est*), meaning that the love by which we reach God implies a form of knowing above ordinary reason.[5] William of St. Thierry put it beautifully in this way: "In the contemplation of God where love is chiefly operative, reason passes into love and is transformed into a certain spiritual and divine understanding which transcends and absorbs all reason."[6] Wisdom is knowledge deepened by love. The wise person knows more deeply by way of love than by way of argument because the eye of the heart can see the truth of reality. Hence the wise person is one who knows and sees God shining through everything, even what seems ugly or despised. Those who privatize love or reduce love to mere sentiment miss out on the radiance of God shining through the world, as Gerard Manley Hopkins wrote: "These things, these things were here but the beholder / Wanting."[7]

The Inward Journey

My journey into God has not followed the beautiful pattern Bonaventure laid out in his "Soul's Journey into God," whereby the divine footprints in nature lead the soul inward to the center of love and upward into union with God. My journey has been more like a flight delayed on the tarmac for several hours due to mechanical problems, finally reaching the anticipated destination only to discover that I have no ride to the hotel and it is freezing rain outside. And thus once I land inside the hotel room I have two choices: I can either allow my cold, tired body to rebel against all the forces of nature or I can simply be thankful for a safe arrival and the

---

4. For example Bernard McGinn, who writes, "Love and knowledge are intertwined in Augustine's mystical consciousness." See Bernard McGinn, *The Foundations of Mysticism: Origins to the Fifth Century*, vol. 1 of *The Presence of God: A History of Western Christian Mysticism* (New York: Crossroad, 1994), 235.

5. Bernard McGinn, *The Flowering of Mysticism: Men and Women in the New Mysticism—1200–1350*, vol. 3 of *The Presence of God: A History of Western Christian Mysticism* (New York: Crossroad, 1998), 82.

6. McGinn, *The Flowering of Mysticism*, 82.

7. Gerard Manley Hopkins, "Hurrahing in Harvest," https://www.bartleby.com/122/14.html.

warmth again of a roof over my head. And if I allow myself to think from my heart then I know it is you, Lord, who constantly knit me in this crucible of love, wherein the joy of a moment can be mixed with the suffering of cold and misery.

Dag Hammarskjöld once wrote, "The longest journey is the journey inward."[8] The inward journey is the most difficult journey because there are few props to rely on and there is no protection against the harsh realities of the human heart. The inward journey is dark and light all at once, sorrow and joy, unresolved questions and peace. I learned how to navigate this inward journey beginning as a Carmelite and then as a Franciscan, and it has now become the royal road of my lifelong journey. As I hold still in the darkness of my heart, I sense the presence of God who is deeply entwined, a presence of eternal love in this moment of experience I call "my life." The "I" is wrapped up with God, like the double helix of a DNA molecule, in a seamless flow of life, in this dynamic complex of "God-life/my-life," embedded in the ongoing creativity of cosmic life. Inwardly I travel over and over again into the farthest corners and mysterious pockets of my thoughts and feelings.

Deep within the cave of my heart, a depth that belongs to me alone, I recognize a fire that burns brilliantly and glows with warmth. Through that glowing fire I see the outline of a face, the face of Christ, but I also see my face, and then I begin to see Christ's face as my face. Sometimes I cannot tell Christ's face from my own face, and all at once I recognize a single face whose eyes are looking inward and outward. The word "God" simply doesn't capture this infinite depth of my soul that stretches toward an endless horizon. By its sheer unlimited being I know it must be divine life, because it is life other than my own and yet entangled with my own life.

I then begin to know that this strange thing called "self" that scientists want to convince me is nothing more than wires and chemicals embedded in a complex informational universe is something more than what can be measured. These wires and chemicals cannot explain *my* experience of this other-than-intimate presence, which is me but not me because—in truth—I simply cannot account for my

---

8. Dag Hammerskjöld, *Markings* (New York: Knopf, 1971), 58.

own existence. How can the configuration of wires and chemicals make a conjugate called "self" when in fact the more I try to know myself in this inward journey, the more I encounter another presence I call God; and the more I travel inward, the more God there is than self, and, truthfully, the further I go the less I can speak of either God or self; there is simply an entangled fire of love. In the search for who I am I find God, and in finding God I find my "self" as no separate self but being itself, flowing into and out of an unquenchable power of divine love.

Dying into Love

When I was a child I wanted to make a famous discovery that would solve human suffering, but when I grew older and entered a religious way of life I had to accept that the most important discovery I could make was to know the suffering of my own self. And this was the hardest type of knowledge to gain because the mind, the emotions, and the ego often collaborate in a secret scheme to prevent access to the true knowledge of oneself. Only when I began to realize all the plots set up to prevent true self-knowledge did I realize, O God, that you are constantly inviting me into the inner chambers of love through the doors of suffering and death.

I have pondered Bonaventure's words for many years, "No other path than through the burning love of the crucified," and I have come to realize that love is the highest form of death and death is the highest expression of love. There are all kinds of deaths and all kinds of loves, and thus only the death of God can show us the type of love that leads to freedom. We have made such a mess of God, either trying to figure God out like a math problem or competing with God for power that it is difficult to really fathom the truth of God on the cross. Teilhard spoke of an irresistible center of absolute wholeness at the heart of everything, and Bonaventure said that the truth of this irresistible center is the burning love of the crucified Christ. God did not become something less than God on the cross; rather, the cross is the revelation of divinity. God is not the power of a monarch or a king; God is love unto death for the sake of new life. The cross reveals what divinity is, the power of divine love to give itself completely to the other and be a helpless love. On the cross God shows us the cost of freedom in love and the power of love to set free.

Teilhard thought that God's self-involving love is the heart of all nature; all creation sings praise to God. God empties into "element" and draws all things through love unto the fullness of being, a fullness that is always dynamically suspended between death and life. Zachary Hayes wrote, "Isolated, independent existence must be given up in order to enter into broader and potentially deeper levels of existence."[9] The environmental philosopher Holmes Rolston said that sacrifice and suffering are integral to a world grounded in love.[10] If this is true, then love is the cause of happiness and the cause of sorrow, for when we refuse to live in love and absorb love into our contracted egos, we live in death. Hell is where love is swallowed up into the darkness of our black-hole lives. But even in nothingness, love seeks to be set free so that it may grow ever more in love, for on the cross death has been conquered by death. We have the eternal capacity not to cling to darkness but to get up and live once again in the freedom of love.

I have come to realize that death without love is destructive and freedom without love enslaves us in lifeless things. True freedom is gained when love willingly undergoes death for the sake of greater love. Not all relationships are lovable or good or worth holding on to, of course. One must desire to be a person, to want to die into love and thus into freedom. Death is a vital part of life. To die into love means to let go and make the hard decisions to move into new relationships in order for love to flourish unto freedom. Creative love needs the truth of freedom to nurture human growth. There is no real freedom without love unto death and no real love without freedom. This "dying into love" that many of the great mystics speak about is a dying into freedom by which one becomes fully alive in God, a freedom that begins in this earthly journey of life and flowers in the eternity of life, that is, the whole of God's eternal love.

---

9. Zachary Hayes, OFM, *A Window to the Divine: Creation Theology* (Quincy, IL: Franciscan Press, 1997), 91.

10. Holmes Rolston, "Kenosis and Nature," in *The Work of Love: Creation as Kenosis*, ed. John Polkinghorne (Grand Rapids, MI: Eerdmans, 2001), 57.

Living from Within

All that I speak of here is not constrained by a personal search for God. Rather this trinity of love, death, and freedom is the hidden scaffold according to which life itself evolves. I have been engaged in the area of science and religion for years, but when I attend conferences where the question is raised on how science and religion work together, I find long-winded essays that fail to satisfy the longings of the heart. It occurred to me one day that we are asking the wrong questions. To ask how science relates to religion is a futile question unless one lives in a Cartesian self that is divorced from nature. But is this not the crux of our problems? The Cartesian self is a self-thinking self who has self-imposed powers to ask any question. Modernity is based on the Cartesian self, and we are deluged with questions, entangled in infinite questions to the extent that we live in the perpetual darkness of entangled questions. The result of all our questions is fragments of meaning dispersed amidst an endless sea of ideas, which can do no other than support a fractured world of struggling life.

Teilhard did not buy in to the Cartesian self. He did not propose models of relating science and religion. Rather, he was more in line with the ancient wisdom tradition, which basically says that genuine self-knowledge makes for true knowledge in all other matters. Teilhard saw the outer world within and the inner world without. Science and religion, he said, "are the two conjugated aspects or phases of the same complete act of knowledge—the only one that can embrace the past and the future of evolution in order to contemplate, measure and fulfill them."[11] The path into the world of meaning and truth is the path into the human heart. If you want to know how science and religion are related, first come to know the deepest truth of your self.

This is what I realized when I looked into the nighttime sky: I saw myself in the stars and the stars within me. The God who created the heavens is the same God who is alive and active in my heart. God who is the absolute power of love, the power of my life, is the power of the future.

---

11. Teilhard de Chardin, *The Human Phenomenon*, 204.

15

Love as Techne

I HAVE SPENT MANY YEARS in higher education, and although I can speak the jargon and follow the rubrics that yield optimal performance, I think our sophisticated educational system is failing the world. We have divorced the mind from the heart and knowledge from love, forcing knowledge into contrived systems of power. The medievalists knew that knowledge without love is lame and that love without knowledge is blind. Teilhard also understood the role of the heart in shaping the mind. To think, he said, is to unify, to make wholes where there are scattered fragments, not merely to understand concepts but to form new horizons of insight that draw us into love. We seek to know so as to fall more deeply in love. It does make a difference how we know what we know because, in truth, we become what we love.

I was sent to study theology only because it was an expedient way of keeping me out of trouble, or at least occupied. When I discovered the medievalists, especially the School of Chartres and the Franciscans, however, I realized a unified wholeness of heaven and earth, a "catholicity" that I had never encountered before. It was like gazing into the night sky and seeing the breadth of the cosmos for the first time. Bonaventure opened up for me the beauty of the cosmic Christ, the intertwining of suffering and love, and the study of theology as the road to holiness. His paradoxical path of knowledge was to proceed by way of love:

> But if you wish to know how these things come about ask grace not instruction, desire not understanding, the groaning of prayer not diligent reading, the Spouse not the teacher, God not man, darkness not clarity, not light but the fire that

totally enflames and carries us into God by ecstatic unctions and burning affections.[1]

Teilhard de Chardin was theologically kin to the Franciscan theologians, and he brought together Franciscan cosmic Christology and evolution in a way that turned my head around at least one hundred and eighty degrees, from longing for heaven above toward longing for the future unfolding within me and drawing me beyond this moment.

I originally set out to study science as the path to true knowledge, but something changed in me in a deep, incarnational way. My life was interrupted by the powerful love of God, who broke in unannounced, seized by God in a moment of chaos. Instead of examining the details of nature in the search for truth, I set out to know God because I could no longer settle for mere data or facts. Knowledge itself became a quest to fill the deep hunger for God in my heart. Teilhard helped me understand that thinking contributes to the wholeness of life when ideas become inchoate seeds of a new world. The knower is like the artist who is attentive to the world of experience and ponders what is seen within the eternal fields of the mind, bringing forth new ideas onto the canvas of life and shaping those ideas into meaningful realities. Study and the pursuit of knowledge, therefore, became a way that I could participate in the unfolding beauty of the world, shaping my life as an artisan of the future.

I constantly search for truth, sheer transparent being that radiates life, and this search for truth also leads me to know that I am not alone; that what I am is of God, and that what God is, is wrapped up in me, and that this insuperable mystery of God's intertwining love is truth, and this truth is in the universe itself. Hence, when I look out from this inner cave of my heart I see *my* universe because I see the cosmos in me. From this inner cell of incarnational love, I see the world in all its splendor: the world of physics and astronomy, biology and neuroscience, quarks, black holes, and entangled realities all dynamically flowing through fields of divine spiritual energy and consciousness, constellations of energy in discrete units we call persons, who are part of this incredible whole and yet in a mysterious way contribute to the

---

1. Bonaventure, "The Soul's Journey into God," 7.6, in *Bonaventure*, trans. Ewert H. Cousins, 115.

whole. Only from this inward journey can I make sense of the outer world, defined as it is by "science" and "religion" but limited by these categories because intellectual theories and analyses leave out the core axis of integration, which is the heart, where love nourishes the fields of the mind. Seeing through the eyes of love, I find the world as a unity, a dynamic unfolding oneness of rich and diverse beauty; the beauty of the stars, the pine trees and the deep woods, the beauty of the ocean and blue dolphins jumping into the sky, the beauty of the carbon atoms bound to their communities of molecules; all of these beauties dazzling like the lights of the northern sky wrapped in the flesh of the human face. And in the beauty of each human face I see the poetry of God, the word of eternal love.

Love is born of God because God is love (John 4:13), and thus every moment of my life, and every life, is being renewed in love. I have come to this reality by smashing through glass doors of doctrines and mandates and cultural labels and name calling and blog bashing, and all the hideous things humans do in fear and distrust. The truth is, God cannot be outdone in love because God is the name of the incomprehensible mystery of love, at once close and embracing and yet ahead, beckoning each of us onward: "Though the mountains be shaken and the hills be removed, yet my unfailing love for you will not be shaken nor my covenant of peace be removed" (Isa 54:10).

I return over and over again to the song of my heart: "Who is this coming up from the desert *leaning on her beloved*?" (Song 8:5). As I lean into God I hear the words: "Let us run together, my Beloved; let us not hide behind the fears of patriarchy, the labels of gender, the slurs of race, the colors of skin, the walls of division." My God is ever newness in love, ever faithful in love, the eternal fire of love that creates, destroys, rebuilds over and over unto eternity because love is invincible, mysterious, and eternally creative. I do not fear the dangers of patriarchy or linger on the moments of rejection or failure. These are inconsequential in the face of love's power.

Reborn in Love

And, yet, I am concerned that this fire of divine love can become choked and smoke filled in the sensational newsfeeds that breed hate, division, and conflict, or in the apathy that lingers in the malls, as we self-indulge in overpriced items while millions of factory workers in out-of-sight countries labor as slaves to make our goods. I am deeply concerned that the Catholic Church excels in secrecy and cannot muster enough humility to name its own sins or break its chains of patriarchy and imperialism or move beyond a theologically weak argument of priesthood and apostolic succession. Many people wonder, is the Catholic Church still related to Jesus? For Jesus was a boundary crosser, a chain breaker, a leper lover, a friend of women and tax collectors, a revolutionary of love.

"Love is patient and kind," Saint Paul wrote. It is not fixated on doctrines, formulas, canon laws, regulations, threats of expulsion, divisions, or smoothing over the crisis of sexual abuse. A church grounded in the core reality of God's love must be a church living from the center of that love, which is why the church can survive into the future only if it opens wide its doors to all those it currently excludes: women, laity, gay, binary, transgendered, divorced, and remarried, and in the not-too-distant future, artificially engendered persons and posthuman persons. In a spirit of humility, the church can learn from the LGBTQ community how to be transparent and authentic, for God's ways are not our ways, and God's thoughts are not our thoughts, and God's love cannot be controlled by human power.

Our postmodern world has failed in love or rather has tossed love into the sea of emotions or simply has not yet learned the art of love. All systems and all relationships that structure our lives have eradicated love: the church, the academy, government. We live in a world bereft of love; we have trafficked love, sold love into the slavery of unbridled patriarchy, power, and passions. And for this reason we are blindly destroying ourselves and the earth and its royal beauty. However, nature's elusive life will not be destroyed and will seek new ways to renew itself. For nature lives in the transparency of truth. A tree does nothing other than be a tree, and thus a tree lives in the freedom of love. Because nature is free and lives in truth, nature will always find ways to recreate itself unto the newness of life. The art of nature, its *techne*, is love, the creative art of relationships unto beauty and more life. And it is because of love and the unity of love at the core of life that we are unwittingly reinventing ourselves through technology and artificial intelligence—not to become enhanced but to become ensouled, unified in a depth that draws us onward. The cyborg is a symbol of hope that signifies we are not imprisoned in our broken, selfish human boxes of flesh; rather, flesh is world and world is *techne*, the art of creating unto life. We will transcend ourselves in a new species, and we can help shape this new species into one of love and compassion, a more loving earth community, if we develop our technological lives along these lines.

We are in the midst of an enormous scientific-technological paradigm shift in culture and society. The early stages of transhumanism are leading to posthuman life, that is, human life electronically embedded in systems of information. How to harness the soul of posthuman life will be the challenge for religion in the future. Religious communities themselves must think more broadly and share their resources with local entities that are striving for a new religious evolutionary way of life. Institutions do have value if they can use their resources to empower networks of smaller communities. Creating local webs of relationships will be essential to the way religious life and the life of the church unfold into the future. Teilhard spoke of "planetization" as the need for the ongoing encounter of religions and the convergence of centers of consciousness. Only by gathering the energies of the sacred and secular into new wholes will we evolve into new life or, as Teilhard called it, ultrahuman life.

Every human life is the cosmos winding its way into the future. Every life makes a difference to the life of the whole. I have come to know that the fire in my heart is the fire in the heart of the universe and that its flames will not be extinguished. This fire will destroy that which is not God and forge what is God into an ever-radiant new presence of God because God is forever being born within us. In this life, at this moment, I allow all that has shaped my life to be summed up in this seamless mysterious breath of life. I let go over and over again and jump into the lap of God's loving embrace. Every moment I am falling in love with God. For God knows me in a deep way, a way that I still hardly know myself; and it is this endless inscrutable depth where love burns brightly that I learn to trust my thoughts, my words, my actions. For I am named for a mystic and a prophet who stood before the idols of Baal; I am named out of fire and the silence of love. I have a mission because every person has a mission—to be the truth of who they are so that God can be God in them. The path to truth demands patience and trust, and this path is an open road within every human heart.

And so as I come to the end of my story (for now), from the covered cradle of Catholicism to the wild chaos of cyborg Christian life, I know that transformation is possible and that we live many lives in the course of our existence. Every time I died I was born anew: reincarnation and incarnation, not as returning life but rebirthing life, as Word becoming flesh: a spiraling incarnation, by which I have begun to glimpse a bit of heaven and the grandeur of God stretching before me.

To those who are searching for happiness and peace or the fullness of life, such life will not be found outside the heart, for that secret place of the heart is our link to eternal life. Instead of getting lost in malls or in endless webs of information, get lost in your heart where lies the infinite depth of God's love. Travel inward by way of unknowing, and you will know the world in its truth; turn from what is unloving toward that which is love, and you will know yourself loved. And if you want to be someone special, try not to be anything but yourself. You and I are divine Love incarnate—in the flesh—as we are and no other—the hidden love of God from all eternity in this particular body, in this particular moment. Trust the power of love within you, and let go of everything that crushes love. Let love take you by the hand and lead you into a world of promise and future life; there I am sure you will see the face of God. For the days are coming, says the Lord, when I will raise up a new people for a new planet, and they will know me in their hearts and minds, and we will be one in love.

That day I saw beneath dark clouds,
the passing light over the water
and I heard the voice of the world speak out,
I knew then, as I had before,
life is no passing memory of what has been
nor the remaining pages in a great book
waiting to be read.

It is the opening of eyes long closed.
It is the vision of far off things
seen for the silence they hold.

It is the heart after years
of secret conversing,
speaking out loud in the clear air.

It is Moses in the desert
fallen to his knees before the lit bush.
It is the man throwing away his shoes
as if to enter heaven
and finding himself astonished,
opened at last,
fallen in love with solid ground.[2]

2. David Whyte, "The Opening of Eyes," in David Whyte, *River Flow: New and Selected Poems* (Langley, WA: Many Rivers Press, 2012), 31.

Index

Sandberg, Carl, 28
Santangelo, Mrs., 12, 13
Sasinowski, Frank, 182, 183
Schmidt, Michelle, 92, 94, 97, 98, 102, 126
scholars, nature of, 110, 111
second axial period, 108, 191
self, and God, 202, 203
Seton Hall University: graduate studies in biology at, 39–43; teaching theology at, 125
sexuality, 152, 153, 154
Shields, Mother Marija, 50, 53, 56, 60, 65, 66, 69, 70, 72, 73, 75, 82, 83, 86, 90, 92, 94
Sister Servants of Mary Immaculate, 18
Sisters of Saint Joseph, 129, 130
spiritual direction, 66, 67
Spoto, Donald, on eremitical life, 119, 120
Stang, Sister Dorothy, 144
Stapp, Henry, 169, 170
Stein, Edith, 75

Taft, Bob, 52
techne, and nature, 181, 182
techno sapiens, 193
technology: and evolutionary life, 181; as extension of nature, 187
Teilhard de Chardin, Pierre: on consciousness and attraction, 170, 171, 172, 174, 176, 184; on evolution, 133; and Franciscan theologians, 207; and integration of religion and evolution, 169, 170, 173, 175, 176; on knowledge and evolution, 177; on love and sexual energy, 154; on love as cosmic energy, viii, 170, 171, 198, 199, 200, 204; on nature, 181; and planetization, 210; theology of, 114–17

Terasem, 183
Teresa Ilia of the Trinity (Carmelite name/identity of Denise Delio), 75
Teresa of Avila, Saint, 57, 66, 73, 75, 76, 77, 94
theology: incarnational, and experience of God, 153, 154; patriarchal, 147; as a science, 103
Thérèse of Lisieux, Saint, 57, 58, 59, 60, 81, 82, 199, 200
transgendered persons, 182, 183
transhumanism, 168, 210
Trinity College (Hartford, CT), teaching at, 127, 128, 129
Trotsky, Leon, 40
Turing, Alan, and machine thinking, 180

Unisphere, 183, 184
Ursuline nuns, 100, 101

Vanier, Jean, 8, 38
Vasto, Adelaide del, 2
Vatican II, and modern science, 133
Villa Maria (German Franciscan nuns), 89, 90, 118, 122, 123, 125
Villanova University, teaching at, 178
Vladia, Sister Andreja, 73
vow of poverty, and religious community, 157, 158, 159, 160, 161

Ward, Susan, 35, 38, 39
Washington Theological Union: and education of seminarians, 147, 148; teaching at, 127–29, 140, 164
Werr, Antonia, 89
Wilders, Max, 176
William of St. Thierry, on love, 201
Woodstock Theological Center, 166–78
world religious, emergence of, 108

Yakshe, Paul, 38, 39